D1602160

Corpus Christi

Picture Research by Margaret Walberg,
assisted by Sally Robeau
and Anita Eisenhauer
"Partners in Progress" by Grady Phelps
Foreword by Dan Kilgore

SPONSORED BY NUECES COUNTY HISTORICAL SOCIETY AND
CORPUS CHRISTI CHAMBER OF COMMERCE

WINDSOR PUBLICATIONS, INC.
WOODLAND HILLS, CALIFORNIA

Corpus Christi

The History of a Texas Seaport

Previous page: In the 1940s Charles Berkeley Normann, assisted by Geneva Flores Hart, painted this rendition of the Corpus Christi waterfront. The painting emphasizes Captain John Anderson's wind-powered mill, which was used to grind salt and corn, as well as to furnish power to cut wood. Anderson, a Swedish-born seafarer, brought his family to Texas in 1852. Courtesy, Corpus Christi Museum

Following page: Howard Norton Cook was commissioned to paint these two murals for the old Corpus Christi Post Office by the Work Projects Administration, Post Office Fine Arts section, in 1939. The top painting depicts the marine side of Corpus Christi industry, with docks, fishermen and shrimpers, boats, and the old Bascule Bridge. The bottom represents the major landed industries in the area, oil, ranching, and farming. Both paintings now hang in the Nueces County Courthouse. Courtesy, Nueces County Historical Society

Windsor Publications, Inc.
History Books Division
Publisher: John M. Phillips
Editorial Director: Lissa Sanders
Administrative Coordinator: Katherine Cooper
Senior Picture Editor: Teri Davis Greenberg
Senior Corporate History Editor: Karen Story
National Sales Manager: William Belger
Marketing Director: Ellen Kettenbeil
Production Manager: James Burke
Design Director: Alexander D'Anca
Art Production Manager: Dee Cooper
Typesetting Manager: E. Beryl Myers

Staff for *Corpus Christi*
Editor: Annette Igra
Designer: Alex D'Anca
Text Editor: Taryn Bigelow
Picture Editor: Laurel H. Paley
Sales Manager: Marcus Black
Editorial Assistants: Todd Ackerman, Susan Block, Phyllis Gray,
   Gregory Harris, Karen Holroyd, Doris Malkin,
   Mary Mohr, Susan Wells
Layout and Production Artists: Cheryl Mendenhall, Lisa Sherer
Typographers: Shannon Mellies, Barbara Neiman

Library of Congress Cataloging in Publication Data

Walraven, Bill, 1925-
   Corpus Christi: the history of a Texas seaport.

   Bibliography: p. 166
   Includes index.
   1. Corpus Christi (Tex.)—History. 2. Corpus
Christi (Tex.)—Description. 3. Corpus Christi (Tex.)—
Industries. I. Title.
F394.C78W34 1982   976.4'113   82-19976
ISBN 0-89781-043-0

FOR PROFESSOR JOHN E. CONNER,
ALMOST IN HIS 99TH YEAR AT THIS WRITING,
WHO INSPIRED A HUNGER FOR KNOWLEDGE
OF TEXAS HISTORY.

Above: A view of Corpus Christi from the first decade of the 20th century reveals a sleepy town about to become a thriving city. Courtesy, La Retama Library

Contents

Foreword

The appearance of a new history of Corpus Christi provides a fresh look at our past and is an appropriate occasion to review briefly the earlier histories of the city.

The Story of Corpus Christi by Mary A. Sutherland was the first and came out in 1916. While not a comprehensive history, it is an invaluable reference to the city's early years, based on the recollections of the author and many other early settlers. The Corpus Christi Chapter of the Daughters of the Confederacy published the work, and the Civil War clearly remained a burning issue.

Coleman McCampbell's *Saga of a Frontier Seaport* appeared in 1934. A collection of episodes and vignettes, it provides a human-interest approach to many facets of the development of the city and area. A revised and enlarged version, *Texas Seaport, The Story of the Growth of Corpus Christi and the Coastal Bend Area,* was published in 1952.

Corpus Christi: A History and Guide, a volume in the American Guide Series, came out in 1942 and is the first overall history of the town. Based on original research compiled by the Works Progress Administration of the 1930s, its contemporary photographs and "Corpus Christi Today" section present a view of the city emerging from the Great Depression and gearing up for the war effort. A condensed version with an added chapter on the King Ranch appeared as *Corpus Christi:*

100 Years in 1952 to commemorate the centennial year of both the city and the ranch.

The *History of Nueces County,* published in 1972 by the Nueces County Historical Society, contains much on the city's history. A cooperative 20-year effort by the society's members, it is somewhat uneven in scope and style but presents the results of much serious research, especially into the early years of Nueces County and the city.

Bill Walraven is well known to Corpus Christi readers through his years as a daily columnist for the *Corpus Christi Caller* and the *Corpus Christi Times.* The historical sketches of pioneer residents, interviews with those who helped make local history, and stories of obscure events in the city's and area's past that appear regularly in his column give him wide background to prepare this new look at our Texas seaport. Longtime business writer Grady Phelps relates the growth of participating businesses and organizations in the context of the city's history. Pictures researched and gathered over a wide area by members of the Nueces County Historical Society portray the changes from a frontier cowtown to a modern, dynamic city of today. So take a fresh look at our past.

Dan Kilgore

Introduction

I am not a native of Corpus Christi, but I feel like one. Among my early memories is standing on the backseat of a touring car coming down Leopard Street into town. Our game was to look down the street between the buildings and be the first to sight the bay. Just the view of the water brought screams of delight. Corpus Christi was the fun place with the magic water. The smell of saltwater, fish, boats, fuel, and creosote pilings somehow got mixed in with a wonderful emotion. Water particularly intoxicates those born away from it.

The old Bascule Bridge was a nemesis to motorists trying to cross the ship channel. But the noise of the great siren announcing its opening gave us goose bumps. To little people the raising of the black span was one of the wonders of the universe. Ships passed within touching distance, hissing and smoking, and tugboats tooted—there was no better show on earth.

North Beach was another world—the midway: popcorn, cotton candy, dodge'em cars, skating rink, Ferris wheel, and ghost house. The wet cypress wood of the saltwater swimming pool, where people went when jellyfish were plentiful in the bay, had a tangy smell like no other. The bay seemed saltier when a windy afternoon comber sent us tumbling and filled our sinuses with water. After the swim, the big treat was yet to come. Aunt Pearl always staked claim to a cabana early for our picnic. No feast could compare with her table as she unloaded boxes and baskets of chicken, ham, salads, chips, eggs, cookies, cakes, pies, and drinks.

A trip to North Beach was like Christmas and Thanksgiving all in one, under the palm trees on the soft, warm sand. It was long remembered—the cool afternoon breezes, the cries of the laughing gulls, brown pelicans perched silently on each piling, and the sound of the wind whipping through the tall palms at water's edge in front of the bathhouse, mingled with the music and screams from the carnival.

Half a century later I am still transfixed by that bay. I can still sit and look at it for hours, still feeling some of that childhood happiness. Perhaps I do so because I did not grow up in an area town, where some came to look upon Corpus Christi as the big kid on the street. It was the City, and they were still the Country. I never felt any of that resentment. When I came to Corpus Christi to live, I felt I had come home. That was 30 years ago. There were other places and other opportunities, but there was no place I would rather live. So I stayed.

The city's past has always been of great interest to me. Talking to old folks and listening to their recollections of the early days whets the appetite for more knowledge of the area and its people. The old natives remember a

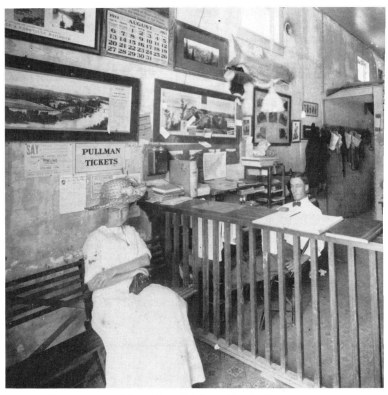

Above: This interior of the railroad ticket office in Corpus Christi, Texas, was photographed in 1911. Courtesy, La Retama Library

Opposite page: When the Nueces Hotel was planned, a company was formed with Herman Cohn as president and H.G. Sherman as secretary. They incorporated and sold stock in the company in shares worth $100 apiece. Courtesy, D.W. Grant family

village where everyone was known and a handshake was a bond. Those who moved to Corpus Christi remember how delighted they were to first see the town and the bay. They, too, found a home they never wanted to leave. It was a town that endured wars, storms, waves of immigration, and growing pains.

Some say it is growing too much. They fear that growth will cost the city some of its charm. It won't. A lot of history has passed through the bay, and the old charm is not gone. Look at the water—the charm of this Texas seaport will never fade.

Bill Walraven

During the Christmas holidays Corpus Christi glows. Boats in the marina decorated with lights add to the festiveness. Courtesy, Corpus Christi Caller-Times

The Beginning

Historically, Corpus Christi is a young city, only 138 years of age. Geologically, the land on which it is built is infantile. And ironically, Corpus Christi—known for its warm, temperate climate and cooling summer breezes—owes its existence to a massive ice cap of another age.

In the Pleistocene Ice Age, which started about a million years ago, snow and ice piled up into mammoth glaciers, hundreds of feet thick, over much of the northern portion of the North American continent—scooping, scraping, moving, and shaping the prehistoric land mass. As the ice sheaf grew, moisture was drawn from the atmosphere and the oceans, dropping sea levels as much as 500 feet. The sea bottom was exposed and the Gulf shoreline was many miles east of its position today.

The ice was melted by four major and several minor thaws, with the final thaw beginning only about 18,000 years ago. As the atmosphere warmed, huge rivers were formed that cut canyons through the rock leading to the coast and into the delta bottom. The rising seawater backed up into the river canyons, washed out the steep sides, and deposited silt and material from the ocean, forming wide river valleys about 7,500 years ago.

Deltas that formed along the mouths of the seven major Texas rivers overlapped to create the flat lowlands that today make up the Coastal Plain. Inland the rivers meandered—clogging with sand and mud, making new channels, and pushing up new riverbanks. (Excavations for buildings on the 35-foot bluff overlooking downtown Corpus Christi have uncovered rich deposits of pure, coarse river sand. Traces of the ancient river were also evident during construction of the Crosstown Expressway some distance to the west of the bluff.)

The river valleys continued to fill in with sediment until the water stabilized near its present level 2,500 years ago. The filling process created the characteristic rounded bays of Corpus Christi and others along the Gulf Coast. Nueces Bay at one time extended inland 10 miles. Smaller creeks carved out Baffin, San Antonio, and Lavaca bays and Cayo del Oso.

When the sea approached its present level, eroded sand and submerged deposits formed shoals and bars that became the barrier islands. These islands have been shaped and reshaped by hurricanes over the past 2,000 years. But only in the past 150 years have the islands begun to show a trend of erosion rather than accretion.

The Bureau of Economic Geology at the University of Texas at Austin in a 1976 study said that further changes for both the outer islands and inner bays may be in the offing because of the innovations installed by man. Channels that have been dredged in the bay trap deposits transported by currents, thereby increasing natural erosion. Dams inhibit the flow of water and river sediment. Artificial barriers installed to protect beachfront structures alter nature's stabilizing influences. Drained wetlands, or tidal flats, inhibit the growth of sea life. The University of Texas report carried the following warning:

Geologists are aware that the Coastal Zone is underlain by sedimentary deposits that originated in ancient but similar coastal systems. These sediments were deposited by the same natural processes that are actively shaping the present coastline.

The entire coastal zone has been the locus of dynamic processes and events for thousands of years and unless these natural systems are understood and respected, man can cause irreversible change in this important area of natural resources.

Through the ages the prickly pear cactus, pictured beside Aransas Bay, has served the inhabitants of this region quite well. It served as food for the early human residents of the area and has always provided food, moisture, and habitat for wildlife. Courtesy, Texas Highways

Top right: About 20,000 years ago at the end of the Ice Age, the first inhabitants of North America crossed from what is now Siberia to what is now Alaska. These were the ancient ancestors of the early coastal Indians. This painting of the moment of *The First Americans Crossing the Bering Strait,* by local artist Dick Turner, hangs in the Corpus Christi Museum. Courtesy, Texas Highways

Second from the left: Wild turkeys have been a source of both nourishment and recreation for hunters for many years. They are among the wariest and craftiest of game creatures to catch. Courtesy, Texas Parks and Wildlife Department

Below: Sea oats and wild morning glory ramble over the dunes of Padre Island. Courtesy, Texas Highways

Third from the left: The javelina, which has a propensity to hide in the dense brush thickets of South Texas, is a frustrating challenge to the hunter. This piglike creature is the subject of many tall tales. If properly prepared, a meal of javelina is edible. Courtesy, Texas Parks and Wildlife Department

Second from the right: The Spanish must have been amazed by the bizarre plants and animals they found in America, but none could have been so strange to them as the armadillo. The animal eats insects and small animals that it finds in the ground. Courtesy, Texas Parks and Wildlife Department

Right: The jackrabbit prefers a sparsely vegetated environment, so an abundance of jackrabbits indicates that the range has been overgrazed by livestock. Under normal conditions large birds of prey and such carnivores as coyotes, foxes, and bobcats keep the rabbit population under control. Courtesy, Texas Parks and Wildlife Department

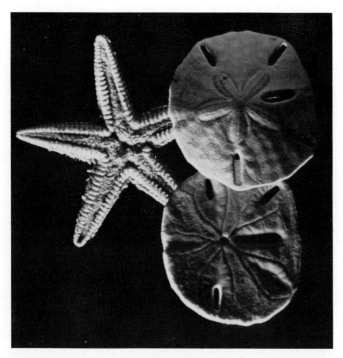

Top: When it was alive, this sand dollar was covered with tiny movable spines that created a velvety texture. The mouth on its underside had five tiny teeth that remain inside the sand dollar's skeleton. The starfish, with its five armlike extensions, feeds on mussels, clams, and oysters. Courtesy, Texas Highways

Above: The tarpon fish is one of the few remaining species of the "decadent" family Elopidae, which was represented by numerous genera and still more numerous species during the Cretaceous epoch. William Dampler wrote in 1675, "the tarpon is a large scaly fish, shaped much like a salmon, but somewhat flatter. 'Tis of a dull silver color, with scales as big as a half crown." Essentially a warm water fish, the tarpon may be found in the waters of the Gulf during the spring and summer, swimming south to the tropics for the cooler months. From Theodore Gill, "The Tarpon and the Lady-fish and their Relatives," *Smithsonian Miscellaneous Collections*, volume XLVIII

The First People

While the low-lying Gulf Coastal Plain was being created, the land was populated only by giant bison, early versions of the horse and camel, elephant-like mammoths, huge land tortoises, and glyptodents—armadillos that stood nearly five feet tall.

Some 8,000 years ago a people who used flint spears and tools moved into the Gulf Coast area and hunted the prehistoric animals. Little is known about these early residents except that they hunted in groups with spears. They apparently left the area about 5,000 years ago during an extremely dry climatic period.

People of the archeological complex known as the Aransas Focus moved into the Corpus Christi region from the Edwards Plateau in West Texas during the Archaic Stage 2,000 to 4,000 years ago. Their burial sites dot the area and indicate that they depended heavily on shellfish, snails, and small animals for food. Campsites have yielded small spear points, large knives of good workmanship, and conch-shell tools.

These Indians abandoned the Gulf Coast during another dry spell about 1,200 years ago. The Coastal Plain was uninhabited for 100 years before Indians of the Rockport Focus moved in. This was learned from excavations of mounds in which the burials of the two groups were divided by several feet of clay.

The Rockport representatives were the Karankawa Indians (there are more than 50 ways to spell the name), who populated the region west of Galveston Island, to Baffin Bay, south of Corpus Christi. The Karankawas may have been descendants of the Aransas Focus people; the burial mounds of both groups are found around Corpus Christi.

Roaming the Coastal Plain in small bands, the Karankawas were fearsome warriors with their six-foot height and war paint of red and black. Nor was their popularity enhanced by their habit of smearing their bodies with bear, shark, skunk, and alligator grease mixed with mud to keep the mosquitoes off.

The tribe lived off deer, javelina, clams, oysters, fish, and berries. They followed the trail of the cactus fruit and pecans when in season. Karankawa warriors carried cedar bows as tall as themselves and could hit game at 100 yards. They could shoot fish that nobody else could see in the water. They also tamed baby wolves and trained them as hunting dogs. The name Karankawa, in fact, means "dog lover."

The Karankawas had finely chiseled features, and both men and women were heavily tattooed about the face and body. They punctured their lips and breasts with slivers of cane and flattened the heads of their young on carrying boards. They were intelligent, but different. They spoke in an odd gutteral without moving their lips or tongues, giving the impression that they were extremely bored or condescending. Europeans, who came to the virgin land seeking riches, instead were greeted by the Karankawas, whose only wealth was their freedom to roam the coast in their own peculiar way.

The Kronks, as Texans were to call them later, likely threw a party for Alonso Alvarez de Piñeda in 1519, as the Spaniard sailed 900 miles along the Gulf Coast, mapping its bays, rivers, and inlets and collecting information about the inhabitants (such as how many gold bracelets they might be wearing). Piñeda traded with and brought gifts for the natives. While the tribesmen inspected the gifts, he stabbed a flagpole into the sand and formally claimed the land in the name of the King of Spain.

On an icy day in February 1529, the dark eyes of the Karankawas watched with stoic good humor as boatloads of soggy, miserable Spaniards in crude homemade barges plopped onto their beaches. These men were the remnants of an expedition led by Panfilo de Narváez that had landed in Florida, missed connections with its fleet, and made the barges in an effort to reach Mexico. The Karankawas built fires and carried the dazed explorers to *ba-aks*, or open teepees. They fed and nursed the explorers and danced and celebrated their welcome all night long. Later, after Narvaez and two others were swept out to sea in the last barge, most of the Spaniards attempted to walk to Mexico.

Alvar Núñez Cabeza de Vaca, treasurer for the expedition, was ill and could not join the trek south. He reported that the Karankawas were horrified to learn that the Spaniards, in desperation, turned cannibalistic and ate their companions who dropped from hunger and exhaustion. Padre Island expert Louis Rawalt believed the Karankawas learned cannibalism from watching the unfortunate Spaniards. Like other tribes, the Karankawas practiced a ceremonial cannibalism against enemies killed in battle, to draw magic from their slain or captured foes. Later they were to employ the practice as a form of revenge against invaders of their land.

The Karankawas were undisturbed for another 150 years, until the fleet bringing René Robert Cavelier, Sieur de La Salle, also received a friendly welcome from them on the shores of Matagorda Bay in 1685. But the French committed a breach of etiquette. They demanded that goods the Indians had stolen be returned, and they

Below: The Karankawa Indian who made this war club showed considerable ingenuity in its design. The club is made of one irregular piece of ironwood, with the burl at its head. Ironwood is exceptionally hard and strong, so although it weighs only a pound, this piece is a quite effective and extremely rare weapon. Courtesy, Department of Anthropology, Smithsonian Institution, Washington, D.C.

Bottom: These wax sculptures of a man and woman of a Karankawa tribe, destined for the Corpus Christi Museum, are the work of local artist Sue Rees. The figures are based on a drawing, made about 1827, by the Mexican artist Lino Sánchez y Tapia. This drawing in the Gilcrease Institute of American History and Art is the only known contemporary picture of Karankawa Indians. Courtesy, Nueces County Historical Society

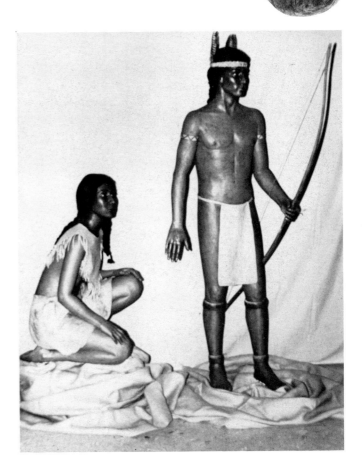

Frenchman René Robert Cavelier, Sieur de La Salle, landed at Matagorda Bay in 1685 to colonize Fort Saint Louis. La Salle mistakenly thought that he had found the mouth of the Mississippi. Initially welcomed by the Karankawa Indians, later the French colonists were at war with them. From Anna J. Hardwicke Pennybacker, *A History of Texas*

took the Indians' canoes without permission. These actions started a war that wiped out La Salle's colony at Fort St. Louis, and 75 colonists died in a massacre.

The threat of French colonization on the Gulf Coast brought a flurry of activity from the Spanish, who brought priests, traders, and soldiers to establish missions. While the Karankawas joyfully accepted the offer to be Christianized, they listened only so long as there was free food and clothing. Their religion was the sunset. Warriors would stand in a trance watching the red sphere of the sun sink into the bay. (The Karankawas buried their dead facing the east, apparently signifying their hope for immortality after death.) Even as residents of missions, where they refused to work, they continued their old habits of stealing, robbing, and killing. Even with full stomachs they would wander back to their hunting grounds, where they could wear their own uniform, which was absolutely nothing but the ornaments in their hair.

They never could understand the concept of individual ownership of good-to-eat animals that roamed loose about the countryside. An animal should belong to the hunter who killed it, they reasoned. This was all right when the Mexicans were in control; they only used the land for pasture and weren't troubled by the loss of a cow or two. But when the Texas settlers came, they tilled the soil, erected fences, and considered cattle theft a heinous crime, punishable by death. The Karankawa's days were numbered, for he could not change his ways.

Empresario Stephen F. Austin issued orders for the extermination of the Karankawa people. They could no longer flee to the mission, for they had frustrated the padres into giving up on them. They could only retreat and die. In 1845 General Zachary Taylor's army reported a band of 50 of them on south Padre Island.

The remaining Karankawas eventually sought asylum in Mexico; but their robbing, stealing, and killing got them in trouble again. They fled across the Rio Grande, where they were attacked and killed in 1858 by Juan Nepomuceno Cortina (who then, before he became a famous bandit, lived in Texas) and a band of rancheros at a place called Tampacuas, 20 miles north of the Rio Grande.

The tribe that had thwarted efforts of the French to colonize Texas, frustrated Spanish efforts to Christianize them, fought Jean Lafitte and other filibusters, and substantially delayed Anglo-American efforts to settle this portion of the Texas coast was no more.

The sun the Karankawa worshipped had set for him.

The Explorers

Corpus Christi may have been discovered a hundred years before the first English colonists landed at Jamestown, Virginia, in 1607. If it was, no one was impressed enough to make note of it. The Spanish, French, English, and Italians likely passed by—there was no gold or promise of riches to bring them ashore. If they landed, it wasn't by design. Often it was to their great misfortune.

According to local legend, Alonso Álvarez de Piñeda not only discovered Corpus Christi Bay, but also named it, after the Feast of Corpus Christi, the day he claimed the territory for his king. He did sail along the Texas coast in 1519 under orders from the Spanish governor in Jamaica, Francisco Garay, who had sailed on Christopher Columbus' second voyage. Piñeda was to look for a passage to the Spice Islands of the Pacific. Actually, it was a move by Garay to horn in on Hernando Cortés' territory south of the Rio Grande and get a share of the Aztec gold.

Piñeda arrived at Veracruz on August 15, 1519. Cortés left the business of conquering Mexico long enough to try to capture Piñeda. He waylaid a landing party and Piñeda sailed back north where he spent 40 days reworking his ship's bottom at what is believed to be the mouth of the Rio Grande. It is unlikely that he was off the Corpus Christi coast on the religious holiday. Although he stopped to talk to the natives and stake Spain's claims to the land at various points along the coast, there is no evidence that he actually saw Corpus Christi Bay. Piñeda's map showed only two marked rivers—the Panuco, at present-day Tampico, Mexico, and Rio del Espíritu Santo, the Mississippi. Four other rivers were not labeled.

Piñeda took back some gold to Governor Garay and told him there was more to be had. He also said some natives were nine feet tall and others three feet tall. He added that the natives were "very friendly." In 1520 Garay attempted to establish a town named for himself near the present site of Brownsville. The "friendly" natives attacked in a flotilla of canoes, inflicting heavy losses and routing the expedition led by Captain Diego de Camargo. Although Cortés never gave up the idea during his lifetime, settlement would not come for another two centuries.

Piñeda is generally credited as the first European to sail past Padre Island, but he may have been the second. Historian Dan Kilgore says a South American scholar, German Arciniegas, claimed that Amerigo Vespucci of Florence, Italy, drew the first maps showing the outline of the Gulf of Mexico. Vespucci would have had no earlier map to copy, since his voyage was in 1498—21 years before that of Piñeda. German cartographer Martin Waldseemuler, who copied Vespucci's maps, assumed Vespucci had discovered the new land and labeled the continent America on his 1507 maps. Waldseemuler omitted the name America from his 1513 maps, but he had already named the land.

The first European visitors to Corpus Christi likely were the survivors of the Panfilo de Narváez expedition that had been stranded in Florida. In September 1528, 242 Spaniards set out across the Gulf in crude barges, hoping to reach Mexico. The vessel commanded by Alvar Núñez Cabeza de Vaca was shipwrecked somewhere near Galveston Island and another of the barges was wrecked nearby. All but four of the refugees perished while attempting to reach Panuco, at present-day Tampico. Cabeza de Vaca was employed as a slave for six years by a tribe of Indians who frequented Corpus Christi and Nueces bays.

Andrés Dorantes de Carranca, Estevanico the Moor, and Alonso del Castillo Maldonado, survivors from the other wrecked barge, were abused by their Indian owners, so they slipped away and joined another tribe to the north. There they met Cabeza de Vaca. (After years of captivity Cabeza de Vaca learned that one other barge, which had been separated from the others in the voyage from Mobile Bay, had landed on Padre Island just south of Corpus Christi, with probably the first Europeans to land there. Indians of the Camoles tribe, however, fell on the weakened Spaniards and killed all 48 of them.) The four Spaniards made their escape in October 1534, while the Upper Indians gathered cactus fruit just west of Corpus Christi, and arrived in Sonora in Northern Mexico in March 1536. They walked west and north, avoiding the fierce tribes of the south who were enraged by reports that thousands of Indians had been enslaved by Spaniards as far north as the Rio Grande.

Some of this same anger may have been directed toward the unfortunate survivors of a treasure convoy that was driven across the Gulf by a fierce April storm and dashed over the sands of Padre Island in 1554. Conquistadores, churchmen, slaves, prisoners, and others were returning to Spain from Veracruz. Instead half of them drowned in the surf and fewer than 300 made it ashore.

The Indians offered sympathy and food but suddenly attacked without warning, starting a terrible retreat toward Mexico, which the victims figured was only a few miles away. They were wrong by about 200 miles. Two of the party were captured and returned

unharmed but stripped of their clothing. To humor the warriors, the entire party—men, women, and children—removed their clothing.

The attacks continued. A priest lost a packet of crossbows as the group rafted over an island pass, and they were completely defenseless. Arrows cut down stragglers. The strong led the march and were shot from ambush. The refugees suffered from hunger, thirst, exhaustion, and severe sunburn. When the few survivors of the trek did reach the Rio Grande, those who ran ahead to drink the fresh water were slaughtered by a hail of arrows from the bushes. One group actually crossed the river. Fray Marcos de Mena, pierced by seven arrows, was left buried in the sand to die somewhere above the Panuco River. He regained his strength and found his friends all dead. He survived and was helped by friendly Indians near Panuco.

Francisco Vásquez, a soldier, turned back after the massacre at the Rio Grande and stayed by the wrecked ships until a salvage fleet arrived two months later. He became wealthy from a share of the treasure and was a leading citizen of Mexico, known for his generous charities. Some 36,000 pounds of silver and some gold were recovered. Another 51,000 pounds remained on the Gulf floor to become a center of a 20th century controversy between the State of Texas and a private salvage firm.

Meanwhile another fleet of crude homemade boats under the command of Luis de Moscoso de Alvarado had sailed by in 1543, stopping occasionally to reprovision. This was the remnant of Hernando De Soto's gold-hunting expedition that had roamed Florida, Georgia, South and North Carolina, Tennessee, Alabama, Mississippi, Louisiana, Arkansas, Missouri, Oklahoma, and possibly Kansas.

During the three-year march that started in Florida in 1539, De Soto, the first European to cross the Mississippi, was harassed by hostile Indians, perhaps angry husbands. (He is said to have kept six maidens among the 100 or so Indians he had enslaved along the way.) A herd of hogs accompanied the expedition. The razorbacks of Texas, Arkansas, and the South can claim those as ancestors.

De Soto died of a fever on May 21, 1542, and was buried near the Mississippi. His lieutenant, Moscoso, tried to lead the column across Texas. Then he turned back to the Mississippi and ordered the building of boats for the return to Mexico. Only 320 of the original 600 soldiers remained. The weary soldiers may or may not have landed on the beaches of Corpus Christi. If they did, they were in no shape to appreciate them.

Frenchman René Robert Cavelier, Sieur de La Salle, was likely another early day tourist. Historian Hobart Huson says Henri Joutel, La Salle's aide who walked back to Canada with five others and returned to France, carried a map of the Texas coast. On it were the major rivers, one of which was the Nueces, called Rio de Oro (River of Gold). The name most likely was a reflection of the river at sunset, since little gold ever flowed down it.

La Salle and some 275 of his people died. But the most significant effect of the La Salle expedition was its impact on the Spanish. They quickly organized expeditions preparatory to colonizing Texas with mission-forts, called *presidios.*

Alonso De León, on his second attempt to find the French colony, may have approached Corpus Christi Bay. Twice he reached impassable waters and turned back. Local surveyor Carl L. Duaine, who has translated journals from the expeditions, believed De León reached the bay without realizing it was the mouth of the Nueces River, which he was to name on his third trip. On April 4, 1689, De León crossed a stream at a beautiful pecan grove southeast of present-day La Pryor and named it *Nueces,* Spanish for "nuts."

Corpus Christi Bay was not officially noticed until 1746, when the vast coastal area from Tampico to the San Antonio River, extending 300 miles inland in some places, was designated the State of Nuevo Santander, and José de Escandón was named governor. Wishing to secure Spanish claim to the territory, Escandón sent Joaquin de Orobio y Basterra, captain of the Presidio and Mission of La Bahía del Espíritu Santo, which was then located on the Guadalupe River, to check the area to locate sites favorable for colonization.

Basterra found Nueces and Corpus Christi bays ideal for such settlement. He also discovered that the Nueces River emptied into the bay, not into the Rio Grande as they had supposed. He named the bay San Miguel de Arcangel. He found the fresh water, abundant supply of fish, sources of salt and fertile soil would make an excellent location for a city. However, the suffering he and his men endured in the Desert of Death on the way back to the Rio Grande didn't do much for the local chamber of commerce.

The bay had yet another visitor in 1720. Frenchman Jean Beranger had been aiming for Matagorda Bay, but sailed through Aransas Pass and set up camp on Live Oak Peninsula on Copano Bay. He studied the Indians, their language and their habits. He also studied the country, for he was interested in reclaiming the territory for France. He saw a 15-foot snake and killed a seven-

Opposite page, top: Alvar Núñez Cabeza de Vaca, a member of the ill-fated Narváez expedition, was one of four survivors of the shipwreck. He lived among the "savages," becoming a trader and shaman. Cabeza de Vaca, or a member of his party, crossed Corpus Christi Bay at least twice during his sojourn with the Indians on the Texas coast. This drawing by Tom Lea depicts Cabeza de Vaca bringing Christianity to the Indians. From *Calendar of Twelve Travelers*

Opposite page, bottom: Published in Spain at about the time of Coronado's explorations, Cabeza de Vaca's famous book *Relación,* 1542, the first book ever written about Texas, was an honest narrative that chronicled the Indians' customs before the introduction of European culture. Courtesy, University of Texas Barker Texas History Center, Austin

Below: These Spanish silver coins (4-*reál*) were recovered in 1967 from a wreck believed to have gone down around 1553 off Padre Island. On one side is the quartered shield of Imperial Spain, showing the castles of Aragon and lions of Castile. On the other side are the Pillars of Hercules. Courtesy, Texas Highways

Top: Nueces County derives its name from the "River of Nuts" or *Rio de las Nueces,* so designated in 1689 by Alonzo de León when he found pecan trees in abundance on the banks of an unknown stream. Courtesy, Texas Highways

Above left: René Robert Cavelier, Sieur de La Salle, sailed past the Mississippi River where he was to establish a French colony, and landed at the head of Lavaca Bay in Texas. There he established Fort St. Louis, from which he made journeys west in search of gold and silver. Courtesy, University of Texas Institute of Texan Cultures, San Antonio

Above right: In 1747 José de Escandón submitted his plans for 14 settlements along and two settlements north of the Rio Grande, with one, Villa de Vedoya, on the north bank of the Nueces River. Escandón was never able to settle colonists on the Nueces River; the exploring party that was to locate a site for the colony returned unfavorable reports, and the plan was abandoned. Courtesy, La Retama Library

foot rattlesnake, which eagles carried away before he could render the fat. Beranger left five men along the shore, promising to pick them up the following year. But back in New Orleans he learned he had, indeed, been in Spanish territory. His crewmen joined the other Europeans who had come to grief on the Texas shore, for their captain never came back.

Much earlier three Englishmen did not perish on the beach. Their survival has to be one of the more remarkable feats of mankind. They were from a British man-of-war in a fleet commanded by Sir John Hawkins, the famous English privateer.

Ten ships put into San Juan de Ulua near Veracruz in September 1568, because they were low on water. A Spanish fleet appeared and sent a note of peaceful intentions. But then the Spaniards entered the harbor and opened fire, sinking eight of the ten English ships. Hawkins in the *Minion* and his cousin Sir Francis Drake in the *Judith* escaped. The Spaniards excused the action, saying the English had conducted slave and other trade in their waters and were, therefore, pirates. This treachery started friction which led to war between the nations. It also made dedicated privateers of Hawkins and Drake.

The two ships, with survivors from some of the other vessels, were badly overloaded. More than a hundred seamen volunteered to take their chances on land, at a point north of Tampico. Many of them were caught by the Spanish, who dealt with them as pirates. Others were killed by Indians. Only three, ordinary seamen David Ingram, Richard Browne, and Richard Twide, survived. Theirs was a fantistic adventure, swimming rivers, escaping Indians, passing by treasure, and walking through all types of terrain and climates.

After a year of hunger and danger they made their way to Canada. They roamed the region until, miraculously, they found an English ship in the St. John River, New Brunswick, in 1569. Thus they returned to England with their tale. The death and capture of their shipmates had been a terrible loss, but loss of their captains would have been far more tragic. If 111 men had not been sacrificed after that obscure naval engagement off the Mexican coast, the last two ships might have been destroyed by the Spanish. Had Sir John Hawkins and Sir Francis Drake died in 1568, the British likely would never have built a fleet capable of defeating the Spanish Armada.

The Spaniards kindled an anger in both men that was to drive them to fame and fortune, robbing and destroying Spanish shipping. Largely because of them the Spanish Empire began its decline. Without Hawkins and Drake, North America might never have been colonized by the English and the Texas coast, where three Englishmen trod the beaches of Corpus Christi four decades before Jamestown was founded, today could be a province of Mexico.

The Spanish Failure

Despite all the shipwrecked sailors, gold-seeking explorers, marching conquistadores, and missionaries, no one seriously considered moving to Corpus Christi until 1746. That was when Captain Joaquin de Orobio y Basterra named the bay San Miguel de Arcangel on which a town, Villa de Vedoya, was to be planted. The nice little village by the bay would be overlooked by a mission called Nuestra Señora de Soto. The settlement was the idea of José Escandón, governor of the newly created State of Nuevo Santander. Escandón was highly successful in colonizing the area south of the Rio Grande. But on the north side of that river only two of his settlements would take root—Laredo and Dolores, a few miles downstream.

The bells of Mission Soto were not destined to ring over the little village of Vedoya. At first colonists wouldn't volunteer. They had heard too much about the bad desert south of the Nueces. But, with the inducements of pesos and equipment, 50 families were recruited. They were to suffer from a snowstorm, smallpox, and the loss of their horses to disease before they even left Mexico. Then they were caught in a terrible drought and suffered greatly as they waited to be moved to the new colony. Finally, the governor relocated them to the south at the mouth of the Soto La Marina River, where they continued to suffer because they were herdsmen who knew nothing of the life of fishermen. They likely would have been happier beside the Nueces where there were game, fish, wild mustangs, cattle, and prime pasturelands. Unfortunately there were bands of Lipan Apache, crowded into South Texas by fierce Comanche on the Upper Plains.

No colony was established at Corpus Christi, but more adventuresome Spanish ranchers from south of the Rio Grande were attracted by the rich grasslands of the Nueces country and began to apply for grants of land.

The coastal prairie, at the time a vast plain of grass with few trees, was populated with herds of wild mustangs and a variety of game, including migrating buffalo. Cattle were also wild and difficult to control, but they multiplied rapidly, making the Nueces Valley the cradle of the cattle kingdom. Ancestors of the hundreds

Above: The reddish egret is a medium-sized gray heron with tough, reddish feathers on the neck and head. Plume hunters almost completely wiped out the reddish egret, but under the protection of the Audubon Society the species has recovered. While feeding, the bird dashes around as though drunk. Courtesy, Texas Parks and Wildlife Department

Above: Although bison lived mostly in the Great Plains region (the "plains bison"), their known range extends almost to the borders of the continent and as far south as Mexico. This 1680s engraving of an American bison was made by Father Jean Louis Hennepin, a Flemish Recollet friar. Hennepin knew and traveled with La Salle, and returned to Europe to write a number of books (of questionable accuracy) about his experiences in America. From the Windsor Archives

of thousands of longhorns that were later driven up the trails to the Kansas railheads scratched their horns on the thickets of the Nueces.

Among the first of the Spanish landowners was Blas María de la Garza Falcón, captain of Camargo, who established Rancho Santa Petronilla 15 miles south of the mouth of the Nueces River. He brought people, cattle, goats, and seed corn. Other ranchers from Camargo received grants and pushed northward into the grazing land as their herds continued to grow. Grants were issued one to a customer, but often several family members applied, creating large tracts of property. Marriages between landholder families further increased the size of some of the holdings.

Most of the owners were military or civil officials who did not live on the ranches, but left them to be run by a foreman, sometimes one of their sons, and worked by distant relatives, servants, *vaqueros*, and Indians. (José Antonio de la Garza Falcón apparently ran his father's spread on the Petronilla.) Some of the ranchos were little more than a ragtag collection of crude huts. Others were built as fortresses against Indian attack. Stock was generally permitted to roam from place to place as pastures were grazed over. Therefore there was often little attempt to improve the property.

A rumor of an English settlement on Padre Island in 1764 brought Colonel Diego Ortiz Parilla and his troops. (Some have speculated that Governor Escandón himself started the rumor to foster interest in the area.) Blas Falcón's son, José Antonio, explored the length of Padre Island. He found wrecked ships (including a 16-gun ship, which he burned), little water, and not a single Englishman.

The younger Falcón prepared a report, submitted under Colonel Parrilla's name, that carried a map of the coast with a sketch of little tents labeled *Camp on the Beach of Corpus Christi*. This is the first written reference to Corpus Christi. The Falcón family is generally credited with the naming of the bay, hence the city. How or why that occurred is not recorded.

In 1794 the bay was briefly considered as the site for relocation of Refugio Mission, then located on Goff Bayou near the Guadalupe River in Calhoun County. Instead the mission was located on Rancho Santa Gertrudis, owned by Juan Barrera, on the Mission River.

In the 16th century Spain had been the most powerful nation on earth. Two centuries later the Spanish empire was the feeblest in Europe. The empire had begun to fade after the defeat of the Spanish Armada in 1588. It reached its nadir after the British defeat of a combined French-Spanish fleet at Trafalgar in 1805 and the occupation of Spain by Napoleon three years later.

The reasons for the failure of Spain in Texas are largely those of that country's failure as a colonial overseer: strict and tyrannical government with a tolerance of graft among officials; long lines of communication and a lack of understanding of the frontier; the feudal nature of the colonial society; commercial practices that forbad trade with other nations; monopolistic control of the economy that caused prices to be four times those in Europe; extremely heavy import and export duties that made smuggling profitable; low pay of army officers, an inducement to graft; exploitation of the people and stifling of thought and speech by church and government, which brought liberal revolt and incursions into Texas; and an unyielding and unresponsive government that refused to admit that the *presidio*, or mission, system would not work in the northern provinces.

In the end, however, it was not only a failure of government. Rather it was the indomitable Plains Indian who harassed the Spaniard out of Texas. The land was frequently abandoned for considerable periods of time as Indians swept across the area, looting, burning, killing, and driving rancheros and their people back south across the Rio Grande.

These were mounted Indians, mostly Lipan, but sometimes Comanche, who had not frequented the area earlier. The Spanish could not conquer, convert, or exploit them. The reduction program had worked well with the sedentary Indians of the humid lands. But the Indians of the arid plains preferred the warpath to evening prayer and the buffalo chase to dry-land farming.

However, a new type of adventurer was arriving, forerunner of a new type of colonist who would move across the Texas frontier as inexorably as a glacier. These colonists would not consider the land mere pasturage. They would learn to ride like the *vaqueros*, fight like the Comanche, and turn to the plow. They would take possession of the land in such a sure and orderly manner that it would never be wrenched from them.

Yet the Spanish culture would forever be imprinted on the fabric of Texas life in its laws (principally those involving women's property rights), architecture, place names, and the people, descendants of colonies the Spaniards had planted.

Below: This seven-foot bronze statue of Padre José Nicholas Ballí is located at the foot of the Queen Isabella Causeway on south Padre Island. The sculpture, by Roman artist Tomás Concepción, was formally dedicated in December 1981. The King of Spain granted the island to Padre Ballí in the early 1800s, and Ballí established a ranch and mission there. After Padre Ballí died in 1829, the island became his nephew's family's possession until the mid-1800s. Courtesy, Texas Highways

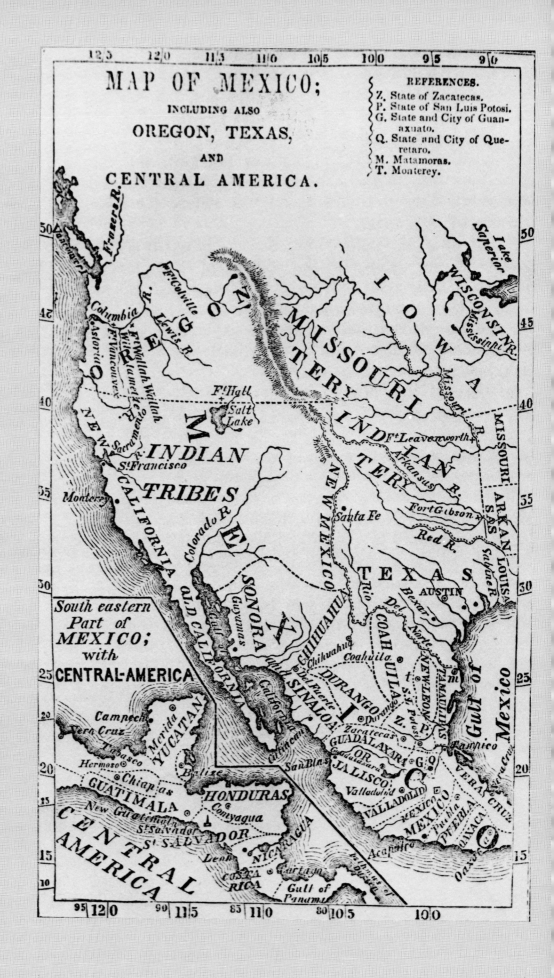

MAP OF MEXICO;

INCLUDING ALSO

OREGON, TEXAS,

AND

CENTRAL AMERICA.

REFERENCES.
Z. State of Zacatecas.
P. State of San Luis Potosi.
G. State and City of Guanaxuato.
Q. State and City of Queretaro.
M. Matamoras.
T. Monterey.

OREGON

MISSOURI TER.Y

IOWA

WISCONS.N R.

Lake Superior

INDIAN TERY

MISSOURI

ARKANSAS

LOUIS.A

NEW MEXICO

INDIAN TRIBES

Salt Lake

St. Francisco

Monterey

CALIFORNIA

Santa Fe

Fort Gibson

Red R.

TEXAS

AUSTIN

COAHUILA

NEW-LEON

TAMAULIPAS

Gulf of Mexico

South eastern Part of MEXICO; with CENTRAL-AMERICA

SONORA

CHIHUAHUA

DURANGO

SINALOA

ZACATECAS

GUADALAXARA

JALISCO

VALLADOLID

MEXICO

PUEBLA

VERA CRUZ

YUCATAN

Campeche

Vera Cruz

Tabasco

Hermoso

Chiapas

GUATIMALA

CENTRAL AMERICA

HONDURAS

Comayagua

NICARAGUA

COSTA RICA

Gulf of Panama

Acapulco

OAXACA

First Claims to the Nueces Strip

The brushland of South Texas was the birthplace of the cowboy. He was the Spanish or Mexican *vaquero* who carved out a new way of life astride a horse on dusty, arid plains.

The *vaquero* adapted to the harsh conditions and made them bearable by designing clothing and equipment for the job. The leather chaps protected him from mesquite thorns. A broad-brimmed hat shielded him from the broiling sun. A kerchief was a dust filter, sweatband, tourniquet, calf tie, and occasionally a handkerchief. His boots and spurs helped him tame and stay on wild mustangs. The lariat made him an artist at his trade and master of the longhorn cow—the meanest, wildest domestic creature ever invented. His job nomenclature and his skills of horsemanship would be copied and perfected by farm boys from Georgia, Arkansas, Alabama, and Tennessee, until the word "cowboy" became known the world over.

Isolation, a sea of grass, animals that could take care of themselves, and a breed of tough, wiry men created vast pockets in which the ranchers were kings of their own empires—with operations and methods later arrivals would copy and appropriate. The Spanish names are spread across the land maps of modern-day Texas—Farias, Villareal, Falcón, Montemayor, Garza, Ballí, De León, and a hundred more. Some grants were issued by the Spanish Crown, others by the new Republic of Mexico.

The ranchers between the Nueces and the Rio Grande were left alone and the cattle multiplied like flies. Until 1820 even the Indians were no threat, as they were occupied with fights and raids to the west. The area was so remote that it was affected little by the revolution fired at the Mexican pueblo of Dolores on September 16, 1810, by an obscure priest named Miguel Hidalgo y Costilla, who led a bunch of impoverished Indians on a rampage against a corrupt and uncaring Spanish system.

The ranchers were not touched by the ill-fated expeditions of Philip Nolan, Augustus W. Magee, Bernardo Gutierrez de Lara, Dr. James Long, and all the other filibusters pushing into the upper reaches of Texas. The wave of Anglo-American colonization swept over Louisiana, which Spain had lost to France, which in turn had sold it to the expanding new republic to the north. The Americans were pushing west again. They came for horses, Indian trade, loot, and empire. Some came to join liberal revolutions against the Spanish Crown.

Nolan was killed and his men captured in 1801. Magee and Gutierrez defeated a Spanish Army in 1812, but the Royalists came back and exterminated most of the ragtag army of Americans, Mexicans, Frenchmen, and Indians. Long's men were routed in 1820 and many were sent to Mexican prisons while Long was trying to enlist the services of pirate Jean Lafitte at Galveston Island.

Nothing changed on the range when King Ferdinand of Spain was forced to reinstate the liberal Constitution of 1812, causing the conservative ruling class of Mexico to join with the clergy in a bloodless revolution that gave the republic its independence on February 24, 1821.

In fact, the ranchers had little contact with Spain, or even Mexico. Spain had forbidden trade with foreigners and Mexico continued the ban. The policy created a brisk business for smugglers, whose prices, minus customs fees, were lower than domestic Spanish-Texas prices. The beach on Corpus Christi Bay became a trade mart where tobacco, sugar, and firearms were traded for

---

A map drawn in the 1840s shows Mexico and what was to become the Western United States. The boundaries are from the days before the annexation of Texas. The region from the Pacific Ocean to "New Mexico" was still in Mexico's possession, and Texas was an independent republic. From Marcius Willson, *American History*

Top: This engraving, circa 1890, illustrates how American settlers might have looked as they entered Texas in the early 1800s. From Anna J. Hardwicke Pennybacker, *A History of Texas*

Above: Longhorn cattle are descendants of cattle left in Texas by early Spanish explorers; wild herds roamed much of South Texas before the mid-18th century. The use of this hardy breed helped save the state from post-Civil War economic collapse. Courtesy, Texas Parks and Wildlife Department

Opposite page, bottom: This watercolor by Lino Sánchez y Tapia (after an original by José María Sánchez y Tapia) illustrates a male and female Lipan Apache Indian. The Spanish gave the generic name of Apache to many tribes, like the Tontos, Chiricahuas, Gileños, Mescaleros, Lipanes, and Navajos. Courtesy, The Thomas Gilcrease Institute of American History and Art, Tulsa, Oklahoma

silver, gold, lead, and other goods.

Mary Sutherland, in her history *The Story of Corpus Christi*, tells of an Anglo-American, the sole survivor of a shipwreck on Padre Island in 1824, who said that several Mexican families lived on the beach and followed the smuggling trade. However, John J. Linn, early day trader and colonist, tells in *Reminiscenses of Fifty Years in Texas* of spending a week on a schooner in the bay in 1829 without seeing anybody except Indians until two Mexicans from Camargo appeared. He mentions no residences or town.

The following year, 1830, some 20 Mexican troops refused to allow Linn to land his cargo at Corpus Christi, because there was no customshouse on the lower coast. Instead he took it through the customshouse at Goliad and sold it in Victoria. The same year General Manuel de Mier y Terán, commander of the Interior Provinces of the East stationed at Matamoros, suggested that frontier towns and forts be established along the Nueces to "wipe out the Lipans." Terán was also worried about the flood of Anglo-American immigrants. He recommended that immigration from adjoining countries be eliminated. The unstable Mexican government ordered the flow of colonists from the United States stopped, but the rule was never obeyed and was abolished three years later.

The congress of the Mexican state of Tamaulipas, competing with the state of Coahuila for control of the Texas territory, proposed that *poblaciones*, or settlements, be established at the mouth of the Nueces. Generous offers were made to attract settlers, but none came. European efforts to establish settlements also met with little success. Dutch nobleman Baron Johan von Raknitz attempted to establish a colony of Germans on the Nueces in 1838, but a French blockade and a shipwreck thwarted his plans.

An ardent American abolitionist, Benjamin Lundy applied to establish a colony on Corpus Christi Bay for free slaves. His efforts failed from a lack of funds. John Purnell and Benjamin Drake Lovell, two U.S. citizens living in Mexico, received a grant in 1825 to settle families on the Nueces, but Purnell fell overboard and drowned at Matamoros while boarding the schooner that was to take him to Corpus Christi.

Stephen F. Austin and the other empresarios passed through the Nueces Strip many times on trips to the Coahuila state capital at Saltillo. None seemed impressed with the country, for their people were tillers of the soil and the grasslands looked dry and inhospitable for homes, farms, and towns. Most of the empresarios' attention was addressed to the area west of the Nueces.

General Terán apparently favored a line of settlements and forts along the western border of the river—a buffer zone against further American encroachment. The Mexicans thought that two colonies of Irish Catholics along the western border of the river, located there by chance, would also be a buffer.

They were wrong.

Irishmen Colonize the Wilderness

The Lipan Apache warriors looked ferocious, and the little band of Irish colonists was terrified. The colonists had never imagined a country like this, with wolves and other wild animals, and painted savages. Empresario John McMullen, who had organized the men into a militia unit, ordered them to show their muskets. The Lipans were not frightened. They made strange cries and threatened to let their arrows fly. McMullen told Captain Kelly to fire the cannon. The explosion sent the Indians flying.

The experience had a depressing effect on the colony McMullen and James McGloin were trying to start. John McMullen had immigrated from Ireland to the United States, then to Matamoros, where he became a merchant. James McGloin, who had missed a boat to Australia, met McMullen at an English port, accompanied him back to Mexico, and became his partner. McMullen and McGloin, later to be McMullen's son-in-law, received an empresario contract in 1828 to introduce 200 families along the left bank of the Nueces River. They personally accompanied the first 58 families, landing in October 1829. The colonists wanted to stay near the crumbling mission of Our Lady of Refuge, which was originally established off Goff Bay in Calhoun County in 1793 but was removed to Refugio in 1794 by the Franciscan Order. It was only 16 miles from the port at Copano if they had to flee by sea.

Christmas of 1829 was a miserable time. The immigrants were homesick for their country, even if they had been hungry there. By spring many had deserted and sailed for New Orleans. Some wouldn't leave the mission. Others followed the empresarios into the wilderness to establish San Patricio de Hibernia on October 24, 1830, on the site of Martin De León's old Santa Margarita Ranch. Within the year a church would be built there.

By 1834 San Patricio was becoming a stable colony. Crops were good. There were wild cattle, game, fish, and clear water. For the first time the Irish began to see the beauty of the new land and feel a sense of belonging to it.

Above left: General Don Manuel Mier y Terán led the Mexican *Comisión de Límites,* an expedition into Texas. With a staff including a small corps of scientists and the artist José María Sánchez y Tapia, the *Comisión* collected data on the geography, natural resources, and wildlife of Texas, as well as on the customs of the Indians. After the expedition, in 1829 Terán led Mexican troops to repel the attempted Spanish reconquest of Mexico. From the Windsor Archives

Above right: Stephen F. Austin was a central figure in the history of Texas. Establishing a colony of Anglo-American settlers in Texas, Austin acted as liaison with the Mexican authorities. After he had been falsely arrested and imprisoned, he fought in the Texas Revolution (which had already begun) and served as one of three commissioners seeking the United States' recognition of the Republic of Texas. From the Windsor Archives

Lipanes.

Lipans Du Texas inférieur et des rives du Rio Grande.

Above: This is Empresario James McGloin's second home near old San Patricio at Round Lake. Now owned by the Corpus Christi Area Heritage Society, it combines the Neoclassical elegance of columns with dormer windows. Courtesy, Corpus Christi Caller-Times

Top: Dougherty house is at Round Lake near old San Patricio. Rachel Sullivan Dougherty and Robert Francis Dougherty conducted an academy on the second floor and later taught at Hidalgo Seminary in Corpus Christi. Courtesy, Bill Walraven

Above: The Merriman-Bobys house was built of hand-sawed native lumber in 1851 on land from the original Spanish land grant of 1831. It was used as a hospital during the Civil War and the 1867 yellow fever epidemic. The house was on South Broadway. Courtesy, Corpus Christi Caller-Times

But the year was one of horror for another group of colonists from Ireland, who left Liverpool shortly after Christmas 1833. Empresarios James Power and Dr. James Hewetson had acquired territory stretching from the Guadalupe to the Nueces. Hewetson, a young Irish medical doctor, had met Stephen F. Austin in New Orleans on Austin's first trip to Texas in 1821 and joined the party. He continued on to Saltillo, Mexico, married a wealthy widow, and engaged in mining and mercantile activities there. He formed a partnership with Power, another Irish emigré, in Mexico in 1826 to establish a colony in Texas. Their grant adjoined the land of the San Patricio Irish, which was up the Nueces.

Power appealed to relatives, friends, and neighbors to join him. The climate was "delightful," he said, and "gold is so plentiful you can pick it up under the trees." Their ship *Prudence* was pounded by storms and arrived in New Orleans in the midst of a cholera epidemic in which people died so fast they could only be buried in trenches. The colonists departed for Copano. The schooner ran aground inside the Aransas Pass bar. Cholera broke out and the dead were thrown overboard.

Rosalie B. Hart Priour wrote that her father nursed the sick and buried the dead until he, too, became ill. He had a short walk on the promised land, and died.

There we were, [Mrs. Priour wrote,] in a strange country, thousands of miles from our friends and relations, on a sand beach exposed to the burning heat of summer or drenched by rain . . . surrounded by wild animals, not knowing the minute we would be drowned. Then there were thousands of naked savages even more to be dreaded than the wild beasts, and a company of Mexican soldiers on guard for the purpose of preventing us from moving from that place under two weeks time for fear we would spread the cholera.

Some of the earlier colonists were still at the mission, which had walls two feet thick.

The inside was the richest I have ever seen in my travels. The railing in front of the altar had a band of silver all along the banister . . . there was a statue of the Blessed Virgin with the infant Jesus in her arms and I think it was all gold . . . a shame that the space that would accommodate the congregation was filled with corn by the Mexicans.

Within weeks most of the colonists were ill, and many would die of dysentery. The Hart family was taken in by the Robinsons on Papalote Creek, 35 miles from Refugio. There they were happy until they had to abandon ripening fields of corn because Tonkawa

Indians had become hostile.

It seemed that the Irish had weathered the worst, yet another wave of misfortune was about to engulf them. Mexican relations with the Irish had been good, and the Irish were too busy to worry about the brewing revolt in the colonies. When General Perfecto de Cos appeared in September 1835 with 500 troops, some Irish welcomed him enthusiastically. Others were distressed at such a display of power.

Refugio Irish were active against the Mexicans in the taking of Goliad and Fort Lipantitlan. The jailing of two Irish messengers prompted Irishmen to volunteer in the Texas cause. They signed the Goliad Declaration of Independence and marched under the Irish Flag of Texas Independence.

San Patricians, formerly indifferent to the aims of Texas, abandoned the Mexican cause when they abandoned their homes as General José Urrea's army approached. Destroyed in the battles, both Refugio and San Patricio had volunteers with Fannin, with whom 14 Irishmen died. Eleven Irishmen died in the Alamo and several fought in the Battle of San Jacinto.

Some of the refugees of the two destroyed towns settled near Victoria, some in East Texas, others in Louisiana, and a few in the Rio Grande Valley. McMullen said later "some men in this place disaffected to our cause, but I am happy to say their number was small. On hearing of Santa Anna's defeat, they fled after doing all the injury possible. The conduct of these men gave a bad name to the place and was the cause of many men suffering . . . ."

The Irish had paid a high price for their citizenship. Refugio and San Patricio counties were among the first created following the revolution, appropriately enough on St. Patrick's Day, March 17, 1837.

Texians Struggle for Independence

The early skirmishes of the Texas Revolution were easy victories achieved at slight loss. However, when the Mexicans would return, their sting would be deadly.

One early Mexican stronghold was Fort Lipantitlan, 25 miles from the mouth of the Nueces, across from San Patricio. With its earthen embankments and dirt-covered timbers, it was to John Linn "a second-rate hog pen." Captain Nicolas Rodrigues, commander of Fort Lipantitlan, confiscated San Patricio's cannon, stirring up the Irish colonists as those at Gonzales had been when a Mexican patrol demanded their little cannon. The Gonzales colonists had fought off the Mexicans, firing the first shots of the revolution on October 2, 1835.

Texians under command of George Collinsworth took Goliad on October 10. While the Mexicans were en route to retake Goliad, Phillip Dimmitt, who had taken command at Goliad, sent Ira Westover and his men, who captured Fort Lipantitlan without firing a shot on November 4. Irishman James O'Reilly persuaded the 21-man garrison to surrender, freeing five prisoners, four Irishmen and an Englishman.

Captain Rodrigues heard of Westover's move and returned to the fort from his march toward Goliad with 80 men, including several San Patricio residents. The Texians, using the Nueces River bank and timber for cover, repulsed the Mexicans, who charged across an open field. The Mexicans suffered 28 casualties. Among the Mexican wounded were the Irish alcalde, judge, and sheriff of San Patricio. The Texians' only casualty was a man who lost three fingers while loading his musket.

Under a flag of truce, the Mexican wounded were treated at San Patricio the next day. Lieutenant Marcellino García, second in command at the fort and a friend of many of the Texians, died of his wounds. Most of the Mexican garrison retreated to Matamoros to return in February as scouts for General José Urrea's forces.

The Irish were divided in their loyalties. They cared little for the Anglo-Saxons, but they supported the liberal Constitution of 1824, placing them in opposition to Antonio López de Santa Anna's Centralist government. Mexico had no tradition of strong local government. It had no concept of rule by the people and no electorate in the Anglo-Saxon context. But Mexico did make a pretext of having a republic. The Federalists' Constitution of 1824 was a rough copy of the United States model, although it made no provision for trial by jury or for religious freedom. A democratic republic could never exist with opposition from the large landowners, the clergy, and the army. The Federalists continued the struggle for a Mexican democracy, but the Centralists prevailed.

Many of the colonists, however, were content to function as Mexican citizens so long as they were left alone to practice their traditions. There was a considerable peace party that hoped to continue under Mexican rule. Among the native Texas Mexican population, many retained their liberal beliefs and fought alongside the Texians at the Alamo and at San Jacinto. Others joined forces with the invading Mexican armies and tracked down many of the Texian escapees from Refugio, San Patricio, Goliad, and Victoria.

Capture of Fort Lipantitlan prevented the Mexican recapture of Goliad and interfered with the communication with General Perfecto de Cos at San Antonio de Bexar, contributing to the fall of Bexar on December 10, 1835. The Mexicans had been driven out of Texas. The Texians and the Tejanos (Texas Mexicans) planned an expedition to Matamoros, which they felt would inspire the other Federalists to resist Santa Anna's Centralist government. They still had hopes of remaining a Mexican state, for they were too few and too scattered to resist an invasion by a major army.

But events had already forced the issue. Santa Anna was eliminating the liberals in Mexico, and the war radicals in Texas were now joined by moderates who saw no other choice but to fight. Santa Anna was able to convince even his enemies that the Texians were out to steal Mexican territory. Mexicans, Centralists and the liberal Federalists alike, were united in their distrust of United States' intentions after U.S. Ambassador Joel R. Poinsett ineptly attempted to purchase Texas. President John Quincy Adams, who believed that the Louisiana Purchase extended to the Rio Grande, had sent Poinsett to offer Mexico one million dollars for Texas in 1825. Andrew Jackson had raised the ante to $5 million. Both efforts had insulted Mexican pride and widened the gap between the two cultures.

The clash may have been inevitable. The Americans had a long history of self-government. They abhorred the military enforcement of civil law, the garrisoning of troops among them, unreasonable taxation, church influence in government, and sudden enforcement of laws after long laxity. The complaints were similar to those colonists had made against England in 1776. And the American frontiersmen bowed to no one, a trait that would cost them dearly as they fought among themselves as Santa Anna marched. The government was paralyzed by dissension.

Sam Houston managed to convince most of the 450 volunteers who had arrived at Goliad not to march on Matamoros. But Francis W. Johnson and Dr. James Grant wouldn't give it up. They had stripped the Alamo of its supplies for the venture, leaving its defenders short of food, shot, and powder.

Johnson was caught asleep at San Patricio at 3 a.m. on February 27, 1836, with no pickets posted, by General Urrea, who arrived unexpectedly after a long, forced march from Matamoros. Ten of Johnson's men were killed and 18 captured. Five, including Johnson, escaped. Dr. Grant was surprised by Mexican cavalry as his men herded wild horses at Agua Dulce Creek on March 2.

Antonio López de Santa Anna, dictator of Mexico and bloody victor at the Alamo, was captured at the Battle of San Jacinto on April 21, 1836. After Texas had thus gained independence, Santa Anna retired, only to be called back to duty. He led troops against, and was defeated by, American forces under Generals Taylor and Scott during the Mexican War. His dictatorial regimes in Mexico finally ended with the 1854 revolution. From the Windsor Archives

Grant and 13 of his men were killed.

As he prepared to retreat from the advancing Mexican army, Colonel James Fannin sent Amon B. King from Goliad to evacuate Refugio and San Patricio residents. Attacked by local rancheros near Refugio, King sent for help. Lieutenant Colonel William Ward and 100 men came to his aid and drove off the attackers. But King pursued them and was captured by Urrea. Captain King and most of his men were shot. Ward fought Urrea and escaped to Victoria, where he was captured by Urrea's men. The indecisive Fannin made a fatal delay in waiting for King and Ward, and his army was surrounded, cut off from water, and forced to surrender at Coleto Creek. Although Urrea opposed the executions, Fannin, Ward, and 352 other men were shot to death by order of Santa Anna on March 27, 1836, three weeks after the fall of the Alamo.

Eighty-six Tennessee volunteers escaped massacre after they were captured at Copano, just after the Battle of Coleto Creek. After being cooped up aboard ship for several days, they dived into the water, swam and frolicked their way to the beach, into the hands of the Yucatan Battalion. Santa Anna's decree had stated that any foreigners bearing arms were to be shot. General Urrea spared them because they were not carrying weapons when they waded ashore.

Meanwhile, families of colonists fled before the bloody invasion in the famous Runaway Scrape. The countryside was empty and Mexican troops looted homes that had not been burned.

Santa Anna reaped the rewards of the bloodletting, however, as 918 Texians attacked his at least 1,300-man army at San Jacinto on April 21 with a devastating frenzy. He was captured and ordered his armies to retreat beyond the Rio Grande. His men suffered on the retreat from lack of supplies. At the same time three Mexican ships were captured at Copano in a comic affair that was to give Major Isaac Burton's mounted rangers the nickname "horse marines."

Major Burton signaled the first Mexican ship to send a boat ashore. The Texians waylaid the crew, rowed out, and captured the ship. Using the captain as a decoy, they captured the other two ships. The vessels were taken to Velasco, where the provisions were distributed among the hungry Texian soldiers, who were on the verge of mutiny. The "horse marines," some of them from San Patricio, may have prevented an uprising that would have destroyed the young republic.

The Mexican army straggled through Nueces County as it made its tortuous way home. It stopped at San Patricio and Colonel José Enrique de la Peña entered the dateline "Corpus Christi" into his journal on June 2, 1836. That day Texians who had been held prisoner in Matamoros were returned.

Two natives appeared "saying those [Mexican] families who could not follow the army . . . are being forced by the enemy to go toward Victoria after being deprived of their oxen, beasts of burden, carriages, and arms," De la Peña said. "I urged them to complain to the commander-in-chief with the greatest possible force about their experiences, but I have purposely chosen to ignore the outcome, for the ill-fated agreement [Santa Anna's surrender] provides no guarantees for Mexicans."

As the beaten army limped across the Rio Grande, the entire Nueces Strip was left unpopulated. There was danger to any who would enter. It was truly a no-man's land and no place for the faint of heart.

The Land Belongs to No One

As the Texas Revolution ended, there was no need for a program to tell the good guys from the bad along the Nueces. They were nearly all bad. Mexico was convulsed by a series of revolutions. The government of the infant Republic of Texas was teetering on the brink of bankruptcy. Neither was able to police the borderland.

Texians, because of the agreement with Santa Anna to remove his troops beyond the Rio Grande, assumed that river to be the border. Mexico, which never ratified the agreement, believed the boundary to be the Nueces, and that only until the border could be permanently established at the Sabine.

Keeping the peace was left to volunteer companies on both sides of the no-man's land. The first order of business when such companies were organized was to establish the guidelines for dividing any booty they might capture. In effect, the ranging companies became legalized pirate bands. Many continued to rob and kill free-lance after they were officially disbanded.

The first "Cow Boys" were outlaws whose specialty was stealing horses and cows. Mexicans drove Texas cows south and Texians drove Mexican (and Texian) cows north. And Indians terrorized them all. Trading was prohibited by both governments as a traitorous activity. But the lure of gold and silver from Mexico in exchange for cloth, tobacco, and manufactured goods was an incentive too strong to resist. Caravans of traders were pillaged indiscriminately by outlaws from both countries.

This young Texan posed in what probably was his finest suit of clothes. Those were dangerous times; he also sports a pistol, a dagger, and a rifle. From Anna J. Hardwicke Pennybacker, *A History of Texas*

Texas adventurers, offered pay and spoils in Mexico, marched in the Federalist cause without sanction of the Texas government. The Federalists were very close to winning a revolution when the tide turned and their cause failed. Enlisting Texians was not popular in Mexico, and politicians made great propaganda of it. When the politicians wanted to draw attention away from their failures, they called for punitive expeditions into Texas.

Raids from one side or the other brought retaliatory attacks. The 350-man Santa Fe Expedition was ordered by President Mirabeau B. Lamar to establish jurisdiction over territory the Texas Congress claimed in 1836, to open a more favorable trade route to New Mexico, and to win popularity Lamar so desperately desired. The wagon train left a camp north of Austin on June 19, 1841. Lamar did not win his popularity, because the starving, thirsty survivors of Indian attacks were easily captured by forces of New Mexico Governor Manuel Armijo. The prisoners were treated brutally as they were sent in bondage to Mexico.

Citizens and the Texas Congress were furious at Lamar because such an expedition had been discussed but never approved by the congress. Only because his term expired was the president saved from impeachment for exceeding his authority. Lamar had wanted to force Mexico to recognize Texas' independence, even if it took war to accomplish it.

The expedition merely served to convince Mexicans that the Anglos had further designs on their territories. Mexican forays into Texas included the capture of San Antonio by General Adrian Woll and raids on San Patricio, Refugio, and Goliad. Texians countered with the ill-advised Mier Expedition in 1842, which ended in the capture of the Texians who were not killed.

Captain Enrique de Villareal, former commandant of Fort Lipantitlan, commanded a troop out of Matamoros that eliminated several groups of cowboys in the Nueces Strip. He had Spanish and Mexican grants for land on which Corpus Christi now stands. Villareal had vacated the land earlier because of Indian attacks. Late in 1839 he located a squatter on his land—another adventurer, Colonel Henry L. Kinney.

After a confrontation with Villareal, Kinney agreed to buy one league of land from him and take an option on nine other leagues stretching from the Oso to the Nueces. The agreement was reached January 14, 1840. Kinney was the first Anglo-American to establish a foothold west of the Nueces. In so doing, he founded a community and vastly influenced the history of Texas, Mexico, and the United States.

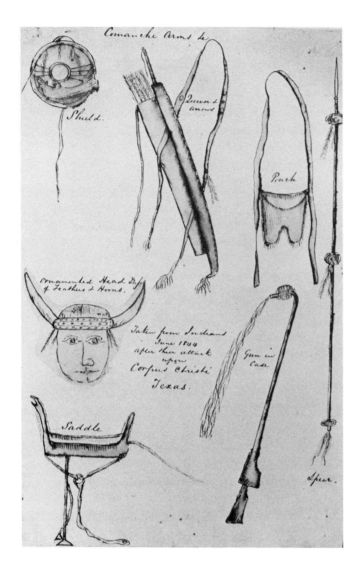

Above left: The Comanches were being slowly pushed out of their land, and they retaliated by sending small parties of their young warriors to harass the settlements from Red River to Corpus Christi. William Bollaert sketched these objects that were captured from a Comanche war party that raided Corpus Christi in June 1844. From the Edward E. Ayer collection. Courtesy, The Newberry Library, Chicago

Above right: A colonel he never was, but that title has always been associated with Henry Lawrence Kinney. Kinney served in the Mexican War, enlisting as a private and then serving General Zachary Taylor as a quartermaster and courier. His other accomplishments included operating his famous trading post, promoting Corpus Christi—as a route to the California gold fields and, in Europe, as "Naples of the Gulf"—to attract settlers, and serving as state senator and state representative. Many of his business ventures failed, and Kinney was deeply in debt when he died. Courtesy, La Retama Library

Colonel Henry L. Kinney's Town

Central plazas in many cities are dominated by a statue of their founding father. Look as you will, you will find no statue of Corpus Christi's founder, Henry Lawrence Kinney.

A founder should be a heroic figure. Kinney desperately wanted to be such a figure. He faced physical danger bravely, was intelligent, and was a leader, but his character was flawed by moral weaknesses that were to deprive him of the heroic image. He projected himself as a suave, swashbuckling gentleman who was also something of a lady killer. Failure, however, would dog him all his life. After each failure, he launched a new and more daring venture that would bring him to the depths of even greater failure.

Hortense Warner Ward, who made an exhaustive study of Kinney's life but died before completing the biography, dispelled many of the popular myths surrounding the man. For example, Kinney was never a real colonel. He never signed his name with the title, but he never discouraged its use. It apparently came from the Black Hawk Indian Wars in the Midwest although he did not participate in them. He also did not fight in the Seminole Wars in Florida or filibuster in Cuba as claimed by various biographers.

Born in Bradford County, Pennsylvania, in 1814, Kinney worked in his father's store from the age of 10. At 19, involved in a scandal with a townswoman, he left home. By 1835 he was in Peru, Illinois, an accomplished and glib promoter, dealing in land sales in conjunction with the construction of the Illinois-Michigan Canal. He was worth a fortune on paper, but the transactions were in scrip. As financial panic threatened, banks called in the paper, the canal project collapsed, and Kinney, faced with bankruptcy, headed south.

In Houston and Galveston Kinney met most of the important men of the new Republic of Texas. He knew Sam Houston, but sided politically with Maribeau B. Lamar. Kinney knew the family of Daniel Webster in Illinois as well as President Franklin Pierce, General Zachary Taylor, and many others. Quick of wit, Kinney had the knack of quickly making friends with strangers. Upon a single meeting he was able to convince Easterners to advance thousands of dollars to support his schemes. He liked the role of perfect host, was generous to friends and acquaintances, and habitually lived beyond his means.

Kinney opened a store on Live Oak Point in mid-1838 with his first partner, Alabaman William P. Aubrey. As a newcomer he led the citizens of Aransas City in opposing moving the customshouse to Lamar, an idea favored by President Lamar. The lure of quick profits in supplying the Mexican Federalist forces moved the partners to the shores of Corpus Christi Bay in September 1839. A crude shack housed the post until a permanent building was erected in December on the bluff. A ranch and fort was established near the Oso, guarded by a 12-pounder cannon and a private army of 30 to 60 men.

Early communications from the post were signed "Kinney's Rancho." But the Matagorda Bulletin referred to "The Port of Corpus Christi" and "Corpus Christi" in 1838, the latter concerning the possible location of a Mexican customshouse there. By 1841 Kinney was using "Kinney's Rancho at Corpus Christi," then "Corpus Christi Rancho," and finally, "Corpus Christi, Formerly Kinney's Rancho." Possibly "Corpus Christi" emerged as Kinney's standing with Texians hit a new low and he preferred a lower profile.

Kinney was the only "neutral" party in the disputed strip between the Nueces and the Rio Grande. He was a sort of double agent, supplying information to both sides. He was a confidant of President Lamar; yet he was in constant communication with General Mariano Arista of the Centralist party and commander in chief of the Northern Army of Mexico, as well as with Arista's Federalist opponents. As a result, some Texians began to voice suspicions of double dealings on Kinney's part.

One of these Texians, Phillip Dimmitt, wrote authorities and accused Kinney of treason. Dimmitt, a fomentor of the Texas Revolution, helped prepare the Goliad Declaration of Independence in 1835, was present at the capture of Goliad, and even designed a revolutionary flag. He was high on the Mexican "enemies list."

Lieutenant Vicente Sánchez and his troops captured Dimmitt at his newly established trading post on the Laguna Madre side of Padre Island on July 4, 1841. The blame for the capture was leveled at Kinney and Aubrey, since Kinney had been assured by Arista in June that his post would not be molested, and because Dimmitt was Kinney's personal, as well as business, opponent. In addition, at the time of the capture, the raiders visited Kinney's Rancho and were given food and whiskey for the journey back to Matamoros.

Dimmitt's capture threw Texas into an uproar and for a while there were outraged demands that the prisoners be released by force of arms. In the face of the wrath, Kinney promised President Lamar that he would go to Mexico to seek the prisoners' release as he had done for others. Kinney, however, never left his ranch. As Dimmitt and his captors headed for Mexico City,

This is the earliest known illustration, circa 1845, of the town of Corpus Christi. From John Frost, *Pictorial History of Mexico and the Mexican War.* Courtesy, University of Texas Institute of Texan Cultures, San Antonio

some of the prisoners escaped. The Mexicans threatened to shoot Dimmitt if the escapees did not return. Dimmitt committed suicide to prevent this from happening.

Kinney and Aubrey subsequently were tried for treason at Victoria and were acquitted. Kinney denied that he had engineered the capture. A witness said that Dimmitt had been warned of the Mexicans' approach, but had refused to take refuge at the Kinney Rancho. Dimmitt was not there to testify. There was some indication that President Lamar, not wishing to lose his observation post west of the Nueces, may have used his influence with the court.

The trading post at Corpus Christi survived numerous invasions by Mexicans, Indians, and renegade Americans. (Kinney himself was wounded in one desperate battle with Indians.) Despite the attacks, trade at the post flourished, a situation that was probably the result of Kinney's diplomacy. Years later Kinney said, "When Mr. Mexican came, I treated him with a great deal of politeness, particularly if he had me in his power. When Mr. American came, I did the same with him, and when Mr. Indian came, I was also very frequently disposed to make a compromise with him."

Kinney's business judgment, however, was not always sound. He purchased the land near the bay from one owner, then had to buy it again from Captain Enrique de Villareal. Years later another promoter would get a court judgment against the same property, claiming still another prior owner, and landowners were forced to pay for their own property again. Kinney amassed vast blocks of land, but was unable to hold them. He mortgaged property for loans and sometimes mortgaged it again without the knowledge of the first lien holder.

In 1852 he held the first fair in Texas, ostensibly as a land promotion to attract colonists. He personally provided financing, advertising, and the ballyhoo for the project. Some historians believe the show was a mere scam to promote another revolution for the Republic of the Rio Grande, a scheme to form a new country from states of Northern Mexico. (Kinney favored revolution, for fortune smiled at him only during times of war.) Although the fair was a financial disaster for Kinney, the

20,000 handbills he sent out all over the world did succeed in attracting a great many European colonists to settle near Nuecestown. But his creditors began to press. John P. Schatzell, his principal financial backer, died, and payment on some $60,000 in debts was demanded.

The gold rush of 1849 had brought an influx of people, whom Kinney outfitted, but the gold fever also caused a drop in population. In 1851 he founded a hide and tallow plant on Corpus Christi Beach with Clement P. Hopson and others. It failed, too. It was 50 years ahead of its time.

Kinney decided to recoup his fortune in a filibustering expedition to Nicaragua in 1854. There he was shipwrecked and again showed his bravery, but once more he faced failure on a grand scale. He returned to Corpus Christi physically ill and with a heavy reliance on brandy, which did not improve his state. He was welcomed home by Corpus Christians, who elected him to the state legislature.

As the Civil War approached, Kinney again saw an opportunity for riches. He offered his services to Abraham Lincoln. Getting no answer, he made the same offer to Jefferson Davis with the same result. He saw a chance to recoup his fortune in war trade, resigned from the legislature in 1861, and moved to Matamoros, where he found death instead of wealth. Still the romantic, he went to pay a social call at 3 a.m. He was met, not by his ladylove, but by two blasts from a pistol. He died on March 3, 1862, and was buried in an unmarked grave.

War profiteer or patriot? Politician or double-dealer? Rascal or prince? Promoter or swindler? Whatever Kinney was, he did lay out a townsite, encourage European settlers, promote Corpus Christi all over the world, dredge a channel to allow ocean-draft schooners to enter the bay, lobby for railroads, vote (as a Texas congressman) for annexation to the United States, and above all, establish a Texas beachhead in a disputed territory.

No monument was erected over his grave and none marks his achievements in the city he founded. He wanted only to be an important man. And he probably was. The City of Corpus Christi is Henry Lawrence Kinney's monument.

A City is Born

Colonel Henry Lawrence Kinney's toehold on Corpus Christi Bay was at best a precarious one. His post was subject to raids by Texas freebooters who ran off with his "Mexican" cattle, Mexican troops who suspected him of harboring border pirates, and Indians who didn't care whom they raided. Kinney even had been jailed for a time by Mexican authorities who suspected he was a Texian spy. He had used his influence to free Texian prisoners.

He appealed to President Mirabeau B. Lamar for help when adventurers took over his fort. He complained to President Sam Houston when volunteers sent to protect the fort took supplies and weapons and deserted. Kinney and Aubrey abandoned the post in 1842 in the face of growing Mexican raids. Sam Houston urged them to return as they represented the only physical claim Texas had to the Nueces Strip. And Kinney was Houston's only reliable source as to Mexican movements.

In June 1844 an English traveler, William Bollaert, said of Kinney's post:

On May 27 this place was visited by 25 Lipans to steal horses, etc. [They] wounded Col. Cooke thro the eye. There were only eight men at the Rancho. Thirty went in pursuit. Ten came upon and recaptured the horses, killed and wounded five Indians. Indians pursued. Then came a desperate fight. Three of our party killed, five wounded. Twenty of the Indians killed and wounded.

In 1853 three lots were purchased from Henry L. Kinney to construct the first county courthouse. In the 1870s a second courthouse, right, was added next to the first; the first was then used as a jury room. The second courthouse was sometimes called the "Hollub" courthouse for the civil engineer who designed it. On the far left is the jail. All three structures were torn down to build the 1914 Courthouse. Courtesy, La Retama Library

Of the settlement he said:

At the present there are 30 to 40 fighting men, a few cannon and Col. Kinney's house fortified. It is supplied with water from a spring, the course of which is dammed up, a presa, or reservoir, and Col. K's plantation makes a good shew of Indian corn, pumpkins, melons, sweet potatoes, beans, tomatoes, chiltipins and sea-island cotton . . . Generally there is a want of streams, but in the valleys or gullies of the lomas are springs . . . and in the vicinity good crops can be obtained.

The town in embryo called 'Grayson' one mile northwest, was laid off on paper only, Corpus Christi being the only settlement. There are some half dozen American stores, including a German and a grog shop or two. All appear to be on good terms with each other.

(Peter William Grayson was a candidate for Texas president when the area was surveyed in 1838. Another surveyor named Live Oak Point "Lamar." Grayson committed suicide and Mirabeau Lamar was elected without opposition. Lamar rewarded his namesake town with a customshouse. Had Grayson lived and been elected, Corpus Christi could have been named Grayson.)

By the early 1840s annexation of Texas had become the center of a bitter struggle in the United States. Some did not want to give slave states a balance of power in Congress. Others feared that annexation would bring war with Mexico. The slave states welcomed Texas, while expansionists believed that God willed the United States to cover the continent. President John Tyler negotiated an annexation treaty with Texas in April 1844. In June the Senate rejected it.

Texas became a Presidential election issue that cost Martin Van Buren the Democratic nomination, to dark-horse James K. Polk. In the general election Polk defeated Whig Henry Clay, an opponent of annexation. Lame duck President Tyler saw this as a mandate from the people and placed the annexation issue before Congress.

Tyler argued that Britain would get Texas if the United States did not. Annexation was approved by joint resolution, an unorthodox maneuver.

Texas President Anson Jones called a special convention to decide the issue. Annexation was overwhelmingly approved on July 4, 1845. Henry L. Kinney was a delegate.

On July 31 American general and Indian fighter Zachary Taylor, under orders from Secretary of War William L. Marcy, landed at Corpus Christi. For a few months, the eyes of the world were on a place that suddenly became a town. Here Old Glory flew over Texas soil officially for the first time. Corpus Christi was on the map as the springboard to the Mexican War.

America Takes the Nueces Strip

The Mexican War has been called the least justified but the most materially rewarding war in United States history. Arguments against the war were heated, some sounding as if they were written at the height of the Vietnam War 125 years later. Lieutenant Colonel Ethan Allen Hitchcock, one of the first soldiers to land in Corpus Christi with Zachary Taylor's army, said, "My heart is not in this business. I am against it from the bottom of my soul as a most unholy and unrighteous proceeding. But, as a military man, I am bound to execute orders." An Ohio editor wrote, "The devil has governed and guided all our actions."

The war had popular support despite heavy newspaper opposition to it. Henry Clay termed it "unnatural and lamentable." Daniel Webster said it was "unconstitutional in its origin." Both were to lose sons in the conflict.

But to troops landing on the pleasant beach, Corpus Christi was a vacation spa. Young Lieutenant George Gordon Meade praised the cooling breezes and the beautiful bathing surf at the edge of the beach campground. The soldiers feasted on oysters, crabs, fish, turtle, and shrimp. Their only complaints were about the brackish water and the lack of firewood. The wood shortage grew acute with a cold, wet winter when the tents leaked and the men could not keep dry. Even the most elementary sanitary procedures were ignored and soon the entire camp was one vast hospital filled with troops suffering from dysentery.

The little village of fewer than 200 souls had owed much of its existence to supplying military ventures of one sort or another in Mexico. Now catering to the needs and whims of 3,000 soldiers became the business of a town suddenly grown to 2,000 civilians. Saloons, bordellos, gambling houses, and an opera house were soon in operation. Samuel Bangs, pioneer printer and newspaperman of both Texas and Mexico, established the *Corpus Christi Gazette* with General Taylor's blessing.

Hitchcock said, "Kinney seems to have a government of his own here. While an object of suspicion to both Texans and Mexicans, he seems to be regarded as a man of power by both sides and capable of serving both sides. He seems to have no concealments, but frankly declares that the Texans have no right to go (or claim) to the Rio Grande . . ."

Hitchcock was the founder of Old Bayview Cemetery, resting place of many of the city's prominent pioneers. He wrote:

Yesterday Sept. 12, 1845 brought us a disaster. A small old steamer, the Dayton, employed for a few days by the government, burst her boiler a few miles from here near McGloin's Bluff [Ingleside] and killed seven men and wounded 17 (three others died the next day). . . .

Sept. 14. A military funeral took place today at the burial ground which I selected. It is on the brow of the hill northwest of the camp and commands a view of the Nueces and Corpus Christi Bay. It is a beautiful spot. . . .

Of camp life, he said, "New Year's Day, 1846. Mild and balmy. The day will go as other days—drinking, horse-racing, gambling, theatrical amusements. A ball is advertised for this evening in Corpus Christi. . . . There are no ladies here and very few women. I take no part in the amusements or dissipations of the place. . . ."

There were rumors and alarms of a Mexican attack. Taylor had been ordered to take a position near the Rio Grande, but the mouth of that river was too treacherous for a sea landing. One hundred and fifty miles away, Corpus Christi was the nearest settlement. And it was within the disputed territory. Taylor refused to march to the Rio Grande until he received direct orders to that effect. So he bided his time and reconnoitered the land and water passages for the move to the south.

Taylor's army was joined by Texas Ranger volunteers. Their lack of military bearing and manners was abrasive to the army professionals, but the Texans taught the officers and their men to ride. Colonel James Love said of them: "The feats of horsemanship of our frontiersmen are most extraordinary. I saw one of them pick up from the ground three dollars, each 50 yards apart, at full speed, and pass under the horse's neck at a pace not much short of full speed."

Some of the 250 officers in the camp were later to win fame in various commands of the Civil War. Two, Ulysses S. Grant and Zachary Taylor, were to become U.S. Presidents. Others who would rise to prominence included Don Carlos Buell, Braxton Bragg, Joseph Hooker, Albert Sidney Johnston, James Longstreet, John Bankhead Magruder, Kirby Smith, and George B. Thomas. Before the war's end, 5,000 Texans would be among the 78,000 Americans participating in the war. Texas Governor J. Pinckney Henderson took leave to command two Texas regiments of infantry and two of cavalry.

On March 8, 1846, Taylor and his army began the march from Corpus Christi to the Rio Grande. He ordered the civilian population of camp followers to stay behind. If they didn't follow, they didn't stay in Corpus Christi. The town was nearly a ghost town.

The army would march on to victory because of its superior weapons and gunpowder, and its revolutionary use of mobile artillery. Most important, leadership from among the 1,000 graduates of the U.S. Military Academy at West Point was the world's best. The Army defeated a nation that had wallowed in anarchy and pillage since the revolution against Spain. The Mexican soldier fought bravely in a number of battles, but he was outgunned and was a victim of poor leadership.

Henry Bamford Parkes, author of *A History of Mexico,* deplored the American action but concluded that the Treaty of Guadalupe Hidalgo, which ended the war and took 500,000 square miles of Mexican territory in exchange for $15 million and other considerations, "was bitterly resented in Mexico, but it had not deprived her of any territories over which she ever had any real control: their absorption into the United States must, sooner or later, have been inevitable."

Less than a month after General Taylor left Corpus Christi, the Texas Legislature passed an act saying, "that portion of San Patricio County lying between the Nueces and the Rio Grande is hereby incorporated into a county by the name of Nueces." The Nueces Strip—that rough,

Left: Before Texas was annexed to the United States, the treasury department of the Republic of Texas issued its own currency. The illustrations on this $20 bill suggest the dual relationship that settlers had with the neighboring Indians. The figure of Texas is at peace with the Indians, as illustrated in the upper right; and below is Texas armed for battle with the attacking Indian, who is poised on the left drawing his bow. From the Windsor Archives

Below: A petition was written, requesting new uniforms, by the officers of Zachary Taylor's troops, stationed in Corpus Christi in December 1845. The men were awaiting orders to move to Mexico. Of the 164 men who signed the petition 28 were killed (three later in the Civil War) and 79 were cited for gallantry. Some of the men who signed it were Ulysses S. Grant, Braxton Bragg, J.J. Reynolds, W.E. Merrill, T.L. Chadbourne, H. McKavett, John F. Reynolds, and J. Bankhead Magruder. Courtesy, Corpus Christi Museum

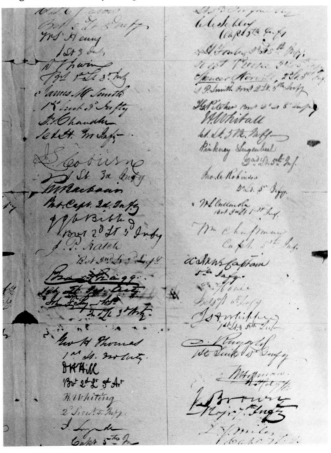

depopulated, lawless area — was now Nueces County. And Corpus Christi was soon to become the county seat of this vast district.

The town was all but dead. But there was a glimmer. The boom the Army had brought showed the way. With shipping and commerce, Corpus Christi could come back. The newborn city was weaned almost from its birth. It was now on its own.

The "Naples of the Gulf"

"Hustler of the Wilderness" was the way Tom Lea, chronicler of the history of the King Ranch, described Henry Lawrence Kinney. Indeed, a hustler and promoter was exactly what the town needed to survive, for the world soon forgot the exaggerated importance the Mexican War had placed on the mudhole that was Corpus Christi.

Kinney, a courier for Zachary Taylor, a staff officer for the Texas Command, a participant in the Battle of Monterrey and above all, an opportunist who could supply the needs of any army for a price, was home and ready to do business. He bought surplus Army wagons and parts for use in trade ventures he planned to Mexico and other Texas cities. Aided by partners in mercantile and maritime businesses, he was ready to make the fortune of his dreams, but few trade routes materialized and the town continued its dusty decline.

Kinney's failure in this venture might have come sooner had not gold been discovered in California. Companies were formed all over the country by men willing to pay for a chance to strike it rich. They wanted to get there quickly, and Kinney promised them the shortest route. The village again throbbed with activity as horse traders, blacksmiths, merchants, and others made wagon trains ready for the trip to the gold fields.

John H. Peoples, editor of Kinney's *Corpus Christi Star*, was Kinney's voice in advertising the gateway to the gold fields. He was so enthusiastic that he sold himself on making the trip. Peoples had won a measure of fame by sending firsthand dispatches from the Mexican battlefields. Newspapers across the country printed his stories. He was one of the first war correspondents.

Peoples also wrote accounts of his journey along the Southern Emigrant Road to California as he accompanied the second contingent known as "Kinney's Rangers." Unfortunately, he drowned in a boating accident in the Gulf of California.

Kinney knew that few of the gold seekers would

stay. The town lost population as permanent residents got gold fever. He advertised in Europe to attract colonists to the "Naples of the Gulf." He would sell land to any who would pay one dollar per acre for at least 100 acres and would buy 10 cows at $10 per head, a yoke of oxen, and a horse, payable on shares in 10 years. It was a good move, for by 1850 the gold rush had all but died out. But Kinney had land to sell, enough land to relocate entire nations. He acquired much of the land on December 3, 1849, with the aid of tax collector J. Benton Johnson and Sheriff William Rogers. Johnson declared taxes delinquent when they were as little as one year overdue. Then Sheriff Rogers sold the land at auction.

Many of the landowners, some issued bounties for service in the Texas Revolution, had never occupied their lands. Others, including grantees of Mexican and Spanish governments, had temporarily abandoned the land because of Indian and other depredations. Indian troubles got so bad that year that the governor stationed 225 Texas Rangers in Corpus Christi.

Sheriff Rogers announced the land sales at the courthouse door. Joseph W. Kinney, the colonel's brother, successfully bid for most of the vast acreages. Some of Kinney's friends (including the sheriff) were also successful bidders. Seventy-two cents purchased one 940-acre tract. Three dollars paid for one-third of a league of land. Kinney paid $26.77 for 3.8 leagues owned by Don Vicente Ynojosa. (Book D, Volume I in the Nueces County Deed Records lists hundreds of similar purchases.)

In 1850 Kinney was selling downtown lots for $350 each and his overseas advertisements had begun to pay dividends. The 1850 Nueces County Census showed that the town had 689 inhabitants living in 151 dwellings. There were no churches and no schools. More than half of the population was "born in Mexico." Of the others, 51 were from Germany, 32 were from Ireland, 53 were born in Texas, 47 were black slaves, and one was a freedman. The county had 108 more males than females, and 149 people were listed as illiterate. In 1852 immigration hit its peak and the community of Nuecestown was founded, near present-day Calallen, by settlers from Scotland, Wales, England, Ireland, and Germany.

The City of Corpus Christi recognizes 1852 as the year of its birth, for that was when the first City Council was elected and Benjamin F. Neal was installed as mayor. (Some argue that the founding date should be September 1839, when Aubrey and Kinney set up shop. Others say the city actually started with the arrival of Taylor's army on August 1, 1845. The first post office opened March 23, 1846, with Aubrey as postmaster.)

The city was created officially by an act of the legislature on April 18, 1846, "under the direction of Colonels H.L. Kinney and William Mann. The limits embraced a square of four miles fronting on Corpus

Christi and Nueces Bays," according to the first official city charter, in 1873. The first recorded ordinance was not passed until January 15, 1879. It prohibited hogs and goats from running at large in the city.

The town hit a growth streak in 1852. Red brick from clay in the bluffs was considered too expensive by most residents, so most of the city was built of wood imported by sea. The boom ended with the yellow fever epidemic of 1854. Entire families were wiped out as death touched practically every home in town. Later that year Kinney left, leaving the town leadership to others. By the mid-1850s, a school was in existence, but teachers were scarce, for they had trouble collecting their pay. Also, Catholic, Methodist, Presbyterian, and Episcopal churches were organized during the decade.

Frederick L. Olmsted's book about his Texas travels predicted that a great city would grow on the middle coast as the "sea gate to Western Texas." He mentioned as likely candidates Indianola, Lavaca, and Saluria. Olmsted could not foretell that hurricanes would someday rule out that section of Texas coast. The Army declined to locate a military depot in Corpus Christi or establish a military road to the city, largely because of the inaccessibility of deep water over the Aransas bar.

It wasn't that Corpus Christians weren't aware of the problem. Kinney had ordered a steam dredge as early as 1849. By 1857 the city had appropriated $50,000 for the project. Dredge operator Dean Howard was unable to complete the project, and it was turned over to a New York financial group that agreed to sell half a million dollars worth of bonds in exchange for the right to

Left: The W.S. Rankin grocery store was located at the corner of Mesquite and Peoples streets in the 1800s. Across Peoples Street and facing the Rankin store was the Furman building. Courtesy, La Retama Library

Below: Advertisements from the February 5, 1846, edition of the *Corpus Christi Gazette* give an interesting view of what life was like in Corpus Christi during the 19th century. Courtesy, Corpus Christi Area Heritage Society

Above: St. Patrick's Church, completed in 1880, was the second Catholic church in Corpus Christi with the same name. In 1912 the Corpus Christi diocese was created, and St. Patrick's was designated the cathedral. Courtesy, Daughters of the Republic of Texas Library at the Alamo, San Antonio

Right: These Corpus Christi residents from the 1800s seem to be ready for a stroll. Note the man's Prince Albert coat and bow tie, and the woman's wide, edged lapels, high collar, and feathered hat. Courtesy, Nueces County Historical Society

collect tolls on shipping. Colonel James Moore began the project anew, but it ended when Federal troops burned his dredge to the waterline.

The town was alarmed by rumors of an impending attack by Juan N. Cortina in 1859. It never materialized. Excitement also ran high over the possibility of a railroad to Mexico. It did not materialize either. By the close of the 1850s, transportation had become the major civic challenge for Corpus Christians. Without a channel, the sea gate to Western Texas would locate elsewhere.

War Clouds

As 1860 opened, few in Corpus Christi would have considered disunion. People were unhappy that the federal government had not helped dredge a channel. And they were dissatisfied with the government for its failure to provide protection on the frontier. But Corpus Christi was remote and the April 12, 1861, attack on Fort Sumter a faraway event.

The population at that time numbered 1,200, almost one-third of whom were foreign born. The county's prime income was from cattle and sheep raising. The town had three teachers, three preachers, and a priest; three shoemakers, two watchmakers, and a hearse driver; and 135 slaves with 35 owners. Many of the slaves had been leased or bought to work on the channel-dredging project.

The winter of 1859-1860 was one of the most severe on record. A number of people in the area died of the cold. By the middle of 1860 there was fear of slave uprisings. A local Castle of the Knights of the Golden Circle was formed. This group favored joining the Southern United States, Mexico, and Central America into a single nation supported by slavery.

As the secession issue grew hotter, most Corpus Christians sided with the South. Local women dressed and conducted a social life like that of the Southern aristocracy. Yet General Forbes Britton and his son-in-law, E.J. Davis, who would be the Reconstruction governor of Texas, spoke strongly in favor of preserving the Union.

Lincoln's election generally was decried in Corpus Christi, and in the vote for the legislature, Britton received only eight votes compared to 650 for P.N. Luckett and H.A. Maltby, both of whom were secessionists. Kinney, back in the legislature, opposed disunion. He resigned from the legislature, pleading ill health.

When secession was voted on in the Texas Legislature, a local meeting loudly ratified it. Dissenting voices were scarcely heard. Many of the foreign-born who didn't want to separate from the United States remained silent. Thomas Noakes, an early English settler who was commissioned a Confederate lieutenant, had his doubts. He wrote in his diary:

This Friday [in May 1861] brought very gloomy news to our community. The rumors are not by any means encouraging.

We are to be blockaded, bombarded and the deuce knows what not by the North. Cortina and his band from Brownsville are going to wipe us out. And Mexico is going to take Texas back again. After that the Indians will finish the rest of wives and children with the tomahawk. If only one of these rumors is correct, we have a poor chance to go on building homes and civilization in this county with only a minimum of food, no farm implements but homemade ones, and steers for ploughing and hauling, only! What if war has begun, and we are not prepared.

It had. And they weren't.

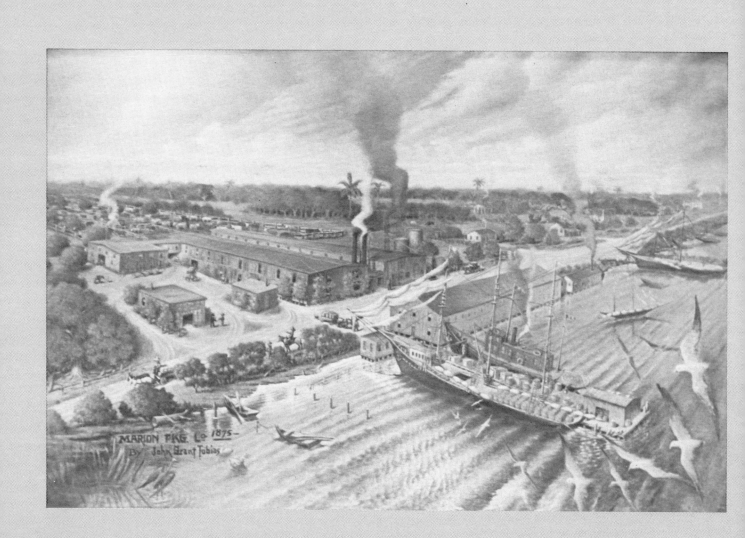

MARION PKG. Co 1875—
By John Brent Tobias

A Baptism

The Civil War soaked the battlefields of the nation with American blood; but in Corpus Christi, save for the suffering of the populace, its effects were relatively mild. Had it not been for the inconvenience of the Yankee blockade, a severe drought, and a couple of unusually frigid winters, the war might have been a lark.

The Battle of Corpus Christi is a case in point. When it was over, volunteer Lieutenant J.W. Kittredge was hailed in the New York press for a major Union victory in the capture of the city. At the same time Confederate Major A.M. Hobby was commended for driving off the Yankee fleet. The Corpus Christi *Ranchero*, in an extra edition dated August 19, 1862, trumpeted, "Bombardment of Corpus Christi; Major. A.M. Hobby Commands; Leads a Daring Charge; Gunboats Beaten! Victory!!"

In the battle a seaman was injured by a flying splinter when a cannonball hit the side of one of Lieutenant Kittredge's shallow-draft vessels, and another was wounded in the thigh by a rifle ball. Private Henry Mote of Captain R.E. Jones' company was killed when struck in the head by cannon grapeshot. Major Hobby himself was wounded slightly on the side of his head by another shot. Otherwise the battle was little more than a source of stories and anecdotes.

Lieutenant Kittredge had patrolled the Gulf for five months before deciding to attack Corpus Christi. His deep-draft bark, *Arthur*, could not enter the shallow bays where cotton, sugar, tobacco, lead, and other goods were being moved unmolested by the Union's Gulf blockade. He had burned and raided Mustang and San Jose islands by cutter but had escaped capture only by abandoning his boats and fleeing across San Jose Island to the safety of his ship. The blockade, however, was causing Corpus Christi acute shortages of many items, such as shoes and whiskey.

The war began to get serious shortly before Kittredge's attack, when four men from Captain Benjamin F. Neal's command on the shellbank of Harbor Island deserted and captured a sloop. One man escaped, another was killed while fleeing, and two others were captured, returned to Corpus Christi, and hanged. The war was losing its glamor.

Corpus Christi, as a village with 1,300 residents, was not important as a military objective. And Kittredge could not have expected to hold the town with his 100 sailors. However, historian Dan Kilgore believes that the true objective of the Union assault was a powder mill being established by George Pfeuffer. Kittredge also would have wanted to stop the flow of salt from Laguna Madre. (Before the end of the war, salt in the Confederacy was selling for $125 a sack.)

Kittredge forced Neal from his makeshift fort in July 1862. The Union commander captured and armed the *Belle Italia* and *Reindeer*. Reinforced by the racing yacht *Coryphus* and the coast-survey steamer *Sachem*, Kittredge was ready to attack. In a defensive maneuver the Confederates loaded three old hulks with chunks of concrete and rock and sank them in the channel entrance to the bay. The *Sachem* easily pulled them aside.

Once in the bay Kittredge chased the picketboat, *Breaker*, until it ran aground near Ingleside. The crew of the *Breaker* set it afire, but the Yankees extinguished the blaze and captured the vessel. According to one legend, the Rebels, in the excitement of the moment, dropped a

---

The Marion Packing Company, shown in this painting by John Grant Tobias, was one of a dozen or more packing companies that operated in the Fulton area immediately after the Civil War. After pickling, the beef was shipped to army warehouses or to ports throughout the world, much of it going to Central America. Ships came in through Aransas Pass, tied up at the packinghouse wharves, and loaded their cargos of hides, bones, horns, beef, and tallow. Courtesy, First National Bank of Rockport

sack of brown sugar into the bilge of the boat and carried a sack of gunpowder ashore, where they wondered why the fire had not set off an explosion.

Defending the town was Captain Neal's battery of smooth-bore cannon—an 18-pounder and a 12-pounder—facing the new rifled cannon on the Union gunboats. The Rebel gun crews had never fired the guns because they had had no powder with which to practice. They would learn the skills in battle.

Lieutenant Kittredge came ashore on August 13, 1862, under a flag of truce. He demanded to inspect Federal buildings. Major Hobby told him there was no Federal property. The Yankee announced that he would bombard the city and gave the Rebels 48 hours to evacuate women, children, and old people.

At daylight on August 15 the Confederates ended the truce with a salvo. They reloaded and fired again, and again, before the Yankees answered. Confederate combat veteran Billy Mann, home on sick leave, had advised Major Hobby to move the cannon from the bluff to the water's edge. The guns had been moved during the night to the breastworks built years earlier by Zachary Taylor's army. The Yankees were not expecting fire from such close range. Return fire sailed over or bounced off the reinforced sand and shell levee.

Felix von Blucher, who had been an artilleryman in Prussia and in the Mexican War, fired the first shot. He also gave the men instructions. One shot punched through the *Coryphus'* mainsail. Another crashed into the hull of the *Sachem*. Young Billy Mann stood atop the parapet in plain view of the enemy to direct fire and to warn of incoming shells. His nonchalance cheered the green troops and demonstrated that the Federal gunners were not the marksmen they were feared to be. (Prior to the truce, Kittredge had sent a 32-pound projectile three miles inland to show what his Parrott gun could do.)

The little Union fleet fired almost 300 shells before withdrawing for the day. The explosions—which filled the refugees at Nuecestown, San Patricio, and Flour Bluff with dread—did little damage. Kittredge did not attack the next day, the Sabbath.

On Monday, August 16, the cocky little Yankee captain sent Master's Mate Alfred M. Reynolds ashore with a party of 30 sailors and a howitzer, flanking the shore battery. The Union ships covered the landing with a barrage of grape, canister, and exploding shells. The Confederate situation seemed desperate until Major Hobby led 25 men on a charge through the curtain of fire and forced the landing party to retreat to the ship. Private Mote was killed in front of the charge at the same time Hobby was wounded. A troop of cavalry came to

assist, but Hobby waved them off, fearing the cannon fire would decimate them.

Kittredge's guns followed the cavalry back into town, shooting randomly at houses in search of the horsemen. Many houses were hit. Old John Dix went to unfurl the Stars and Stripes atop his house to save it from bombardment by showing that he was a good Union man. He was met by his Southern daughter-in-law, Cynthia, with a shotgun. She said she would blow him off the roof if he tried it. James Barnard, bedridden with rheumatism, took to his feet and ran from town when a shot crashed through the wall of his house. Actual casualties included three cows, the Shaw's Newfoundland dog, and a number of grave markers in Bayview Cemetery.

Between 400 and 500 shells were fired at the town that day. Many did not explode. The Confederates retrieved them to salvage gunpowder. (One story says the locals were delighted to find bourbon whiskey in some of them, apparently hidden there by seamen who stole it from Kittredge's private stock so they could have a shot on the midwatch.) For years most Corpus Christi homes had cannonballs for doorstops. At least two of them exploded years later when exposed to heat. One old veteran, who had lost a leg in the war, lost it again when the long-delayed explosion blew off his wooden leg.

The *Ranchero* called Corpus Christi "The Vicksburg of Texas." Vicksburg, the last Confederate bastion on the Mississippi River, was not to fall until nearly a year later.

Kittredge was back on September 12 with a request from Admiral David Farragut that the wife of Colonel E.J. Davis be allowed to leave for New Orleans. Davis was a former Corpus Christi and Brownsville lawyer and judge who had become a Union officer and later would be the Reconstruction governor of Texas. Once told he would get his answer in a few days, Kittredge ventured ashore at Flour Bluff to capture a couple of Confederates. Instead he fell into a trap set by Captain John Ireland (who also would be a Texas governor) and was captured.

Kittredge, who never allowed the Southerners to outdo him in chivalry, was deemed an "honorable" enemy and allowed to receive money and personal effects from his ship. (Kittredge later was paroled. Early in 1863, while in command of the steamer *Wamsutta* off the Georgia coast, he struck a seaman, was court-martialed, and was dismissed from the service.)

On December 7, 1862, John Ireland, with seven infantrymen and three seamen, set out to probe the depth of Corpus Christi Pass in the schooner, *Queen of the Bay*. Three cutters from the *Sachem* bottled it up in the

Above: Captain John Anderson (1813-1898) came to Corpus Christi in 1852 and built a house of shell concrete on Water Street. After the Civil War he erected a "Dutch windmill" and used it to saw wood, grind corn, gin cotton, and grind salt. When the wind was right, it would grind 50 bushels of corn a day. Finely ground table salt was shipped to distant markets, and coarsely ground salt was used to preserve meat and cure hides by the many packing plants that flourished along the coast after the Civil War. Courtesy, University of Texas Barker Texas History Center, Austin

Left: Edmund J. Davis, Reconstruction governor (and the first Republican governor) of Texas, in derision was called the "Carpetbag governor." Davis had come to Corpus Christi from his native Florida in 1848, and soon became known as an able lawyer. He married Miss Anne Britton, the daughter of well-known Nueces County legislator Forbes Britton. Davis was appointed judge of the 16th Judicial District of Texas—a district that embraced the lower Rio Grande Valley, Nueces, San Patricio, Duval, Refugio and Victoria counties—and was acknowledged to be a good judge, even during the tense pre-Civil War days. Still his championship of blacks' rights and Union causes made him unpopular in many quarters. Courtesy, Texas State Capitol, Austin

pass with the *Arthur* and its heavy guns waiting just outside in the Gulf. The Confederates took cover behind a bluff, and the marksmen wounded most of the 19 men in the cutters. One Union soldier and a Corpus Christi civilian, Peter Baxter, were killed. Union survivors straggled back to their camp on Mustang Island.

On December 27 the Confederates attempted to destroy the lighthouse at Aransas Pass because the Yankees had been using it as an observation post. The soldier assigned the job doubled the amount of powder recommended and the explosion sent the spiral staircase flying out the top like a giant spring. Only the top 20 feet of the structure were damaged, however, and it was put back into service after the war. Kittredge's little fleet was dispersed. The *Sachem* was hit and captured at Galveston. The new commander was content simply to blockade the coast.

Benjamin Neal and newspaperman William H. Maltby established Fort Semmes on Mustang Island. But the surrender of Vicksburg on July 4, 1863, freed thousands of Union troops for duty in Texas. Confederate General H.P. Bee panicked when 7,000 troops under Union General Nathaniel Banks landed at the mouth of the Rio Grande on November 1. Although he had time for an orderly withdrawal, he set the torch to Fort Brown. Exploding powder and fire nearly destroyed Brownsville. General Bee retreated and South Texas was left unprotected.

General Banks decided to sweep the barrier islands of Rebel opposition. Some 1,200 combat-tough Federals landed near Corpus Christi Pass and marched 22 miles, dragging their artillery with them. With naval shells landing and troops massed for the attack, Fort Semmes' outmanned garrison ran up the white flag. Captain Maltby did the honors since Major Neal, the commander, was across the bay tending to court.

Perhaps Neal was thinking of the plight of his captured command when he, as judge, ordered Chipita Rodriguez to hang on Friday, November 13, after a jury had recommended mercy. She was the only woman ever executed in Texas. Many have felt the woman was not guilty of the crime, killing a traveler at the Aransas River Crossing and taking his gold.

Morale in Corpus Christi was very low—a far cry from the beginning of the war, when belles in white crinoline and hooped skirts presented flags and tossed bouquets to the troops. The men were gone, many to Union prisons. And the people were hungry, discouraged, and fearful of invasion, either by Yankees or Mexican bandits.

Some of Maltby's men changed sides and became

Opposite page, top: William H. Maltby and his brother Henry, printers and journalists from Ohio, came to Corpus Christi and started the *Ranchero*, whose press had to be hidden during the Civil War. After the war William, the "last ditch Democrat of Corpus Christi," edited the *Advertiser*, championing both the Democratic party and ex-Confederates, and criticizing the Davis regime. Courtesy, La Retama Library

Opposite page, bottom: A civil war in Mexico (the War of Reform, 1857-1861) preceded the one in the U.S., and the liberals' victory brought Benito Juárez, left, to the presidency. Napoleon III of France attempted to rule Mexico, appointing Archduke Maximilian of Austria "emperor." Juárez (still recognized as president by the Mexicans) and Luís Terrazas led guerrilla armies in the north, and Porfirio Díaz in the south, to defeat the French, and in May 1867 Maximilian was captured, court-martialed and executed. Díaz, right, was to rule Mexico later, stopping Juan Cortina and his raids north of the Rio Grande. Courtesy, La Retama Library

Above: Ships were guided by the 1855 Aransas Pass lighthouse for about 90 years. Its lens, imported from France, was buried during the Civil War and kept hidden from the Yankees. The "lighthouse" is now a privately owned vacation home. Courtesy, Charles Butt

armed guides for the Union. Some townspeople passed military information to the 29th Iowa troops garrisoned at the former Fort Semmes, renamed Fort Aransas, after the army moved up the coast to capture Fort Esperanza on Matagorda Island.

The winter was bitterly cold. Union troops came to town for house warmings. They tore down homes belonging to absent Confederates and reassembled them, with help from deserters, on Mustang Island. Their warm billets were furnished with elegant furniture from the same source. Confederates came to town and hauled off houses and furniture of Union "renegades." There was great distrust and suspicion on both sides.

English immigrant Thomas Noakes wrote, "About half the people in Corpus Christi have deserted to the Yankee and when you are talking to your most intimate acquaintance, you cannot tell whether you are addressing friend or foe."

Major Matt Nolan, who had come to Corpus Christi as a 12-year-old bugler with General Taylor, was sent on the trail of Cecilio Balerio. Balerio commanded a troop of Union Mexicans that had captured the King Ranch headquarters and threatened the flow of cotton through San Patricio and Banquete to the Rio Grande, a commerce vital to financing the Confederacy's war effort. Nolan, a Texas Ranger and veteran of battles at Galveston and Louisiana, caught up with Balerio near present-day Falfurrias and defeated him, killing five and wounding many others. Nolan returned to Corpus Christi to skirmish with Union troops loading captured cotton.

In June 1864 Union troops, who had been giving food to the starving population, were withdrawn from the Texas coast. In December the Nueces County Grand Jury indicted nine men for treason, some of whom had been prominent citizens before the war. But they were never brought to trial.

On December 22 Matt Nolan, then sheriff and at the same time a Confederate lieutenant colonel, was shot to death by someone wielding a shotgun as he talked to a man on Mesquite Street. He lived long enough to name his killers, who apparently believed he was going to take action against their stepfather, a former sheriff and a Union sympathizer. Two brothers were indicted, but the war ended a few months later and the indictments were dropped by the Reconstruction government. The stepfather once more became sheriff.

Residents were to refer to the last two years of the war as "The Bad Times." Even weevil-infested cornmeal was scarce. A few miles to the west of town, however, business on the Cotton Road continued to be brisk.

Top: Bandit Juan Nepomeceno Cortina ruled a group of "Cortinistas" who raided far into Texas, driving great herds of cattle and horses to Mexico. Along the road between Corpus Christi and the Rio Grande the Cortinistas kept constant, bloody vigilance. Courtesy, La Retama Library

Above: John Salmon "Rip" Ford headquartered troops in Corpus Christi in 1849 to defend the city against Indian raids. He served in the Mexican War, fought border bandit Juan Cortina, and later commanded Confederate troops in the defeat of Federal forces at Palmito Ranch, the last battle of the Civil War. Courtesy, F.H. de Cordova

European mills were starved for cotton and their buyers in Mexico paid in hard money. The Battle of Palmito Ranch on May 16, 1865, was fought not because the combatants did not know the war was over, but because Union officers saw an opportunity to move in and grab Confederate cotton for personal gain. Colonel John "Rip" Ford thwarted this plan and defeated the Yankees in the last battle of the Civil War.

Confederates, Yankees, Mexicans, and others made fortunes while the Rio Grande was the only source of cotton for the world. At times more than 200 ships would be waiting to load cotton. Fortunes made there would finance a number of private South Texas empires during the bleak postwar years—a time that was more violent in Texas than the war had been.

There would be no peace in the borderlands.

A Decade of Reconstruction

The rankle of defeat in the Civil War and the rancor of Reconstruction were never as severe in Corpus Christi as in the rest of Texas. For one thing, nearly half the citizens were Union sympathizers and a number of Union officers had settled in town after the war.

Antagonisms were further diminished in the summer of 1867 when yellow fever nearly decimated the city. More then 300 of the city's 1,000 residents perished. So many were ill, few were available to bury the dead. Lumber was scarce and boards intended for the new Presbyterian Church were used for coffins. The town's three doctors worked heroically night and day trying to stem the tide of death until they, too, fell ill and died. Most of the wartime antagonists died or lost family members. The survivors were united in a common bond of sorrow.

One of the most dedicated nurses during the disaster was Judge Edmund J. Davis, lately a brigadier general in the Union army. He turned his home into a hospital and personally cared for the sick and dying. This must have earned him respect from such staunch Confederates as William H. Maltby, editor of the *Corpus Christi Advertiser* and critic of Reconstruction and of the *Nueces Valley*, the voice of Reconstruction that grew fat printing government notices. Maltby lost his wife and other members of his family to the plague.

Corpus Christians had been displeased over thefts, drunken brawls, assaults, and indignities suffered at the hands of occupying troops. There was at least one shooting, but no major confrontations resulted. The residents might not have been so riled had the troops been white instead of black. Local officials were appointed by Union officers. Yet their rule, aside from tax assessments that were considered excessive, was not too harsh. Some property owners lost land because they could not pay taxes in U.S. currency.

When the radical Republicans captured Congress, Presidents Lincoln's and Johnson's conciliatory approach to the South was rescinded. Government policy was to punish the Rebels. Carpetbaggers ruled and Judge Davis became governor with the help of Army vote counters. He organized the state police to quell disorders, but they were as uncontrollable as the lawbreakers.

Except for a couple of officials, Corpus Christi was free from gross corruption, partly because of the leadership of the former Union officers, who became citizens, not carpetbaggers. Several married into local families whose politics remained strongly Democratic.

It was also during this era that the great cattle drives were beginning—in two directions. One headed to the Eastern markets. Others, driven by thieves, headed for Mexico. It would take a decade for the state to free itself from Reconstruction. In that time the Union cared little about protecting the frontier. With the Rangers disbanded and the state police unable to act, the Nueces country was helpless.

It was an ideal situation for Juan Nepomuceno Cortina, the red-haired "Red Robber." He had been beaten earlier by John "Rip" Ford and late in the war by Colonel Santos Benavides, the "Gray Ghost of the Border," with his Confederate *vaqueros*. But now Cortina was to have his revenge. He could sit back and send armies for "Nanita's cattle"—stock he felt was rightfully his. He would set the Nueces Strip afire in the greatest burst of violence the borderland would ever see.

No Peace in the Borderlands

At the end of the Civil War a reign of terror commenced. During the following nine years, nearly a million head of cattle were stolen, 2,000 Texas ranchers and workers were murdered, and property losses were placed at more than $5 million. Bandit troubles reached their peak between 1871 and 1875. Not all the brigands were Mexicans. There were Union renegades, unemployed Confederates trained only to ride and kill, freebooters from all over the world, and posses of citizens whose methods rivaled those of the bandits.

The road to Brownsville was all but closed. Captain Richard King traveled with a small army, yet his

Top: Corpus Christi's citizenry lived in shelters of many types. The first residences were built near the shoreline below the bluff. The town's more imposing residences were built high on the bluff. Behind them was a poor area occupied almost entirely by Mexicans living in *jacales*. Well water smelled strongly of sulphur, so citizens collected runoff water from their roofs in barrels. Note the barrel next to this clapboard shack. Courtesy, State Historical Association Collection

Above: In 1876 surveying parties were well armed. In the top row (left to right) are chain carriers R.P. von Blucher and G. Rossiter Crafts, and surveyor in charge C.F.H. von Blucher. In the bottom row are rodman George von Blucher, Phillip N. Fullerton (guest), and hostler Hilario Martinez. Pioneer surveyors carried guns to protect themselves from wild animals, Indians, and bandits. Courtesy, Corpus Christi Caller-Times

Above: The Caller Publishing Company was first located in the old Noakes frame building at 301 North Chaparral Street. Eli Merriman, one of the publishers, can be recognized (third from the left). Nelson Noakes and Adolph Noakes are standing in the doorway, and Mrs. N.E. Noakes is upstairs against the railing. In this photograph the building is decorated for the 1902 Knights of Pythias carnival. From *The Crony Special.* Courtesy, University of Texas Institute of Texan Cultures, San Antonio

headquarters was beseiged several times and assassins made several attempts on his life. Citizens kept firearms near at all times and often took the law into their own hands. Once, a drunken rowdy refused to pay for a pair of boots and shot a Chaparral Street merchant. A vigilance committee was convened on the spot. Some grabbed him while others fetched a hemp rope a block long "so everybody could have a pull at it," and they strung the accused up to the nearest tree. The hanged man's father cut down the body and praised his good fortune at acquiring such a good rope.

Rustlers became so bold that Mifflin Kenedy, Captain King, and D.C. Rachal began fencing vast pastures, but the thefts and killings continued. Four men were murdered at Morton's store on Baffin Bay as they knelt and begged for mercy. Two men, whose loot included a bag of sugar with a hole in it, left a sweet trail, which a posse followed back to Corpus Christi. The two were tried and hanged. Four others were strung up in Duval County. A local editor commended Refugio citizens for promptly lynching half a dozen suspects in the slaying of a ranch family. The raids became more frequent and the bandits were getting more brazen.

In 1873 Governor Davis was deposed and his successor, Richard Coke, reinstated the Rangers. It was an open season on bandits. The *Nueces Valley* complained that "Capt. Wallace caught several Mexicans at Concepción and shot some and hanged the others without so much as a 'by your leave.' Not much will be gained by substituting military for highway robbery."

That sentiment radically changed on Good Friday, March 26, 1875, when 50 of Cortina's men moved toward Nuecestown, capturing prisoners as they went. Among them was Judge S.G. Borden, cousin of the inventor of condensed milk. They hanged one old man who refused to join them.

Driving their captives ahead of them, they entered Nuecestown at dusk and attacked Thomas Noakes' Store. John "Lying" Smith, a customer, made a run for it and was gunned down. Noakes dropped through a hole in the floor and crawled down a ditch to the river. His wife, Marie, didn't follow him. She was whipped with a quirt as she refused to let go of a feather mattress. The raiders burned the store to the ground.

News of the raid panicked townspeople who rushed aboard ships at the wharfs in such numbers that they nearly capsized them. Eleven men rode out from town. Businessman George Swank led a charge that freed the hostages, but he was shot and killed. The raiders retreated across the Rio Grande, leaving one of their wounded behind. He was taken to town and hanged from a carriage gate where his body was left for several days as a warning.

The Nuecestown raid was the final straw. The entire state was outraged. Minute companies fanned out over the countryside dispensing retribution to any Mexican they saw. Five ranch houses were burned. It is said that more were killed than the 630 who died at San Jacinto. Some of the state's leading Mexican-American citizens were killed.

Eighteen new silver-studded Dick Heye saddles had been taken from Noakes' Store. Anyone seen sitting on such a saddle was shot off it. Nine of the saddles were recovered from a band of rustlers killed by Captain Leander N. McNelly's men at Palo Alto. Legend says that Noakes got back seven more saddles than he lost, but he was stuck with them. Nobody wanted to be found astraddle one of those fancy saddles.

McNelly and his men came through Corpus Christi shortly after the Nuecestown raid. Morris Lichtenstein equipped the troop with .50-caliber Sharp carbines and Captain King provided them with new mounts "because the bandits are riding stock from this ranch." McNelly ordered the minute companies to disband or he would deal with them as outlaws. He made it dangerous for outlaws to cross the Rio Grande into Texas. And Mexican President Porfirio Diaz made it fatal for the outlaws to continue their profession in Mexico. He stood them against walls and had them shot.

McNelly also carried the new list of wanted men he had compiled while in the state police. It was as big as a catalog, 227 pages thick with more than 5,000 names. When the Rangers started working on the names in the book, habeas corpus seemed to mean they'd just as soon bring in corpses. A great many unsavory characters in the book didn't like its plot and migrated to New Mexico and Arizona, where many became legendary bad men.

Texans at last could put down their guns and go about the business of settling a frontier.

Cattle Drives Make Cattle Kings

Fort Worth claims to be the place "where the West begins." Actually, the West began about 45 miles southwest of Corpus Christi.

It happened in 1852 when Gideon "Legs" Lewis, who had newspaper, real-estate, and mercantile businesses in Corpus Christi, teamed up with riverboat captain Richard King and set up a lean-to at a spring on Santa Gertrudis Creek. It would be the first successful rancho in the Wild Horse Desert and the beginning of

Opposite page, bottom: John Rabb (1826-1872) was a rancher and Texas Ranger. His wife Martha came to be called the "Cattle Queen of Texas," and one of the earliest showplaces on the Corpus Christi bluff was her "Magnolia Mansion." The Rabb ranch, acquired by Robert Driscoll in 1886, was the foundation of the fortune left by Driscoll's daughter Clara to establish a free hospital for the children of Nueces County. Courtesy, Ella Reagan Sparks family

Below: This building, built in the early 1880s, was the third to serve as the Nuecestown School, the first school in the area. All students from the first to eighth grades attended classes in a single 20-foot-square room. In 1980 James T. Persons, Jr., donated the building to Nueces County to be restored and converted into a museum by the Calallen Junior Historians. Courtesy, Mrs. A.B. Ault

Top: The Corpus Christi fire department of the 1870s was composed of several volunteer fire companies like the Pioneer Fire Company pictured. The first fire fought by the Pioneers (unsuccessfully, unfortunately) was the one that consumed the Baptist Church on January 13, 1873. Courtesy, La Retama Library

Bottom left: Leander H. McNelly, a captain in the Texas Rangers, organized a volunteer militia to quell border strife in 1886. The troops were armed with Sharps rifles by Corpus Christi merchant M.S. Lichtenstein and provided with horses by Richard M. King. Captain McNelly and his men swept the Nueces Strip clear of renegades and bandits. Courtesy, La Retama Library

Bottom right: Mifflin Kenedy did not enter ranching on a large scale until after he had become well established in business. Kenedy's experience in fencing his first ranch, the Laureles, convinced him that he should lose no time in enclosing La Parra Ranch, which he purchased in 1882. When Kenedy completed fencing La Parra, he had the second largest pasture in the U.S. Courtesy, La Retama Library

the "Wild West." It was also the beginning of the modern ranching industry. Lewis was killed by a jealous husband, but King continued to build, first as a partner with Mifflin Kenedy, then on his own as the two men built separate empires.

Men came home from the war to find the ranges teeming with millions of unbranded cattle. Money was scarce, but the industries of the victorious North had created a new market—factory workers who could afford beef. A four-dollar Texas steer might bring $30 in Chicago.

The idea of droving steers north was not new. Thomas M. Coleman, a San Patricio County rancher, had done it for three years beginning in 1857—all the way to Chicago. Later he was a partner in the huge Coleman-Fulton-Mathis Pasture Company. The large landowners organized the biggest drives. The King Ranch sent 17,000 cattle up the Chisholm Trail in one drive. In all, more than five million cattle moved up the trails during the two decades of the cattle drives.

For a time, anyone with a branding iron and a horse could gather a herd. Small operators banded together to drive cattle to the Kansas railheads. The cost of transporting each head was only 50 or 60 cents. The more prudent invested in cheap land. Others thought the free range would last forever. It was a definite incentive to rustlers.

Landowners resented use of their land by squatters and cattle thieves. In 1869 Kenedy built a 36-mile fence, sealing off a huge pasture on his Laureles Ranch. King soon followed suit at Santa Gertrudis. D.C. Rachal fenced in 25 square miles of his pasture, which extended from Banquete to Driscoll to the Nueces River. Much of the property that had been the Rabb Ranch eventually became the Driscoll Ranch.

Cattle were so plentiful that it was profitable to sell the hide, horns, and tallow of the less desirable animals. Rendering plants appeared all along the coast. Kenedy slaughtered 500 head a day at his plant at Flour Bluff. One packinghouse was located where La Quinta Royale is today. Others were on North Beach and along the Nueces River. A few pickled beef in brine, some made fertilizer of it, and still others fed the meat to hogs or threw it into the bay or on the ground. Mountains of bones piled up and the city was engulfed in a noxious cloud of bad odor and green flies.

In 1873, the year the bay froze over and thousands of cattle froze to death in the great "die-up," 208,000 hides were shipped from Corpus Christi. The hide market brought on the "Skinning War" in which ranchers tried to protect their herds from "peelers," who killed the animals, skinned them, and left the carcasses on the prairie. A law requiring a recognizable brand slowed the practice. The hide inspector became an important county office. A financial panic ruined the cattle market for both the honest and dishonest.

By 1875 there was a shortage of cattle. Barbed wire, which had been invented in 1873, was introduced to the area that year. But it was only grudgingly accepted. As foreign syndicates began buying up huge pastures, barbed-wire fences became more widely used. They were resented by most people, and wire cutters caused $20 million in damage in a single year. In 1884 fence cutting became a felony, and to be caught with wire nippers on the range was not healthy.

Fences allowed ranchers to upgrade their breeds and to consolidate and protect their property. Fences also killed the cattle drives. At the same time, they made it possible for railroads to build protected rights-of-way. The railroads would bring immigrants, create new towns, and offer a new frontier.

Willie Hinnant, a Lagarto rancher who still remembers those days, said:

Before folks had fences, they burned off the prairie every year so the grass would come back green. Indians had done that for thousands of years. But folks didn't want to burn up their fences, so they quit grass burning. The fire had killed off the little mesquite shoots before they could get started. In those days there wasn't anything on the prairie you could tie a horse to. They never had any need for root plows.

Cattle couldn't move to new grass and the pastures became overgrazed. Tangled forests of gnarled mesquites took over the pastures and they weren't adequate for grazing. It became profitable to sell brushland to farmers who would grub out the mesquite roots and plant crops in the waxy, black soil.

Barbed wire, windmills, and railroads changed the land irrevocably. And those who brought the railroads were the cattle kings, who were riding high on the ranching frontier. They needed railroads, ship channels, and barge canals to move their stock to market.

Fortunately for Corpus Christi, the town's interests were exactly the same as those of the cattle kings. Other villages were vying for channels and railroads. Corpus Christi needed the cattle kings to become a major city.

The War Against Isolation

Not altogether facetiously, you could say Uriah Lott put the iron horse before the cart. Lott, a diminutive New Yorker with a bulbous nose, was promoting a railroad Corpus Christi had wanted for years; yet some town merchants were afraid that a railroad would hurt the lucrative cart trade with Mexico.

After the days of the cow trails, Corpus Christi became, for a time, the world's largest shipping point of wool. From the mid-1880s until 1893, there were more sheep between Corpus Christi and Laredo than any place in the United States. Wagons brought in 500-pound bags of domestic wool and long trains of Mexican carts, each pulled by two to six pairs of oxen, exchanged wool for merchandise.

It appeared that wool would supplant beef in the economy, especially after the great drought in 1891 killed hundreds of thousands of cattle. But then a plague hit, killing nearly all of the sheep. President Grover Cleveland lowered tariffs, a move more deadly to the sheepmen than disease. The industry revived far inland in arid areas away from the moist wetlands that produced the disease-bearing parasite. Ranchers began to improve the bloodlines of their cattle, and the sheep industry disappeared from the coastland.

The dream of a railroad for Corpus Christi had started before the Civil War, when a charter was granted for the Corpus Christi and Rio Grande Railroad to Eagle Pass. Another aborted scheme was a line up the coast in

In 1910 Rockport was the subject of a far-reaching plan, by the Gulf Coast Immigration Company, to develop a modern city and an elaborate harbor facility called Harbor Island. The harbor, which would have been primarily for receiving and dispensing ocean-going freight, was to be connected by rail to Rockport, the Coastal Bend, and beyond. However the harbors never materialized; the great influx of people never occurred; and the 1919 hurricane dashed the Gulf Coast Immigration Company's plans. Courtesy, First National Bank, Rockport

1866. A third would have connected Corpus Christi with another railway south of San Antonio. Yet Corpus Christi remained almost cut off from the world.

Uriah Lott came to Texas in 1873 in time to contract yellow fever in Brownsville. He founded a business in Corpus Christi, selling hides, hardware, groceries, and Singer Sewing Machines. He was a banking partner of Perry Doddridge and worked to acquire a deep-water channel.

Lott promoted a bond election in 1874 to revive the Corpus Christi and Rio Grande. Nervous businessmen defeated it. Undaunted, in 1875, Lott sold bonds for the project, obtained land grants from the state and a charter from Congress on March 11, and started construction. He was short of cash and seemed doomed to failure when Captain Richard King and Captain Mifflin Kenedy came to his aid.

Colonel Lott drove the first "golden" spike on Thanksgiving Day in 1875, at Mesquite and Cooper's Alley. *Caller* editor Eli T. Merriman recalled:

In celebration of the event was a large number of citizens, including members of the Corpus Christi Fire Department and the Star Rifles, in their bright uniforms, gathered for the ceremonies. William Headen, mayor of Corpus Christi, delivered an address and the Rev. C.M. Rogers offered the prayer. The spike driven by Colonel Lott had been gilded by Charles McKinzie to look like gold. McKinzie's effort at deception was so successful the spike was stolen during the night.

After many difficulties, the line to San Diego, then to Laredo, was finished in 1881. Captain King bought the first locomotive and named it the *Corpus Christi.* The wood-burning engine had to make frequent stops for fuel, and sometimes even the passengers were asked to

Above: David Hirsch was photographed in 1899 in his office at Corpus Christi National Bank. Hirsch was the first president of the bank and served on the first board of directors with other notable Corpus Christi residents. Courtesy, Corpus Christi National Bank

Below left: At age 18 Eli T. Merriman worked as a typesetter for the *Nueces Valley.* In 1876 he and William B. Maltby launched the *Corpus Christi Free Press,* and in 1883 he, W.P. Caruthers and Ed Williams established the *Corpus Christi Caller.* Merriman continued to edit and manage the *Caller* for 29 years, making it one of the outstanding newspapers in Texas. He also worked for the town's port, and later for the U.S. Government. From the *Eli Merriman Scrapbook*

Below right: Uriah Lott is the man responsible for the building of the first railroad in Corpus Christi, the Corpus Christi, San Diego, and Rio Grande Railway. Not stopping there, later Lott also pushed through the San Antonio and Aransas Pass Railroad. Courtesy, La Retama Library

cut wood. The line's service was so erratic that it was sometimes called the "Mañana Line." Lott's backers got their money back as he sold the line to the Palmer-Sullivan syndicate, which changed the road's name to the Texas-Mexican.

In the end, the railroad spelled the end of the cart trade, but the railroad tremendously increased the volume and variety of Corpus Christi's trade with Mexico and emphasized the shortcomings of its shallow-water port. Corpus Christi now had a back door, but it remained a village. The 1880 population of 3,257 increased by only 446 by the turn of the century.

In 1885 Lott began the San Antonio and Aransas Pass line with no capital at all. He bought used track and cars on credit. As before, Captain Kenedy came to the rescue, actually building 500 of the line's 688 miles. Kenedy insisted that the line continue from Aransas Pass to Corpus Christi, and he paid to build the Nueces Bay trestle. Before it went into receivership, Lott pushed the rails to Kerrville, Houston, and almost to Waco. Southern Pacific took over SAAP (called "Sap" by residents), giving Corpus Christi access to most other lines.

Lott's next venture with an Arkansas railroad was a financial disaster for him. But Lott was never one to give up. He convinced B.F. Yoakum, a former clerk for him at SAAP who became a railroad tycoon, to extend a rail line from Sinton to Brownsville, with extensions to New Orleans.

Incorporators included Lott, Robert J. Kleberg, Sr., Dr. A.E. Spohn, Robert Driscoll, Sr., Richard King, John G. Kenedy, James B. Wells, Francisco Yturria, Thomas Carson, Robert Driscoll, Jr., E.H. Caldwell, George F. Evans, Caesar Kleberg, John B. Armstrong, and John J. Welder. Financing came from St. Louis for the St. Louis, Brownsville and Mexico, later part of the Missouri-Pacific system. Some businessmen were miffed because the tracks skirted Corpus Christi, but they were appeased by the fact the Tex-Mex lines connected with it.

Rails reached a camp 15.9 miles west of the city. The camp became Rob's Town (now Robstown) since it was in the middle of Robert Driscoll's pasture. By Christmas the line had reached Driscoll Ranch, where the town of Driscoll started. In May 1904 the rails reached the spot where Robert J. Kleberg had already begun the town of Kingsville while waiting for the tracks. A branch line swung off through the Rio Grande Valley, changing Rattlesnake Junction into Harlingen, and spawning the towns of La Feria, Mercedes, Weslaco, Donna, Alamo, San Juan, and McAllen.

On July 4 the line finally reached Brownsville, and

Above: These children posed in the 1880s, dressed in tucked and embroidered lawn dresses with elaborate ruffled collars. Courtesy, Nueces County Historical Society

Left: The sunny days of Corpus Christi made head coverings a must, from the common sunbonnet to the "coolie" straw hat. This turn-of-the-century photograph was taken on Chaparral Street. Courtesy, Corpus Christi National Bank

Above: Someone snapped a picture of photographer Louis de Planque in costume for Columbus Day. "Don Luis" was well known in Corpus Christi; at 6 feet tall and weighing 200 pounds, he was hard to miss. Mr. de Planque's studio was located on William Street opposite the Masonic Hall. Courtesy, La Retama Library

Below: Early in the 20th century farm laborers (and some city workers) lived in camps similar to this one. The houses were made of grass thatched onto mesquite limb frames, or of mud and grass bricks. Courtesy, University of Texas Humanities Research Center, Austin

Uriah Lott was accorded a hero's welcome. "This is the man who got Brownsville admitted to the Union," the mayor of Brownsville told a huge crowd, as the first train pulled into the station. The little man was given a long, loud standing ovation.

The San Antonio, Uvalde and Gulf Railroad (SAU and G) reached Corpus Christi in 1914. Lott had nothing to do with the "Sausage" line, so called because of the abbreviation of the name. But he had brought Corpus Christi into the Union with three of its four railroads. The little New Yorker could promote for everyone but himself. His rail connections enhanced the city's attractiveness as the location for a deep-water port.

Lott died in 1915, and the Kleberg family installed a monument over his grave in Chamberlain Burial Park in Kingsville. Uriah Lott made the country rich by opening it to immigration and the development of farms and towns halfway across Texas. He died without a penny. But a man like that could never be considered poor.

The Struggle for Deep-Water Transportation

The people of Rockport and Corpus Christi were always being reminded of the difficulties of crossing the Aransas Pass bar to reach the Gulf of Mexico. General Zachary Taylor got stuck on a mudbank trying to get to Corpus Christi in 1845. In 1857, after the channel had been temporarily cleared, a cannon was fired to celebrate the first vessel crossing through.

The City of Corpus Christi had a contract to clear it out again when the Civil War started, but the Yankees burned the dredge boat. Dredging was costly and the equipment of the day was not up to the job. Thomas Noakes bitterly told his diary how he had worked his boat with the dredge and had never been paid.

In 1874 a Morris and Cummings Company dredge cut a full eight feet through the mud west of Harbor Island. When the Morgan Lines steamer, *Gussie*, docked at Municipal Wharf, about 3,000 people turned out to see a real steamship. The editor of the *Nueces Valley* described the visit:

The Gussie *is by far the largest ship that ever came in our wharves—a regular seagoing steamer—built of iron— capable of carrying 480 beeves or 1,000 tons of freight—for watertight cross bulkheads—with fire extinguishers, lifeboats and life preservers—capable of carrying 60 passengers—a full complement of officers and men, 28 in all—and everything in*

Umbrella grass, courtesy Texas Highways

Top left: Seagulls are ubiquitous around the Corpus Christi area. The species has prospered greatly from the presence of the human population. Courtesy, Texas Highways

Bottom left: The sight-seeing boat *Gulf Clipper,* shown with the city skyline visible in the background, takes passengers on tours of the bay side of the city. Courtesy, Texas Highways

Above: Large tankers of as much as 100,000 deadweight tons enter the inner harbor of the Port of Corpus Christi loaded with crude oil. This vessel is being assisted by a tugboat while making its way to an oil dock to have its cargo discharged. Courtesy, Port of Corpus Christi Authority

Top right: This view of the Corpus Christi skyline, with the port in the background and the T-heads and L-head in the foreground, brings into sharp focus the reason for Corpus Christi's epithet "the Sparkling City by the Sea." Courtesy, Port of Corpus Christi Authority

Below right: A sailboat slips gracefully through the waters of Corpus Christi Bay. Courtesy, Corpus Christi Area Convention and Tourist Bureau

Coral bean, courtesy, Texas Highways

Above: Nets are drawn in after a day of shrimping. Extensive marshlands in the region serve the coastal fishing industry as nursery grounds for broodshrimp and other wildlife. Courtesy, Texas Highways

Above right: The brown pelican once was very common along the Gulf Coast, but in the 1960s there were only around 12 or 13 birds left, their drastic decline caused by pesticide contamination. Their numbers have recovered slowly in recent years. Courtesy, Texas Parks and Wildlife Department

Above: A successful day of offshore fishing could result in the catching of a swordfish. This large game fish may attain a weight of up to 200 pounds. Courtesy, Texas Parks and Wildlife Department

Left: The speckled trout is one of the most sought-after bay fish along the Texas coast. Courtesy, Texas Parks and Wildlife Department

Orchid tree blossoms, courtesy, Texas Highways

Top: Pirate maids, parades and pageantry (including throwing the mayor overboard) characterize Corpus Christi's annual Buccaneer Days. The 10-day carnival, which falls in late April or early May, kicks off a long season of summer fun. Courtesy, Texas Highways

Right: Catching shellfish, water insects, and small crabs for food in its spoon-shaped bill, the roseate spoonbill nests in colonies, returning year after year to the same place. Courtesy, Texas Highways

Opposite page, top: This view from Corpus Christi Bay shows the Bayfront Plaza with the Harbor Bridge in the background. Courtesy, Corpus Christi Area Convention and Tourist Bureau

Opposite page, below: A roseate spoonbill glides across the sky above the Texas Gulf Coast. Courtesy, Texas Parks and Wildlife Department

Evening primrose, courtesy, Texas Highways

Above: The Corpus Christi skyline and Harbor Bridge create a
magical scene at night. Courtesy, Texas Highways

Orchid tree blossom, courtesy.

apple pie order. She was a beauty to behold. Some people thought all the bells should have rung a peal of joy. We are glad they did not. It was a respect to the Sabbath. On another day it would have been imminently fitting. . . .

By 1886, however, Morgan liners were dragging too much bottom. They went to Rockport to load Coleman-Fulton cattle, but for Corpus Christi, it was back to lightering. By the turn of the century, goods were still being lightered from Aransas Pass, just as they were when General Taylor supplied his army 55 years earlier.

Time after time, efforts were made to deepen the channel over the Aransas Pass bar, but it kept shoaling over. On November 30, 1876, the steamer *Mary,* loaded with a cargo of new goods—barrels of apples, bolts of cloth, and merchandise to stock Corpus Christi stores for Christmas—went aground on the bar in a squall.

The federal government appropriated money to dredge the bar in the 1880s. The job was taken over by the Aransas Pass Harbor Company in 1890 after a jetty was installed. The firm's engineer, L.M. Haupt, had a theory that one jetty would wash the sand right out to sea. The resulting channel, however, measured four feet instead of the 20 feet he had predicted.

In 1899 Congressman Rudolph Kleberg sponsored a bill to cut the bar down to a 15-foot depth. There was still the problem of the zig-zag channel that curved around behind Harbor Island and joined the channel to Rockport. This route was 32 miles from the city to the Gulf. Corpus Christians wanted to make a straight line through Turtle Cove (as the channel now runs) to Corpus Christi. But the government dredged the straight route just eight feet, so it could be used only as a small intracoastal canal. Other portions of the canal were being dredged on the upper Gulf, but it would be years before they would be connected to the Lower Coast.

The Turtle Cove route would be 10 miles shorter than the one then in use. Most cotton from the area was going by rail to Galveston, an arrangement that made neither farmers nor merchants in Corpus Christi happy. They wanted their own port.

But in 1910 the Army Corps of Engineers decided that Corpus Christi was not developed sufficiently to warrant a harbor (this to a town that needed a harbor so it could develop). The Army approved a port at Harbor Island, near the Gulf, that would require much less dredging. A turning basin was prepared and a rail line run to the mainland. Corpus Christians grudgingly accepted the arrangement, for Harbor Island was much closer than Galveston Island, but Corpus Christi had missed the dredge boat.

Above: Edward Sidney and Minerva Ellen Duncan's children play on an uncommon three-legged windmill at Flour Bluff in the early 1900s. The Duncans were among the early settlers attracted to the area by promoters who posted fliers in West Texas and the Midwest and mailed brochures containing such oddities as tarpon scales. Courtesy, Sidney E. and Ruth Elizabeth Duncan

Below: This train hauled supplies from Robstown to Brownsville in the early 1900s to construct the St. Louis, Brownsville and Mexico Railroad. The capital to finance the line came from a St. Louis syndicate—hence the presence of "St. Louis" in the railroad's name. Courtesy, Corpus Christi Caller-Times

Above: Late in 1888 Colonel E.H. Ropes proposed to cut a channel through Mustang Island and build a city on the island. Ropes purchased the dredge *Josephine* to cut the pass, but the venture was beset by troubles and abandoned. From *Frank Leslie's Illustrated Newspaper*. Courtesy, University of Texas Institute of Texan Cultures, San Antonio

Bottom left: Patrick F. Dunn, known also as "Don Patricio," owned nearly all of Padre Island and operated a profitable cattle ranch there. He also served for two terms as state representative and was a close friend of Vice President John N. Garner. From the *Burton Dunn Scrapbook*

Bottom right: Solomon Melvin Coles was born in 1844 into a slave family in Virginia. After the Civil War he became the first black to enter Guilford Institute in Connecticut, subsequently attending Lincoln University and Yale University Divinity School. Coles served as a minister and educator in Corpus Christi. From Edna Jordan, *Black Tracks to Texas*

The 1916 storm washed out the railroad and damaged the harbor facilities at Harbor Island. It was a sign of things to come. The great storm of 1919 was an ill wind that destroyed the coast and took hundreds of lives. But it would blow Corpus Christi a "safe and adequate" port, the future guideline of the Army for new ports.

Land Boom and Bust

Colonel Elihu Harrison Ropes was probably a man ahead of his time. The slender New Jersey newspaperman, insurance agent, and advertising manager for the Singer Sewing Machine Company, was 47 years old when he breezed into town in 1889 with all the impact of one of Corpus Christi's famous hurricanes. Ropes, attracted by the climate, the rich soil, and the town's proximity to the Gulf, had Eastern financial backing and plans for a deep-water port near the present-day water-exchange pass on Mustang Island. He named the project Ropes Pass, at Port Ropes, leading through Ropesville, from which he envisioned a railroad stretching all the way to South America.

He paid Prokop Hoffman $12,800 for 1,280 acres and subdivided Port Aransas Cliffs and "Flower" Bluff. His 125-room Alta Vista Hotel (at the S-curve) would overlook wide boulevards and traffic circles. Santa Fe, Minnesota, Ropes, Rossiter, and other names remain from his plan. A streetcar, driven by steam, ran from the hotel to town.

Residents of Corpus Christi turned giddy under Ropes' influence. Staid and conservative citizens turned into speculators and invested their life savings in the boom. Land bought for $8 an acre was bringing $1,000. The 1890 population of 4,387 doubled with newcomers and speculators. Ropes' magnetic personality captivated the townspeople.

Ropes' dredge *Josephine* had made little progress on the channel when a financial panic hit the nation in 1893. Bankrupt investors blamed Ropes for their misfortune. He left town "to get more money" and never returned. Like his dreams, the *Josephine* was covered by island sand. The Alta Vista Hotel was to stand forlorn and vacant, except for one brief return to glory and elegance. Then it was abandoned until it burned in 1927.

None of the three Yankee colonel promoters, Henry Kinney, Uriah Lott, or Elihu Ropes, found the fortunes they sought in Corpus Christi. But other promoters would follow, writing extravagant prose about the balmy, healthy climate, cool summers, fertile soil, game,

fish, fruit—a Garden of Eden. These new promoters found ready partners in the railroads, which saw immigrants as customers. The day of the cattle frontier was passing.

Monuments to ranch fortunes towered over the bluff. First was the "Magnolia Mansion" of Mrs. Martha Rabb, "The Cattle Queen of Texas," in the 1880s. There were also Mifflin Kenedy's steam-heated Italian villa, and, most imposing of all, the huge turreted mansion of Mrs. Henrietta M. King.

After the turn of the century, the ranchers needed working capital. They needed money to reclaim vast pastures from the invasion by the tenacious mesquites. They also needed cash after protracted droughts depleted their herds.

The ranchers began to subdivide and sell pastureland to farmers. Robert Driscoll hired George H. Paul of Iowa to sell his land. At 31, Paul was a super salesman, but he was not the high-pressure type. He had 1,100 agents across the country who sent him prospects. He also advertised all over the world. Potential buyers were given free train rides to South Texas and given meals—just to look. Eighty-five percent of them bought land and sold their holdings in the Midwest or East.

Germans, Poles, Czechs, Bohemians, Englishmen, and others were among the immigrants. The German churches at Vattmann and Violet, and the Sokol Hall of the Czech gymnast group are a few of the reminders of transplanted cultures. The Europeans and the Northerners, in a generation, became drawling Texans.

Next Paul was hired by the Coleman-Fulton Pasture Company, the partnership formed by George W. Fulton, Sr., Thomas M. Coleman, and Thomas H. Mathis. Paul changed the name of the operation to Taft Ranch, since Charles Phelps Taft, president of the company from 1894 to 1929, was a half brother of President William Howard Taft. The name helped sell huge tracts of land.

The land was cleared of the stubborn mesquite by Mexican labor. Then huge steam tractors pulled big plows, digging up the roots in the rich, black soil. Immigrants set up tents on their land on the prairie until they could build houses. They had no water or conveniences. Some lived in wagons. In the 20th century, they were truly pioneers on a new frontier.

The names of the promoters still mark survey maps. F.Z. Bishop subdivided the Weil Ranch and established Bishop on the rail line below Driscoll. Theodore Koch subdivided a large section of King Ranch and built a railroad to "The Riviera of the South" on Baffin Bay where a number of German families settled. Other arrivals settled Sinton, Taft, Gregory, Orange Grove,

Robstown, Premont, Falfurrias, and Riviera as the flood of immigrants came to change the land forever. Now cotton, not the steer, would be king.

Cotton made a deep-water port a virtual necessity. Such a port would give farmers more equitable shipping rates. The new crop would also change the ranch-oriented economy of Corpus Christi. But this could happen only if Corpus Christi was the center of cotton shipping.

A Metamorphosis

When Roy Miller was elected mayor at age 29 in 1913, Corpus Christi was still a rural fishing village and tourist resort. Streets were muddy bogs. Sanitation was almost nonexistent. The bluff was an ugly, eroded clay slope that had provided material for bricks and a slick place for children to toboggan on sheets of tin. Miller ran on a ticket of modernizing the town, and he must be given the credit for wresting it into the 20th century.

A crude water system had been installed after much of the downtown area was destroyed by fire in 1892. In three years, Miller's administration paved 12 miles of streets, laid 26 miles of storm and sanitary sewers, installed a modern water system, built a new city hall and municipal wharf, and organized a paid fire department with new equipment.

The Volunteer Fire Department, since its formation in 1871, had been the center of the town's social life. All the leading citizens were members of one company or the other. The annual firemen's ball was the event of the year. Firemen were also the center of parades and competitions with departments from other towns.

The population at this time was around 9,000. The city extended only a few blocks west of the bluff and to Chatham's Ravine (Blucher Park) on the south. Most of the residences were below the bluff and on North Beach.

North of Twigg Street and extending to Hall's Bayou (now the ship channel) was Irish Town. The finer homes were on the bluff, but behind them was the "Hill." This was "Mexican Town" with its jacales and shacks of the Mexican-Americans, as well as some of the better homes of Mexican-American merchants. The Anglo community was fairly well-knit, and the role of the Mexican-American was strictly a secondary one.

A 1914 bond issue provided $100,000 to improve the bluff with white concrete balustrades, wide stairways, roads, and a Confederate memorial fountain and relief statue. The village was becoming a city. The Beach Hotel (later the Breakers) dominated the landscape on North Beach. Downtown, the new Nueces Hotel, with its ballrooms and restaurants, would be a community center for half a century. The Seaside Pavilion on a pier in the bay was still the city's principal recreational attraction. The town had streetcars, electric lights, and by 1919 it would have a natural-gas system.

In 1916 Camp Scurry was established at the south end of town, near present-day Louisiana Parkway, for Texas National Guard units activated into federal service during the border troubles. Cotton farming prospered in the wartime economy and more laborers were available as more people were displaced by the revolution in Mexico. In 1918 the camp was a training ground for the Fifth Engineers and the Fourth Field Artillery. The soldiers found Corpus Christi to be a peaceful town, unfortunately, for prohibitionists had dried up the saloons in an election in March 1916.

Even without a deep-water port, the city was progressing. The 1916 storm was but a minor setback. The bay piers with their dance halls and restaurants were gone and some seaside structures were destroyed. Otherwise the damage was light.

But the churning storm of 1919 was the sudden disaster that was to stun and mangle the town and change its direction forever.

Above left: The "Big House," the magnificent villa at the center of Santa Gertrudis, was built as the family seat by Mrs. Richard King between 1912-1914. Designed—after an hacienda that Robert Kleberg had seen—by Carlton Adams with elements of Spanish, Moorish, and Mexican architecture, the house serves primarily as a guest house and as the location of quarterly board meetings of King Ranch, Inc. Courtesy, Nueces County Historical Society

Below left: Tarpon have long been a prize catch for area fishermen. Fishing for tarpon off Mustang Island, the "Tarpon Capital of the World," even attracted President Franklin D. Roosevelt in 1937, and Port Aransas was known as "Tarpon" in 1900. Courtesy, Nueces County Historical Society

Below: Swimming has always been a popular sport in Corpus Christi. Here we see a group modestly clothed in swimming attire of the early 1900s. Courtesy, Judge Max Bennett

A New Day

Corpus Christians have always marked time reference by hurricanes. Hurricane Celia in 1970, a giant tornado of a hurricane, did half a billion dollars in damage. Its destruction erased much of the memory of the great storm of 1919. Other recent benchmarks include Aubrey in 1957, Carla in 1961, Beulah in 1967, and Allen in 1980.

It has always been that way, with storms in 1945, 1933, 1921, and as early as 1818. The latter storm sank four of pirate Jean Lafitte's ships at Galveston. It also washed a Spanish barkentine up a creek from Aransas Bay and left it high and dry, far out on the prairie. Later its timbers were said to have become a ranch bunkhouse and the ship's bell a dinner bell. The incident gave the creek the name Burgentine, a corruption of barkentine.

In 1875 and 1886 the thriving port of Indianola, located on a narrow strip between Matagorda Bay and Powderhorn Lake just west of present-day Port O'Connor, was wiped out by hurricanes. After the second blow, the town was abandoned and its commerce sent to Galveston and other ports. The gateway to Western Texas was up for grabs.

In 1916 residents had ample warning. On the advice of the local weather observer, people were evacuated from low-lying areas. But cottages on North Beach, a middle-class neighborhood, were unharmed. Sixteen lives were lost, six aboard the *Pilot Boy*, a popular excursion boat that sank off Port Aransas.

The good fortune of 1916 created disaster in 1919. There were warnings. A headline in the September 11

Caller said, "South Florida Prostrated by Gale; Property Loss Appalling. Key West Gets Full Force of Hurricane." The paper on Sunday, September 14, carried storm warnings. There was a hint of a storm as the wind blew slightly west of north. Clouds threatened by 10 a.m., when the weather observer warned people to leave the lowlands.

Automobiles were commandeered to warn and evacuate people, but most refused to leave. Some led their families to safety over the railroad trestle over Hall's Bayou before tidewaters became too deep and swift to cross. Rescuers abandoned some of the automobiles and walked out.

By 1 p.m. winds were 80 miles per hour from the east. Residents then began to move to higher levels to escape the water. The family of 10-year-old Theodore Fuller attempted to cross the trestle. He later recalled:

In 1916 the water reached only as far as the railroad. This time the crest reached the rails the same time we did . . . water was falling with a deafening roar and rushing like a huge swollen muddy mountain river . . . father was searching for a safe house (west of the tracks) for shelter . . . a young soldier from the Army Convalescent Hospital at the Beach Hotel joined our party and broke into a house . . . it was strange breaking into someone else's house. . .

The house to the northeast was being pushed along towards us . . . the family . . . joined us . . . the walls of the house they were in moved slowly back and forth. . . . From time to time there was a collapse in some part of the house. . . . Part of the wall parted. . . . Aunt Doshie was leaning against the wall . . . her hand . . . was crushed when it [the wall] closed . . . three fingers had been severed . . . but she bore the pain stoically. . . . I began to whimper. She comforted us and told stories about heroic rescues . . . our soldier sang happy ditties . . . the water began to rise . . . all exits were blocked . . .

The opening of the Port of Corpus Christi brought a giant celebration and a military parade down Mesquite Street in 1926. None of the businesses that are identifiable in this photograph are still in existence. Courtesy, Port of Corpus Christi Authority

our soldier dived down [and got out of the house] through a window and tore a hole in the roof. . . . We were trapped like rats. Everyone rushed to the outlet . . . the house was starting to roll. . . . Esther [Theodore's sister] yelled. She was diving through the window to get out. . .

We briefly saw our brave soldier drifting away . . . his eyes stared as if he had been injured as he clung to a piece of debris. . . . Aunt Doshie was beside me on a roof when Esther bobbed up at the edge of our heaving raft and climbed on. . . . Waves were now high and our roof turned upside down. . . . I felt my way along the roof under water until I found the edge . . . we watched in horror as Aunt Doshie strangled, threw both arms in the air and screamed. Her voice was piercing even over the sound of the storm. Then Esther said in a tone calmed by resignation, "There goes Aunt Doshie."

. . . the water was warm while the cold spray and wind cut unmercifully. My shirt was ripped off. . . . Esther told me to hold on. She didn't know how much longer she could last . . . her hand was under my chin. For a long time I seemed to hear her only vaguely. I was never completely aware of things the remainder of the night . . . as out of a deep sleep I awoke and saw Esther sitting quietly beside me . . . our raft, and expansive floor, was floating among the tops of some mesquite bushes . . . the water was calm . . . we were on the northeast side of the Nueces River some 18 miles from where we started . . . we were cut and bruised and my body had grown so stiff it was painful to move. . . .

On Friday [four days after the storm] we were taken to the station at Sinton after being cared for by townspeople. . . . A train pulled in and there stood Papa. . . . "Brother is waiting for us in Corpus. He will be eager to see you," he said.

I asked, "And Mama? Is she there, too?"

He looked over me with his eyes on the horizon. . . . "No, son, she is with Aunt Doshie and we won't see them for a long, long time. They are in heaven."

In town huge combers pounded into homes and businesses within two blocks of the bay below the bluff. Bales of cotton, pilings, timbers, and other wreckage crushed structures and dumped occupants into the frothy sea.

Miss Lucy Caldwell, a 37-year-old Terrell, Texas, schoolteacher, was vacationing at the Nueces Hotel during the storm and wrote about it in graphic detail:

After the storm . . . I was assigned to the courthouse by the Red Cross to assist in serving food and distributing clothing, candles, and matches. . . . I saw there Mexicans, Negroes and whites all huddled together, hungry, almost naked, shivering, barefooted . . . women with their hair down, some with toes cut off, hands cut off, teeth knocked out, limbs

broken or cut . . . women shrieking for lost ones, men prostrated from trying to save their families, families with everything they had tied up in a pillow slip, people with fortunes swept away.

Rescue parties came in every hour or two, bringing in corpses from the beach. . . . Sometimes they would have two, sometimes as many as 20. And, oh, the condition they were in. Arms and legs off, heads almost severed, all the hair gone, swollen beyond conception, and black from the oil . . . hair entangled with seaweed and the bodies so mutilated that identification was impossible. At one time there were 83 unidentified bodies in the morgue.

And, oh, the shrieking and hysteria among the refugees as these bodies were brought in. . . . All this time the rain was pouring. And the odor cannot be described in words. . . . Slime, mud, dead horses along the beach, decayed fruits and vegetables, burst sewers, wet lumber, molded dry goods. . . . The streets were so slippery with slime from the oil which floated ashore from the storage tanks which burst at Port Aransas you could not hope to go many feet without slipping down. . . .

There was not a coffin in town until the relief trains could bring in coffins from (army camps). The courthouse lawn was a carpenter shop for making rough wooden coffins. The morgue became so foul and congested that after the third day, the bodies were taken immediately, after a short attempt at identification, to the cemetery and buried in trenches in the pouring rain. Priests and ministers worked day and night in squads. . . .

Relief trains came from San Antonio, Brownsville, Houston, El Paso and Laredo with cars of ice, army cots, blankets, mattresses, pillows, bread, meat, canned goods, army suits, shoes, ambulances, trucks, stoves, engines, coffins, undertakers and 600 soldiers and officers . . . when the U.S. took over on Wednesday, everything became almost as rigid as a cantonment. . . .

Miss Caldwell concluded by saying, "P.S. I have avoided telling many of the most horrible things I saw."

Tides during the storm reached 13.9 feet, with waves on top of that. Whole families disappeared; most of them drowned. For more than a block inland along the bayfront, every structure was destroyed. Some lucky survivors waded or swam to safety before the water rose. One young man rescued three people by swimming across Hall's Bayou until he, too, was swept away and drowned.

Floating wreckage drifted as it was hammered by the waves until it was forged into a huge dam of debris along Chaparral Street, protecting other structures farther inland from destruction. Nearly everything north of downtown was either destroyed or heavily damaged, including the icehouses and electric plants. Gone, too, was the new causeway to Portland.

So many were missing that no accurate count could be made of the dead. The official number was 280, but other estimates ranged as high as 600. Bodies washed up on the beach at White Point across Nueces Bay or were found under collapsed downtown buildings. Many of the victims were vacationers. Twenty soldiers recuperating at the hospital on the beach were drowned. Nothing remained on North Beach but parts of two damaged buildings. One was Spohn Sanitarium, where several nurses and patients had been swept away. Only the Beach Hotel (later the Breakers) survived.

It was a tragedy never to be forgotten. Relief for the survivors came from all over the country. Corpus Christi began to dig out under martial law.

Tourism suffered only briefly and local businesses rebuilt, took their losses, and recovered largely without outside assistance. Catastrophe welded the area in common purpose. On October 10, *Caller* editor Roy Miller wrote a front-page editorial:

> *Corpus Christi, today, now, this very minute, has the opportunity of her existence to fix and secure her future. . . . The one thing . . . which will ultimately place Corpus Christi in the forefront of great American commercial and industrial cities is deep water. . . .*
>
> *. . . Because of the recent storm, the whole question of port facilities in this vicinity is to be reopened and restudied by the Government. . . . In our opinion . . . in the interest of safety for life and property, a safe harbor should be established against the high land. . . .*
>
> *. . . We say to Congress as we say to ourselves. NOW IS THE TIME. . . . The stand is that 100 percent of the population which has not been shrunk by a single quitter since the storm and is on the job and will stay on the job until Corpus Christi gets DEEP WATER.*

Even a dynamo like Miller must have been amazed by the reaction his words brought.

A Protected Port and Oil Boom

For once Corpus Christians found an issue they could agree on. They wanted storm protection, and they knew a city would grow where the deep-water port was located. Robert J. Kleberg called a meeting of all large landholders, merchants, bankers, railroad executives, and professional men and started a drive that won the

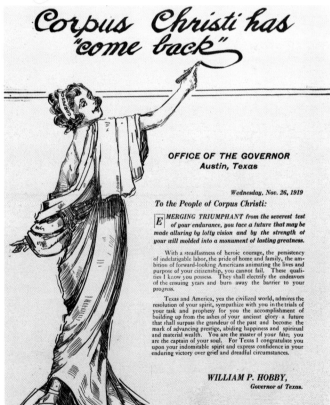

Top: For days after the 1919 storm, every able-bodied man was drafted, along with about 1,200 paid city workers, to clean up the city. Workers are pictured here clearing debris off Chaparral Street. Courtesy, Nueces County Historical Society

Above: This letter from Governor William P. Hobby expressed pride in the way Corpus Christi dealt with a major disaster. Courtesy, University of Texas Barker Texas History Center, Austin

Above: This breakwater off Corpus Christi's North Beach, now used by fishermen and tourists, was completed in 1925. Courtesy, Corpus Christi Caller-Times

Below: Robert J. Kleberg, Jr., is shown on his favorite cutting horse working cattle on the King Ranch in a 1953 roundup. Courtesy, Corpus Christi Caller-Times

political war over deep water for Corpus Christi.

People from Rockport and Aransas Pass argued that a six-mile channel would be much cheaper than a 21-mile channel. But those towns had been devastated by the storm tide. Furthermore, all three railroads at Corpus Christi said they would not extend their lines to either town.

The federal government required storm protection for a port before approving a channel for it. The Texas Legislature passed a bill allowing Corpus Christi to use *ad valorem* taxes from six surrounding counties for 25 years to pay for construction of a seawall and breakwater. Leaders of those counties were solidly behind the project, for a port would lend prosperity to the entire area. San Antonio and other cities also strongly backed the legislation.

Then Congress acted, and on January 16, 1925, the dredge boats *John Jacobson* and *Matagorda* began digging the channel while harbor facilities were being built with Navigation District and state funds.

The port opening on September 14, 1926, the seventh anniversary of the storm, was the biggest party Corpus Christi had ever thrown. Thousands came to help celebrate. Governor Pat Neff, Mayor P.G. Lovenskiold, Roy Miller, and others spoke. Robert Driscoll led officials aboard the USS *Borie*, which steamed through the Bascule Bridge, formally opening the port.

The port was stark and bare on the sand flats. And almost immediately the tiny turning basin was inadequate, for wildcatters were bringing in well after well in Duval, Webb, Jim Hogg, and Zapata counties to the southwest. The oil was there, and the port needed facilities to handle it. By 1927 Humble Oil and Refining Company had established a refinery near the new channel south of Ingleside.

In 1901 a well was drilled for oil in Artesian Square. If there was sulphur in the water, oil must be close behind, local officials reasoned. They struck more sulphur water, which tasted so vile that it was sold as a health nostrum. A well drilled west of the city in 1923 on the Dunne Tract provided an ample supply of natural gas for the city. Discovery of oil in Saxet Field in 1930 brought on a flurry of drilling that slowed somewhat after four straight blowouts and the effects of the Great Depression. Production and exploration boomed again and oil began to soften the effect of hard times.

The opening of the port may be considered the birthday of modern Corpus Christi. The sleepy fishing village on the coast would be transformed forever. Now it was to become the hub of a transportation and manufacturing complex with a varied economy. In rapid order the village was becoming a city.

The decade of the 1920s was marked not only by the advent of industry but by turbulent politics as well. The Ku Klux Klan vied with the established government for control. That's the way it began, but it became a struggle between Catholics and anti-Catholics. The battle moved into the streets and erupted into violence and killings before tempers cooled and the boom of oil and prosperity eased tensions.

Oil companies were pressing for loading docks and facilities when Southern Alkali Corporation established a plant west of the turning basin on September 1, 1930, requiring an extended and deepened channel. The enlargement was one of many that provided space for refineries and heavy industry to sprout along the canal.

However, the collapse of La Fruta Dam at Mathis that same year threatened the source of fresh water for the industries. A wall of water came cascading down the Nueces — fortunately there were no communities in the flood plain. The earthen dam was replaced by Mathis Dam.

Early in 1930 the Texas Air Corporation originated, and the airport — to be named Cliff Maus for its first manager, who was killed in a plane crash — opened to serve the many company and private planes needing accommodations. American Airways, later American Airlines, began service in 1932. It was replaced by Braniff two years later.

By late 1935 the county had 60 oil wells in two oil-fields. Two years later there were 894 wells in 15 fields. The city's population also burgeoned. It skyrocketed from 27,742 in 1930 to 57,301 in 1940.

Farmers and ranchers with new oil wealth built fine homes in town. Young men idled by the Depression came from all over the country to work in the oil-fields and industrial plants. As new subdivisions were constructed, little was done for the poorer sections of the city, where streets were unpaved and pit privies stood behind every house. Yet the Depression never reached the depths in Corpus Christi that it reached in other sections of the country.

Maston Nixon had raised the first skyscraper on the hill with a 12-story office building in 1927. Two others immediately followed downtown. The Plaza Hotel towered over the bluff in 1930, to be joined by the fancy Robert Driscoll Hotel a dozen years later.

A bond election in 1939 was required to finish the $2.5 million seawall on the bayfront. The project was finished in 1940, providing storm protection for downtown. It had taken 20 years for the 14-foot, two-

Above left: On December 22, 1922, the Saxet Company brought in the first producing gas well in Nueces County, John Dunn Number 1. Shown is a later blowout in the Saxet Field, which had both gas and oil wells after 1930. From the Doc McGregor collection. Courtesy, Corpus Christi Museum

Above right: Behind a protective sheet of steel an early-day blowout specialist prepared a charge to explode in the wild well in the background and extinguish the flame. Drilling rigs in South Texas are constantly threatened with the blowout menace. From the Doc McGregor collection. Courtesy, Corpus Christi Museum

Below: June 1, 1932, marked the dedication of the new airfield and the opening of American Airways service to Corpus Christi. A large crowd of Corpus Christi officials and citizens turned out to load the 10-passenger Fairchild with bags of letters promoting the city. Courtesy, Corpus Christi Caller-Times

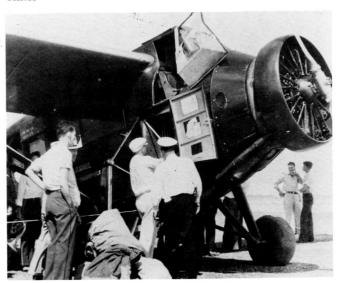

Top: The USS *Constitution,* the Navy's oldest ship, paid an historic visit to the Port of Corpus Christi in 1932 during a tour of ports around the nation. Courtesy, University of Texas Humanities Research Center, Austin

Right: Captain Richard E. Williams became the first black to head a major Navy shore command when in 1977 he was appointed base commander of the Naval Air Station at Corpus Christi. Courtesy, Corpus Christi Caller-Times

mile wall to become a reality, but at last the city had a safe front yard.

Continued prosperity came in the form of an expanding industrial base. Southern Oil and Refining opened in 1936, Taylor Refining and Columbia Carbon in 1938, Pontiac Refinery in 1941, American Smelting and Refining and Sinclair Refinery in 1942, and Celanese Corporation of America started at Bishop in 1943.

In 1931 the tanker SS *Youngstown* sideswiped the Bascule Bridge, disabling it for several days. It was an omen that the drawbridge, the proud symbol of the port opening, would become a "bottleneck"—an impediment to both highway and water traffic and a threat to further growth. The bottleneck would not be broken for 28 years—when the Bascule Bridge was removed and Harbor Bridge opened in 1959.

The Military Factor

From its very beginning Corpus Christi was a military town. It started as a trading post and fort that welcomed and was host to one half of the existing United States Army in 1845.

The town, however, was not such a good host to the U.S. Fifth Infantry and its 112 troopers stationed there in 1850 as protection against Indians. The infantry unit was completely useless in combating an enemy mounted on swift ponies. The citizens were not sorry to see the soldiers go after a brief tour of duty.

Corpus Christi was a Confederate base and a Southern town. It bowed in defeat and was occupied by Union forces. In 1898, during the Spanish-American War, a company of Texas troops camped on North Beach, almost where Zachary Taylor's men had been in 1845. A local militia, the Kenedy Rifles, was organized. The 38 men went to Cuba but did not see combat service. They were given a big welcome when they returned home.

Early in 1916 the Sixth Infantry Brigade, composed of the Second and Third Texas Regiments (National Guard units federalized to combat raids by Pancho Villa and other armed Mexican bands), cleared mesquite in the area between Buford, Santa Fe, Louisiana, and Ocean Drive and established Camp Scurry. There were rows of wooden-floored permanent tents and a large auditorium and assembly hall called the Airdrome. The streetcar line from town ended at the camp. There were 3,000 men in the brigade.

The Second Texas was famous for its football team. It trounced the First New York Cavalry, a team of 26

Top: During his 1941 U.S. Senate campaign Lyndon Johnson made a memorable stop in Corpus Christi. He is shown here, on June 17, talking with ex-Texas Ranger Captain Will Wright and a group of others. Johnson, a close friend of many Corpus Christi residents, helped the city when he served first in Congress, and then as Vice President and President. Courtesy, Lyndon Baines Johnson Library, Austin

Above: The League of United Latin American Citizens (LULAC) was founded and held its first convention in Corpus Christi on May 19, 1929. LULAC has since grown from a Texan to a national organization and has made great strides in advancing the Hispanic community. From the Archives of the League of United Latin American Citizens. Courtesy, University of Texas Mexican American Library Program, Austin

lettermen and seven All-Americans from Harvard, Yale, and Princeton, by the score 69-0. The Texans eventually rolled up 432 points to 6 for all opponents.

Historian Dan Kilgore said streets in the area— Louisiana, Texas, Ohio, and Indiana—were named for states represented by Guard units. Dr. Gordon Heaney remembered that a ditch (now Louisiana Parkway) was used for sewage disposal by the troops. The Guard was disbanded in March 1917 but was recalled to active duty to Camp Travis a month later. The troops saw duty in machine-gun units on the Western Front in France.

The Fifth Engineers of Iowa were in Corpus Christi for a time, and the Fourth Field Artillery closed Camp Scurry at the end of the war. The soldiers hauled shell from North Beach to the road which was thereafter called Shell Road—until the name was changed to Upriver Road.

In 1938, as America's involvement in World War II approached, a Navy survey team came to Corpus Christi. It made no comment, but Senator Tom Connally and a freshman congressman named Lyndon B. Johnson were aware of the Navy's need for 2,000 acres for an air-training base.

The Navy required a sheltered bay and land that sloped to the water for a seaplane base. Two locations were under consideration—one near Ingleside on the north side of the bay, the other near Flour Bluff on the south side. Congressmen Richard M. Kleberg and Tom Connally convinced the Navy that Corpus Christi was the place because the land was vacant and the prevailing breeze was favorable for landings most of the year. A citizens' committee guaranteed roads, water, and housing if the Navy would locate its $44-million base at Flour Bluff. The local cost was $1.725 million.

Corpus Christi was a beehive with construction of the base, housing, highways, and the bayfront improvement. La Armada, now a public housing project, was ready for Navy dependents when the base opened. The station was commissioned by Secretary of the Navy Frank Knox at 11 a.m., March 12, 1941, under military security. Few civilians were invited.

Knox said the base was to teach young men "a new art of war. This station has not been built in the spirit of aggression. . . . I want to dedicate this station not to war, but to peace—the peace of justice and righteousness. Any other type of peace is but a mockery." Members of the House Naval Affairs Committee, ranking naval officers, Governor W. Lee O'Daniel, and other spoke. Strangely, with all those practiced orators on the rostrum, the entire program lasted only 17 minutes.

The base was the largest naval flight training center

in the world. The first pilot training class graduated on November 1, 1941. Thousands more trained to clear the Pacific of enemy planes and ships. Many space-age astronauts received their flight training at the base.

By the end of 1944 more than 20,000 civilians were employed at the Main Base and 20,000 more at satellite fields: Cabaniss, Rodd, and Waldron Fields, the radar training school at Ward Island, and the auxiliary airfields at Kingsville, Rockport, and Beeville.

At war's end, activities were curtailed and other fields were decommissioned. There was a move to close down NAS itself in 1948, but Senator Connally blocked the move in Congress. That year the station was declared a permanent installation. It was expanded with the outbreak of the Korean Conflict and the base at Kingsville and Chase Field at Beeville were reactivated.

On June 30, 1959, the Overhaul and Repair Section, which rebuilt aircraft and engines, was closed, throwing 3,000 civilians out of work. The city reeled in the resulting depression caused by the loss of the $18-million payroll.

However, on April 21, 1961, through the efforts of then Vice-President Lyndon B. Johnson, Congressman John Young announced that the Army would move its helicopter repair service into the old O&R space. The Vietnam War again stepped up both Army and Navy activities, with 6,000 employed by the Army alone at the peak of the war.

Many foreign pilots have trained at NAS, and helicopters refurbished at the Army Depot found their way to trouble spots all over the world. The first female Navy pilots, Ensigns Rosemary Conaster, Barbara Allen, Jane Skiles, and Judy Neuffert, received their wings there in 1974. Captain Richard E. Williams became the first black to head a major shore command when he was appointed base commander in 1977.

In 1978 a national deemphasis on defense led to a move to close down the Naval Air Station. President Jimmy Carter came to the rescue and ordered that the base remain open. Training schedules at the air station were full as Ronald Reagan's Administration gave top priority to defense spending. The Army Depot prepared to enlarge its repair lines in anticipation that the large CH 47 Chinook helicopters would be again repaired at Corpus Christi.

In the 1980s the military remained the largest single employer in the city.

Playground on the Gulf

Colonel Henry L. Kinney first boosted Corpus Christi's virtues as a tourist mecca with his advertisements for the "Naples of the Gulf."

There actually was little to satisfy a tourist in those days, unless he liked to live dangerously, for there were

Opposite page: The master blacksmith in Corpus Christi for many years, Mr. Boemer closed his shop when he retired because he could find no one to learn his trade. His shop was located on Ayers Street near Wynn Seale Junior High School. Once a service in high demand, blacksmithing has become almost extinct. Courtesy, University of Texas Humanities Research Center, Austin

This page: Biel Grocery Store's meat market had just received a shipment of fresh sausage when this photograph was taken. Note the NRA (National Recovery Act) Eagle poster, upper left, and the Christmas decorations. Courtesy, University of Texas Humanities Research Center, Austin

Top left: The Hotel Breakers, the only structure on the beach that withstood the hurricane of 1919, boasted its "own private beach" that was "two blocks long" and "free from undertow" on this postcard from the early 1940s. Courtesy, Houston Metropolitan Research Center, Houston Public Library

Above left: Photographed during World War II, the Confederate memorial sculpture was commissioned in 1914 by the Daughters of the Confederacy. The celebrated sculptor Pompeo Coppini created the allegorical figures of land, right, and sea, left, meeting at and crowning Corpus Christi, the beautiful young woman who stands between them. Courtesy, Corpus Christi Caller-Times

Above: The 14-story Plaza Hotel, center, and the 12-story Nixon building, left, were the dominant structures in Corpus Christi's skyline in 1931. The Nixon was Corpus Christi's first skyscraper (later renamed the Wilson building). The Plaza Hotel was torn down to make way for the 21-story Six Hundred building. Courtesy, Cech-Trefflich family

no roads and the trails were notoriously dangerous. But the coming of the railroads gave the city an opportunity to brag about its cooling breezes and healthful climate. Cabins, cottages, and hotels grew along the water. Great piers offered even more natural air conditioning. Pavilions offered bowling, dancing, drinking, dining, fishing, bathing, and entertainment. Colonel Elihu H. Ropes' Alta Vista Hotel was reopened briefly after the turn of the century with fine food and services, but it could not get enough high-spending customers, and it closed. From 1905 to 1919 "Epworth-by-the-Sea" was headquarters for the annual Methodist Encampment. Special trains from north and central Texas brought thousands to bathe, hear preaching, and loll on the beach.

Corpus Christi abounded in saloons and, with the advent of electricity, dozens of motion-picture houses. In 1915 the city council passed an ordinance requiring all saloons on Chaparral, Mesquite, and Water streets to move to the east side of the street so that ladies could walk the sidewalks without having to peer into the sinful parlors.

The 1916 hurricane dented the tourist business with the loss of the piers, but the city's economy was heavily dependent on the tourist trade until the 1919 storm, which destroyed the facilities. The industry was slow to recover because investors were reluctant to invest heavily on ground so recently devastated.

Sam A. Robertson built the Don Patricio Causeway to Padre Island in 1927. The one-lane, board-rutted bridge opened the island to tourist traffic for the first time. It was destroyed by the 1933 storm.

Bruce Collins, Sr., and John Mosser built the North Beach amusement park that became a landmark and sparked a revival in tourism in the late 1920s. It featured a bathhouse, saltwater swimming pool, roller rink, roller coaster, Ferris wheel, midway, and picnic area. It was the site of Splash Day and beauty pageants.

The Nueces, Princess Louise, Breakers, White Plaza, and Driscoll hotels did much to bring people to town, both as tourists and as conventioneers. In recent years the Hilton, La Quinta Royale, Holiday Inn Emerald Beach, Sheraton, Ramada Inn, Master Hosts Inn and others, plus the easy access to Padre Island and its hotels and condominiums, have made the area increasingly popular as a resort. High fuel costs have made South Texas a winter home for many thousands of Midwesterners and others. Natives considered the

tourist industry a clean industry, preferable to smellier, more polluting enterprises.

In the 1980s inland tourists still are naturally attracted to the water. For those who like to fish, there are the many charter boats at Port Aransas for deep-sea or red snapper fishing. At the Peoples Street T-Head there are bay charter boats whose captains can usually find fish.

For visitors with landlubber stomachs, there are a number of good piers on Padre and Mustang islands, as well as at Cole Park and near the Oso in the bay. The many shallows of Laguna Madre offer the best in wade fishing. And those with heavy fishing gear can test it in the surf of the Gulf of Mexico.

Many attractions in and around Corpus Christi provide tourists with activities throughout the year. At the end of April or early in May Buccaneer Days is the big event in Corpus Christi. It follows the week of the Fiesta in San Antonio, which falls during the week of San Jacinto Day, April 21. Festivities include a carnival, fireworks displays on the bayfront, sailboat regattas, a junior parade and an illuminated parade, the Buccaneer Days Coronation, a beauty pageant, and dozens of sporting events and competitions.

Another festival in Corpus Christi is Bayfest, the first week in October, which features food, drink, live entertainment, artists, historical exhibits, a boat parade, a children's area, and waterfront activities. It was first held in 1976 to celebrate the Bicentennial.

The Annual Navy Relief Festival is held the first week of April, with the Blue Angels, Navy Parachute Team, aircraft displays, and fun, games, and refreshments. From June through August there are bayfront band concerts on Sundays at the Cole Park Amphitheatre. In late June the Texas Championship Billfish Tournament is held at Port Aransas, which also holds the Outboard Fishing Tournament in July, following the famous Deep Sea Roundup, the oldest of all fishing tournaments.

At Taft it is the Boll Weevil Festival in October, at Rockport it is Seafair the first week in October. The Jim Wells County Fair in Alice is in the last quarter of October. Portland's Pioneer Days are in mid-April, as is the Rattlesnake Roundup at Freer. The Goliad Longhorn Stampede is in early July, and Goliad's La Bahía Downs offers quarterhorse races on most weekends in the summer.

The Modern City

Through the highs and lows of the national economic scene, Corpus Christi's energy-based economy had remained relatively healthy. It was a diverse economy with oil and gas contributing 34 percent to the total; the port and manufacturing, 20 percent; government and the military, 19 percent; tourism, 13 percent; and ranching, farming, and fishing, 6 percent.

As the nation entered a recession in 1970, Corpus Christi had a mean visitor—a hurricane named Celia. Like a huge tornado, it did little damage to the waterfront, but it played havoc with the rest of the area. Insurance payments amounted to nearly half a billion dollars. Miraculously, the loss of life was low.

It was not an entirely ill wind, however, for the rebuilding created a mini-boom that extended well into the decade. The economy leveled out for a time, but then the nation was hit by the fuel shortage. After that, new storage tanks sprouted like mushrooms over the refinery area. At the same time many of the refineries and petrochemical plants were expanded on such a scale that the growth was the equivalent to the acquisition of several new industries.

Expansion and the arrival of several new refining operations nearly filled the vacant spaces along the banks of the 12-mile port channel. The Corpus Christi Port Authority worked to create more industrial space in Nueces Bay with landfill dredged in deepening the channel—a plan that met considerable opposition from ecologists.

The oil shortage also brought renewed oil exploration over South Texas and in the Gulf of Mexico.

Hobie Cats on Corpus Christi beach await a race in Corpus Christi Bay. This beach, recently restored at a cost of $3.7 million, is a favored vacation retreat for visitors to the Texas coast. In the background is the Breakers condominium complex, built on the site of the original Breakers Hotel. Courtesy, Corpus Christi Area Convention and Tourist Bureau

Just outside the heavy industrial district, oil-field support industries, service companies, pipe yards, supply firms, and machine shops stretched for miles.

In mid-1982 an oil glut forced prices of petroleum down, causing a temporary recession in the exploration as hundreds of rigs were stacked, waiting for orders to drill. Wildcatters, who had drilled over South Texas for years, were taking a second look and drilling deeper, more expensive wells. Major companies spent millions on offshore exploratory wells. Despite their efforts, the output from the old Nueces County oil reservoirs continued to decline and more wells were depleted than were discovered.

In 1982 the Texas Railroad Commission said that the output from wells in the county had been on a steady decline for the past 10 years. In 1981 total crude oil production was 2,568,036 barrels with 6.73 billion cubic feet of gas. Gas wells produced 114.66 billion cubic feet of gas and 582,377 barrels of condensate.

Regardless of the local production, imported oil continued to flow to refineries equipped with exotic new equipment to remove sulphur and acids from the imported heavy petroleum.

Deeport had been a hotly contested issue that remained to be resolved. Under the plan, the U.S. Army Corps of Engineers would dredge a channel 72 feet deep to Harbor Island, accommodating vessels up to 275,000 deadweight tons. When the first environmental impact statement concerning the superport was issued, it estimated that the dredge material would have covered 3,000 acres of wetlands, bringing a torrent of opposition from environmentalists and others. Under a modified plan, proponents claim only 155 acres would be covered. The proposed port would be just inside the jettied channel from the Gulf of Mexico, across the ship channel from Port Aransas.

The Port of Corpus Christi's first full year of

Above: Named for a city with a proud naval tradition, the *City of Corpus Christi* SSN705 Los Angeles class nuclear-powered submarine was launched in April 1981. The second U.S. Navy vessel named for the city (the first was a twice-commended World War II patrol escort), the submarine's first name proved controversial: some religious officials objected to naming a warship "Corpus Christi" ("Body of Christ"). President Ronald Reagan ordered that the words "City of" be added. The submarine has an overall length of 360 feet, a beam of 33 feet, and a submerged displacement of 6,900 tons. Courtesy, Department of the Navy

operation in 1927 produced 991,621 tons of cargo. In 1981 the total port tonnage was 50.3 million tons. This was down from the 53.5 million tons of the previous year, primarily because of the explosion that destroyed the Corpus Christi Public Elevator on April 7, 1981, killing 11 people. Producers Grain Elevator was being modernized, and the public elevator was being rebuilt, so for a period no grain at all was moving from the port.

With more and more industry locating along the harbor and with increased storage space, there was nothing but growth ahead for the nation's seventh largest port (in terms of tonnage). The port continued as one of the greatest influences on the Corpus Christi economy. Eighteen port-related firms surveyed employed 7,557 employees with a direct annual payroll of $188 million, or an average of $24,900 per worker.

Manufacturing was growing on a large scale on the north shore of the bay, where huge steel derricks were fabricated on their sides. They were loaded on barges and served as legs for oil-drilling platforms in deep water. This industry grew tremendously after the early 1970s.

Other major manufacturers also worked steel in fabricating huge pressure vessels used in refineries and chemical plants. Others built large power plant packages used on the offshore rigs. One built natural gas compressors. Another made farm machinery. Several companies relocated in Corpus Christi to manufacture circuits, electrical components, and instruments. Two firms moved their clothing manufacturing plants south to take advantage of the Sunbelt climate and the favorable labor market. Ore-based industries that produce zinc, chromium, aluminum, and cement were also among the large port operations.

The military was second only to manufacturing in the economy. In 1981 the Army Depot and Naval Air Station employed nearly 5,000 civilians with an annual payroll of $196.4 million. The 1,961 members of the military drew $35 million. Including goods and services purchased, base operating support, and other local expenditures, the economic impact of the base was $283.2 million at the beginning of 1982. Kingsville had 2,400 military personnel and 325 civilians and Chase Field, Beeville, employed 1,458 military and 612 civilians. All three bases were involved in advanced jet training, a business that picks up when troubles are brewing in the world.

Tourism also continued to grow despite hurricanes and gasoline shortages. The Tourist Bureau found that the average winter visitor stayed 6.6 days and the summer visitor 5.2, spending an average of $41.62 a day.

The convention visitor stayed 3.8 days and spent $105 a day. The tourist business increased by a whopping 62 percent from 1977 to 1981. In 1977 visitors spent $57.4 million. In 1981 the figure was $184.3 million. Within a 50-mile radius of Corpus Christi, visitors spent $306 million.

A boon for the convention industry, the Bayfront Plaza Auditorium was opened in 1981. During the portion of the year that it was open, 15 conventions were held there. Convention activity showed a slight downward turn from previous years, but the bureau was undaunted because 64 conventions had been booked for the future and the prospect of additional hotels improved the outlook.

Farming and ranching continued to be a viable industry in Nueces County, which had 904 farms covering 541,056 acres. The average farm size was 466 acres. Depending on market conditions, farmers planted cotton, sorghum, or corn. In 1979 the county produced 409,000 bushels of corn, 5,700 tons of hay, 7.75 million hundred weight of sorghum, and 107,400 bales of cotton. The agricultural population also included 72,000 cattle and 41,000 hogs.

The search for oil undoubtedly will continue in Nueces County, as will the flow of foreign oil into the Port of Corpus Christi for processing into gasoline, fuel oil, heating oil, and dozens of bulk chemicals. Farming may decline, but only if it is crowded out by the growing city. And Corpus Christians can count on people from the rest of the country who will come to see the sights.

A Forward-Looking Community

The skyline of Corpus Christi underwent changes in the 1980s for the first time in several years. There seemed to be no end to the boom in the immediate future.

In addition to the several office buildings already on the bluff, two 16-story towers of the FirstCity Bank were joined with the former Driscoll Hotel, which had been converted into an office complex in the 1970s, by an overhead walkway across Leopard Street. The Upper Broadway Post Office was razed to make way for the 23-story Texas Commerce Plaza, the tallest building in Texas south of San Antonio. Along with the Wilson Tower and Wilson Building, 600 Building, Guaranty Bank Plaza, Petroleum Tower, Atlantic-Mobil Building, and Sun-Texaco Building, the new towers added space for the new energy and petrochemical offices that continued to come to Corpus Christi. On the bayfront Corpus Christi National Bank's new wing filled in the

Below: The Corpus Christi Army Depot repairs and maintains military helicopters and helicopter components. The depot is South Texas' largest employer with about 3,200 civilian and 35 military employees and more than one million square feet of maintenance shops. Courtesy, Corpus Christi Army Depot

Bottom: The GI Forum was founded in Corpus Christi by Dr. Hector P. Garcia on March 26, 1948. It was originally composed of veterans of both Latin and Anglo extraction who met to protest the reduction in the number of beds available to veterans at the U.S. Naval Hospital in Corpus Christi. The GI Forum became a state organization with its first convention in 1949. Courtesy, Corpus Christi Caller-Times

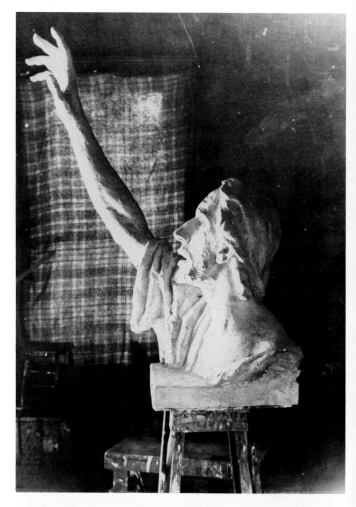

Above: The world premier of the opera "Chipita Rodriguez" was presented by the Corpus Christi Symphony Orchestra in the spring of 1982. The score is by Dr. Lawrence Wiener and the libretto by Dr. Leonardo Carillo, both of Corpus Christi State University. The opera is based on the story of Chipita Rodriguez, the only woman in Texas to be hanged. Courtesy, Corpus Christi Caller-Times

Top right: In 1928 Gutzon Borglum, sculptor who created the Mt. Rushmore National Monument, presented Corpus Christi with a statue of Christ. A large rendition of the statue was to be placed at the harbor entrance, but some residents objected and the plan was rejected. The statue is now on a South Dakota mountain. Courtesy, La Retama Library

Bottom right: The Art Community Center is housed in Corpus Christi's first museum building, the 1936 Texas Centennial building. Since 1972 local artists have held monthly exhibits there, and they gave the city the studio building (on the left) as a bicentennial gift. Courtesy, Art Community Center

lower skyline between its 1960 tower and La Quinta Royale, and the older downtown office buildings.

The rest of downtown, largely abandoned when businesses lost out to competition from suburban shopping malls, also was reviving. Preservation and remodeling of half a dozen older buildings was complete and renovation of others was planned. With the old and new construction, a revitalized downtown was beginning to emerge. The half a dozen hotels interested in building near the Bayfront Arts and Science Park would find financing despite the period of high interest rates, extending the skyline to the north and giving the city a new profile.

Both apartment and home construction increased to keep pace with the flood of new residents. The 1980 census placed the population at 231,999 in the city and 268,215 in the county. With rigidly enforced zoning and planning ordinances, Corpus Christi provides a clean, well-ordered city where residential areas are protected from encroachment by businesses. The bayfront has been vigorously protected as the city's unblemished front yard, and the backyard—industry row—is its workshop.

The growth was all to the south for many years, but developers began building in the far west section of the city in the 1970s. In the past Mexican-Americans were grouped on the "Westside," now in the center of the city. But many moved to the newer sections in increasing numbers as employment opportunities expanded, and the once strictly Anglo "Southside" was no longer solid.

The site of an annual pilgrimage over the Easter holidays by thousands of residents of Northern Mexico, Corpus Christi had 130 churches, representing 38 denominations. Corpus Christi had been known as a town of tolerance after the excesses of the Ku Klux Klan days, but religious differences became a matter of community dispute on two occasions.

In 1928 Gutzon Borglum, a sculptor who created the Mount Rushmore National Monument, presented the city with a statue of Christ. The statue was to be placed at the harbor entrance, but Protestants objected to the "idolatry" and the plan was scrapped. The statue instead was installed on a mountaintop in South Dakota.

The idea reappeared in the 1970s when surgeon-sculptor Dr. Sherman Coleman created another statue of Christ. This time it was the Jewish community that objected on the grounds that a religious icon placed on state property in the bay constituted a violation of the principle of separation of church and state. The statue does not look out over the bay, but it may be seen near the main entrance of Spohn Hospital.

Above left: Members of the 1982 Corpus Christi City Council, (from left to right) Herbert Hawkins, Dr. Charles Kennedy, Bob Gulley, Betty Turner, Mayor Luther Jones, and Cliff Zarsky (missing is Jack Dumphy), pose in front of City Hall. Courtesy, Corpus Christi Magazine

Above right: From left to right, members of the Nueces County Commissioners Court William McKinzie, J.P. Luby, Judge Robert Barnes, Richard M. Borchard, and Carl Bluntzer, pose in 1982 before a monumental sculpture in the Nueces County Courthouse. The three-story sculpture, the work of Lavernis Royal, depicts seagulls circling a shrimping boat. Courtesy, Nueces County Historical Society

Below: Built at a cost of $93 million, the Choke Canyon Dam was dedicated on June 8, 1982. This accomplishment is part of the struggle to keep water pulsing through the lifelines of the Coastal Bend. Courtesy, City of Corpus Christi

Five independent school districts lay within the city limits. In 1982 they had a combined enrollment of 48,906. Higher education was available at Del Mar, a two-year community college, and at Corpus Christi State University, a state-supported, upper-level college. Texas A&I University at Kingsville, 40 miles to the southwest, had more than 5,000 students. Texas A&M University maintained a research and extension center near Robstown, and the University of Texas Institute of Marine Science Engineering and Resources was at Port Aransas.

Corpus Christi had one daily newspaper publishing company, several weekly newspapers, five television stations and cable television, 16 radio stations, and two magazines. The city voted bonds to build a new central library to be the centerpiece for its four satellite branch libraries.

The Corpus Christi Symphony Orchestra, organized in 1946, enjoyed an excellent reputation. The Corpus Christi Museum was chartered in 1956, and was the creation of Aalbert Heine. After several temporary homes, it received an anonymous donation allowing construction of a modern building in the Bayfront Arts and Science Park, the first structure there. It was a museum for all ages, but its curator emphasized the creation of entertaining programs to delight children. The Japanese Art Museum, founded by Mrs. Billie Trimble Chandler as a private collection on South Staples, was renamed the Museum of Oriental Cultures. It was to be relocated in the Bayfront Park.

The Gulf Coast has drawn artists from all over the world. Painters and sculptors had an outlet in the small Community Art Center on Park Avenue. This museum was constructed during the Texas Centennial of 1936. It became the Art Museum of South Texas in 1967, and through the efforts of oilman Edwin Singer, moved into the building in Bayfront Park designed by Philip Johnson in 1972. The new museum featured traveling exhibits, largely composed of avante garde art, while the Community Art Center exhibited more traditional forms.

Other cultural attractions included a number of private art galleries; two theatre groups: Little Theatre at Harbor Playhouse and Encore Theatre at the old Ritz Theater; three ballet organizations: Corpus Christi Ballet Theatre, Corpus Christi Concert Ballet Association, and the Coastal Bend Dance Foundation; and a writer's group, the Byliners, established as the Fine Arts Colony in 1939 by Mrs. Dee Woods and the Corpus Christi Chorale.

In addition to the many cultural attractions, Corpus Christians have not neglected their concern for the quality of their environment. The seawall was constructed in front of the city to serve as a storm barrier, but beautification of the ugly clay fill made Corpus Christi's bayfront a showcase among American cities. Mrs. Armstrong Price was the spearhead who moved the city into action on the project.

Under the Open Spaces Act, large stretches of bayshore were acquired as public park property so that no future building could obstruct the view of the bay along Ocean Drive. Along this area several parks were created by dredge fill, providing more recreational space. With federal assistance, the badly eroded beach north of the ship channel was restored with river sand. Thus, the public was guaranteed access to the two-mile stretch of wide beach. Similar access was assured along the beaches of Mustang and Padre islands. Two county parks, a state park, and the Padre Island National Seashore will never be displaced by commercial development.

Inland, the city had other recreational spots in municipal and county parks and at Lake Corpus Christi State Park near Mathis. Other recreational facilities will be created by the Choke Canyon Reservoir on the Frio River near Three Rivers. The two lakes also will provide industry and communities of the area with ample water for years to come.

Reflecting Corpus Christians' civic pride in their past and in their present, the city motto several years ago was "Port of Play and Profit."

That motto holds true for the future as well as the past.

Prickly pear cactus blossoms, courtesy, Texas Highways

Top left: King Carlos III ruled Texas from 1759 to 1788, serving as King of Spain during the American Revolution. This bronze statue was a bicentennial gift from King Juan Carlos of Spain to Nueces County. Courtesy, Nueces County

Bottom left: This tiny crucifix is the *pièce de résistance* of the treasures salvaged from a sunken Spanish galleon off the Texas Gulf Coast. Barely an inch long and crafted of pure gold, the cross is thought to have belonged to Ponce de León's daughter-in-law. Courtesy, Texas Highways

Above: The lovely mesquite tree is a menace to farmers and ranchers, but it has been useful, providing lumber for fence posts, railroad ties and fuel, and providing beans which Confederates used for "mesquite coffee" during Civil War shortages. Courtesy, Texas Highways

Above: Using nature's lavish palette, a green South Texas pasture blooms with bluebonnets and orange Indian paintbrush. Courtesy, Texas Highways

Above: The Army of Occupation, commanded by General Zachary Taylor, moved from Corpus Christi to the Rio Grande on March 11, 1846, leaving the booming town of 2,000 nearly deserted. Courtesy, Corpus Christi Area Heritage Society

Right: The rope bed in the south parlor of Centennial House sports a handwoven coverlet with the inscription "Made by S. Riegel, German Township, for Joannah Baker, 1847." Coverlets like these were often made by itinerant weavers who would reside with a family for a time and do whatever weaving was requested. Courtesy, Corpus Christi Area Heritage Society

Top left: Charles Berkeley Normann painted this portrait of "Colonel" Henry Lawrence Kinney, founder of Corpus Christi. Courtesy, Corpus Christi State University

Below left: Colonel Kinney held the first state fair in Corpus Christi on May 1, 1852. The prizes included silver urns, pitchers, punch bowls and a "splendid assortment of Rich Goblets, cups, tumblers, etc." Each prize bore the following inscription (with empty space for the winner's name): "From H.L. Kinney, and General Committee of Lone Star Fair, Corpus Christi, May 1852." Courtesy, Corpus Christi Museum

Above: Captain John Ireland with his small land force captured Yankee boats off Mustang Island in 1863, as shown in T.J. Noakes' painting *Battle of Corpus Christi Pass.* Courtesy, City of Corpus Christi

Purple bull thistle, courtesy, Texas Highways

Top left: James Henderson Roark, "the largest truck farmer in Texas" (height 6 feet, 4 inches, weight 388 pounds), organized the Roark Produce Company with T.M. Lawrence and F.V. Woodward. Truck farming was one of the most important trades in the early 1900s. Courtesy, Mr. and Mrs. Atlee Cunningham

Bottom left: Centennial House, completed in 1850, is the oldest house in the Corpus Christi area. It was used as a hospital during the Civil War, and has been a place of refuge from storms and raiding parties throughout its long history. Courtesy, Corpus Christi Area Heritage Society

Above: Eugenia Lavender painted this full-length portrait of St. Patrick for the sisters of the Incarnate Word Academy in Corpus Christi. The picture hung in the sanctuary of the old St. Patrick's Church. Courtesy, Sisters of the Incarnate Word and Blessed Sacrament

Above: The Limoges china pictured, decorated with the initials "PVK," belonged to Petra Vela Kenedy, wife of Captain Mifflin Kenedy. America was in full swing with Victoriana; many different and unusual items were considered not only proper but necessary for decoration of home and table. Limoges table china was quite expensive and fragile; the Kenedys' was probably the only set of Limoges china in South Texas at the time. Courtesy, Corpus Christi Museum

Top: The Sidbury house, built by businesswoman Charlotte Sidbury in 1893, is the last surviving example of High Victorian architecture in Corpus Christi. In 1979 the Junior League of Corpus Christi received a National Trust award for restoring and adapting the house for use as a museum and offices. Courtesy, Nueces County Historical Society

Above: The Gugenheim house, handsomely restored by the Campfire Girls, was built around 1900 by Simon Gugenheim, who was a successful dry-goods merchant in Corpus Christi for many years. Courtesy, Nueces County Historical Society

Bougainvillaea, courtesy, Texas Highways

CORPUS CHRISTI, TEXAS
Under the Salt Cedars,
Seaside Hotel

Above: This postcard view of guests sitting under the salt cedars at the Seaside Pavilion Hotel and Pier was popular in the early 1900s. The hotel was known throughout the United States. Courtesy, La Retama Library

Opposite page, top left: Vacationers swam and enjoyed a magnificent view of the water at the Seaside Pavilion Hotel and Pier. The pavilion was destroyed in the hurricane of 1919. Courtesy, Texas A & I University John E. Conner Museum

Right: The Nueces Hotel's lovely sun parlor, with its wicker furniture and plants, was not only for tourists. People flocked there for informal business meetings. It is said that more business took place in the sun parlor than in any office in town. Courtesy, La Retama Library

Opposite page, center left: The bandstand in Artesian Park, captured on this postcard circa 1908, was the scene of many concerts and political rallies. Courtesy, Texas A & I University John E. Conner Museum

Above: The 1914 Nueces County Courthouse, here illustrated in watercolor by Vava Calahan, is one of the finest Classical Revival structures in the American Southwest. Its most striking feature is the tall entrance pavilion facing the bay, preceded by a broad flight of steps and decorated with columns, terra-cotta figures, and a crowning pediment. The building was given National Register designation in the late 1970s, and there is hope that it will be restored. Courtesy, Nueces County Historical Society

Wild olive blossom, courtesy, Texas Highways

Above: The present Church of the Good Shepherd is at the corner of Broadway at Park. A striking feature of the church is the display of the six flags that have flown over Texas during her colorful history. On the left hang the flags of Mexico, Spain, and France, and on the right the flags of the Republic, the Confederacy, and the United States. Courtesy, Nueces County Historical Society

Right: The Art Museum of South Texas was designed by New York architect Philip Johnson. It features changing exhibitions, films, lectures, art classes, tour guide programs, a library of 2,500 volumes, and a gift shop. The building is owned and maintained by the city of Corpus Christi, while programs are sponsored by the Corpus Christi Art Foundation, which is funded by private donations. Courtesy, Jim Darby

Above: The award-winning *Cotton Pickers*, painted in 1939 by
Antonio E. Garcia from sketches he made in Robstown,
depicts Mexican cotton pickers gathered on Saturday to spend
their meager earnings. *Raspa*, watermelon, and guitar music
help the laborers to relax after their back-breaking work. This
painting was included in a traveling exhibit in 1939; in 1976 it
was selected for the exhibit "17 Mexican-American Painters,"
which was shown in museums from Boston to San Francisco.
Courtesy, Antonio E. Garcia

Above: *Rejoice With Me*, a statue of the shepherd in the
parable of the lost sheep (Luke XV), stands at the Church of
the Good Shepherd. The work was created by Sherman T.
Coleman, M.D., a Corpus Christi surgeon and an award-
winning member of the Southwest Sculpture Society.
Courtesy, Nueces County Historical Society

Bottlebrush, courtesy, Texas Highways

Opposite page, left: One of the Museum of Oriental Culture's dioramas is of a five-story pagoda, a replica of one in Japan. The museum houses the largest collection of Hakata dolls in the United States. Courtesy, Texas Highways

Opposite page, right: Skulls of longhorn cattle at the base of a column and a cluster of flying seagulls at the top come together in this sculpture by Helen Richter Watson of Laredo, Texas. The work graces the planted area in the lobby of the Nueces County Courthouse. Courtesy, Nueces County

Above: The eerie, fantastic beauty of the wind-swept oaks along the shore of Live Oak Peninsula brings many visitors to Rockport year after year. Courtesy, Texas Highways

Top right: Date palm and bougainvillaea. Courtesy, Texas Highways

Redbud, courtesy, Texas Highways

109

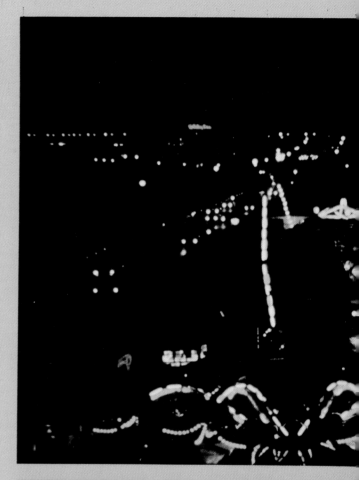

Above: Young and old come to see the Christmas decorations in the popular annual Christmas Tree Forest at the Art Museum of South Texas. Courtesy, Texas Highways

Top right: Traditionally Corpus Christi has had annual celebrations and events during the summer, like Epworth-by-the- Sea and Splash Days. The carnival pictured is part of today's Buccaneer Days. Courtesy, Corpus Christi Area Convention and Tourist Bureau

Bottom right: These shells native to the Texas coast are displayed in a typesetting tray. Courtesy, Texas Highways

Poinsettias, courtesy, Texas Highways

111

The mechanical cotton-harvesting machine, which could
harvest two rows of cotton at a time, was first introduced to
the area in 1948. Early machines harvested about ten acres per
day, or ten bales of cotton. In use today is the four-row
harvester, with a harvesting capability of 30-40 acres per day.
Prior to the progress made in the development of such
machines, cotton was picked by hand with "stoop labor."
Courtesy, Corpus Christi Caller-Times

Partners in Progress

Most of the major cities of America were born along rivers, deep-water coastal ports, wagon-train routes, or rail lines, where they became centers of trade. So it was for Corpus Christi, in a rich region of fertile farmland, limitless pastures for stock grazing, bountiful fishing and hunting, and a delightful climate.

European immigrants were flocking to settle South Texas when Colonel Henry Lawrence Kinney, a 25-year-old Pennsylvania entrepreneur, opened his trading post, or "rancho," in September 1839 atop a 40-foot bluff on the town's crescent-shaped bayshore. Although Corpus Christi was hardly more than a camp at the time, it was an ideal gathering place for Mexican, Anglo, and Indian traders. They brought immense droves of horses and mules, saddles, bridles, blankets, and silver; they took back with them unbleached domestics and tobacco.

The ambitious Kinney's business flourished as he became the city's first real merchant, colonizer, politician, and smuggler and built its first house, fort, and corral. A later achievement was as Corpus Christi's representative in the state capital, promoting the city as both a shipping and wagon-freight center.

The encampment of U.S. General Zachary Taylor's Army troops in 1845 during the Mexican War sparked a burgeoning growth in population, commerce, and as a seaport; the 5,000 troopers spent freely and attracted new trade. In 1849 the California Gold Rush brought more visitors and trade as ranchers sold wild mustangs and mules to gold hunters who came by boat to travel overland to California. Soon a thriving, diversified economy emerged with cattle raising, farming, fishing, assorted-goods shipments, and tourism.

The oil and gas industry opened up in 1914, boomed in the 1930s, and remains today a powerful economic influence. It has its own immense place in history and has ensured the future prosperity of the city, more so than any other single business factor. The energy sources fueled the arrival from the eastern United States of major petro-chemical, oil-refining, metals-manufacturing, and other industries, creating large staff openings and payrolls.

The opening of the deep-water harbor and channel to the Gulf of Mexico in 1926, the Corpus Christi Naval Air-Training Command in 1941, and the Corpus Christi Army Depot in the 1950s added other enormous business, economic, and population developments.

The Corpus Christi Chamber of Commerce, formed in 1905, has provided a steady, active leadership in the expansion of the business community. The Chamber's backbone, of course, has always been its membership of organizations committed not only to a fair profit, but to a strong and viable economy.

Corpus Christi firms take pride in the contribution they have made to the city's outstanding growth. Some have grown and flourished for many years; others have made equally important marks in only a few years of operation. The histories of many of these organizations are presented here as partners in Corpus Christi's progress.

BAKER MARINE CORPORATION

In a world of industrial giants that supply men, machines, and materials to the oil and gas industry, Baker Marine Corporation has emerged as one of the new breed of offshore companies. Even though it is a young corporation, organized in 1972, Baker Marine has made its mark in the worldwide construction of mobile self-elevating offshore drilling platforms and in other areas of the energy industry.

Larry Baker, Sr., has long been known for his uncanny ability to get common people to do uncommon things. The growth and acceptance of Baker Marine Corporation in the offshore oil and gas industry is proof of that ability.

The Baker family built Baker Marine from a one-rig-a-year construction yard into an international energy-related corporation. The total operation encompasses more than 20 subsidiary companies, which have different capabilities that relate to the energy industry. Today Baker Marine Corporation is the largest privately owned manufacturer of offshore drilling platforms and support equipment in the world.

Baker and his son, Larry Baker, Jr., direct the worldwide activities of Baker Marine Corporation from the international headquarters near Ingleside, Texas. It was this location on the North Corpus Christi Bay shoreline that Larry Baker, Sr., in December 1973, came to work for a troubled rig building company, I.H.C. Holland. He ultimately turned it into a winner with his expertise and motivation skills. These skills, along with his ability to plan for the future and work a plan into a reality, have earned recognition for the Baker name.

The firm's key advancements have come in the design, development, and construction of mobile self-elevating offshore drilling platforms. Since the future production of offshore oil and gas lies in the deeper waters of the continental shelf, Baker Marine's newest jack-up rig design is for water depths of up to 450 feet. This new design is for water 100 feet deeper than any other design currently on the market. This is another innovative step by Larry Baker, Sr., to help ensure a way for the United States to obtain a constant and stable supply of petroleum energy. With Baker Marine Corporation's worldwide network of engineering and development personnel,

The first rig built under the Baker Marine Corporation name— a BMC 300 independent leg slot-type offshore drilling platform, designed to operate in 300 feet of water. This photograph shows the rig undergoing a test of the elevating system at the Ingleside, Texas, shipyard.

Larry A. Baker, Sr., chairman of the board of Baker Marine Corporation.

Baker Marine designed and manufactured electro-hydraulic elevating units for mobile self-elevating offshore platforms.

designs for pipelay barges, semisubmersible drilling rigs, and production jackets have been completed. Baker Marine's ongoing research and development department has helped diversify the companies' product line to include a 30-ton crane, 75-ton crane, anchor winch, crane winches, skidding systems, elevating systems for mobile offshore rigs, and a windlass. New innovations, which are still in the research and development stage, include a method of recovery for stationary jacket platforms.

Baker Marine was an outgrowth of I.H.C. Holland-LeTourneau Marine Corporation. I.H.C. Holland was a Dutch shipbuilding firm that specialized in the design and construction of cargo vessels and dredges. I.H.C. Holland wanted to expand its operations to include the mobile self-elevating offshore rig-building industry. In an effort to bring about this expansion, the company formed a partnership with R.L. LeTourneau, nephew of the great industrialist and inventor, R.G. LeTourneau.

R.L. LeTourneau sold three rigs, one to Penrod Drilling, one to Petrobras (the Brazilian National Oil Company), and one to Maersk Drilling. Construction of the first rig, "Penrod 63," was started in February 1971 at the Ingleside yard. During this time I.H.C. Holland purchased LeTourneau's shares and changed the name to I.H.C. Holland Marine Corporation. As construction problems mounted and delivery dates were missed, I.H.C. hired Larry Baker to assume management of the Ingleside fabrication yard. Under Baker's management, agreements were worked out with Petrobras and Penrod. Petrobras purchased the hull that was under construction for Penrod Drilling. The hull was completed, renamed, and christened "Petrobras III" in December 1973. Larry Baker not only directed the completion of the unit to the satisfaction of its owners but also purchased the Ingleside company from I.H.C. Holland. On June 26, 1974, he formed Baker Shipbuilding Corporation, renaming the

venture Baker Marine Corporation the following November 15.

Since the start and completion of Hull 01, Baker Marine Corporation has assembled nearly 60 offshore drilling rigs at its 57-acre facility and at locations around the world. Some of the giant rigs tower above 50-story office buildings and have periodically dominated the Corpus Christi area skyline.

At peak construction periods, the Baker Marine labor force has numbered almost 1,500 persons, making BMC one of the Corpus Christi region's largest private employers. In January 1982 Baker unveiled plans for a mammoth offshore drilling rig service and repair complex, which is estimated to bring a billion-dollar investment and provide more than 5,000 new jobs over its development in the next five years. This project, Baker's Port, Inc., is under development on 3,000 acres which were purchased from National Steel Corporation of Pittsburgh. Baker's Port will mean not only a major expansion of the Baker rig-manufacturing yard, but will also offer dry-docking facilities to accommodate the largest existing pieces of exploration and production equipment currently in use throughout the world. The dry-docking facility will provide a much-needed service to the offshore petroleum interest. All offshore drilling contractors are being required to meet increased industry and federal regulations to ensure maximum protection for personnel and equipment.

Baker's Port is a planned industrial, commercial, and residential development that will allow people and

Construction techniques employed by BMC include the Papa Bear crane. The 800-ton-capacity barge-mounted revolving crane is owned by the BMC subsidiary, Baker Offshore Erector Company, and is shown setting a 10-foot diameter, 300-foot-long leg section for a BMC 250 mat-type rig at the Ingleside yard.

An aerial view of Baker Marine Corporation's yard in Ingleside, Texas.

industry to coexist in an environment that will enhance family life and job productivity. Long-term lease sites for light industrial, commercial, residential, and recreational facilities are included. Development plans call for a golf course, hospital, shopping center, schools, hotels, and condominiums. Deep-water access will also be available for raw and refined product warehousing for import and export throughout worldwide marine markets.

The independent Baker Marine firm has built more than 20 different rig designs ranging from shallow-water drilling barges for inland and protected waterways to rigs capable of drilling in 350 feet of water. In addition to its main fabrication yard near Ingleside, Baker Marine Corporation also operates two related fabrication sites in Corpus Christi, at Cabaniss Field and on Rincon Industrial Channel.

Because of the great demand for versatility in the oil patch, Baker Marine Corporation expanded its operations to include new products and services. The company is divided into six categories of expertise: construction, drilling, engineering, land development, offshore service, and resource transport and recovery. With this diversification, Baker Marine Corporation is able to serve the energy-related industries of Corpus Christi and the world.

Baker Marine's construction facilities include the main yard at Ingleside, Texas. This is where Baker Marine Corporation fabricates the steel components such as side plates, bottom plates, top plates, leg wells, legs, and leg

footings that eventually become a Baker Marine class of mobile self-elevating offshore drilling platform. As an extension of this yard, the Cabaniss manufacturing plant in Corpus Christi fabricates elevating gear units, gears, drill floors, cantilever beams, and mechanical equipment. Other companies that comprise the construction end of Baker Marine Corporation are Art Coles, Inc., in Port Lavaca, Texas; Baker Marine Private Limited, in Singapore; Hart-Baker, Inc., in Lafayette, Louisiana; and Rutherford, Inc., in Fairfield, Texas.

J.F.P. Well Service, Inc., and its affiliated companies comprise the major Baker Marine Corporation subsidiary engaged in the search for reserves of oil and natural gas. They have land-based rigs with a 25,000-foot drilling depth capacity, well-servicing units to meet down-hole problems encountered by older wells, and offshore drilling rigs for use in water depths of up to 350 feet. These large mobile offshore units are capable of drilling to depths of 25,000 feet. Along with J.F.P.'s capabilities, Baker Marine Corporation has partial interest in other offshore rigs around the world.

Baker Marine's engineering experience in all facets of offshore environments has led the industry in new designs and ideas. With the staff of engineers and designers at the Ingleside plant and the corporate efforts of subsidiary companies, new ideas have become realities. Baker Marine's engineering companies include Baker Marine Engineers and Baker Brown Offshore in Houston, Texas; and Self Erecting Platform Management Private Limited in Singapore.

In land development, Baker's Port, Inc., and Baker Agriculture have made a significant economical impact on the Corpus Christi area. Baker's Port will generate new employment opportunities in the South Texas area.

Service to the offshore market, both domestic and foreign, has helped make Baker Marine Corporation the organization that it is today. Baker service companies include Baker Offshore Erector Company, Baker Marine Offshore Services, Baker Marine Technical Services Private Limited of Singapore, and Baker Aviation. The most dominant of these companies is Baker Offshore Erectors with its 800-ton-capacity revolving offshore crane.

In the last area to be considered, resource transport and recovery, Baker Energy Resources Corporation (BERCO) is a firm engaged in the directionally controlled horizontal drilling industry. BERCO provides the pipeline industry with economic and environmentally acceptable means in which to pass pipelines for resource transport, resource transmission, energy transmission, and communications. This system offers an alternative to digging through or building over natural and man-made obstructions.

BOYD-CAMPBELL COMPANY, INC.

It is more than coincidence that the histories of Boyd-Campbell Company, Inc., and the Port of Corpus Christi are nearly identical.

Arkansas-born J.L. Boyd was operating a steamship agency in Beaumont when plans were being made for the Port of Corpus Christi. Born in 1869, he got his start working for the railroads, a common training ground at the time for anyone working in shipping, and had traveled around the Gulf Coast area. The new harbor interested him and he moved here in 1925 with his company, Boyd-Campbell, which his grandsons operate today.

When Boyd was persuaded to take the job as the first director of the infant Port of Corpus Christi, his only son, Tom—who was also in the shipping business in Port Arthur and Beaumont—moved to the area to run his father's shipping company.

Boyd-Campbell was the first local stevedore company and steamship agency to serve as money changer, grocer, fuel attendant, cargo business agent, public-relations expert, go-between, and general problem-solver for the ships that called in Corpus Christi.

Serving as port director until 1930 when Colonel L.M. Adams retired from the U.S. Army Corps of Engineers and assumed the post, J.L. Boyd remained with the port as assistant director and traffic manager until his death

in 1939. His former partner, Steele Campbell, had died two years earlier.

Over the years since 1925, Boyd-Campbell has counted many "firsts." These include the first cargo of cotton in 1926, then initial shipments of bulk sulfur, cottonseed cake, onions from the Coastal Bend, West Coast lumber for the 1930s oil boom, drummed gasoline, scrap iron, bulk-grain sorghum, and assorted bulk ores. During the 1940s war years, the company operated a surplus-commodities depot for the U.S. Navy—discharging vessels, segregating and warehousing merchandise, and loading out cars and trucks.

The organization was the first tenant of Corpus Christi's first "skyscraper," the Nixon Building (now the Wilson Building). Tom Boyd was also the first president of the Propeller Club, Port of Corpus Christi, a position later held by his two sons.

Tom Jr., who joined the firm in late 1945, and James S. (Jim), who became a member in 1955, assumed the leadership of the company after their father's death in 1959. James S. (Sonny) Boyd and David S. Boyd are the fourth generation to be involved in the operation.

Through the years one member whose name seldom appeared in business dealings but whose influence gave stable support, inspiration, and counsel has been the corporation's principal stockholder, Mrs. Tom (Phyllis) Boyd, Sr.

Today Boyd-Campbell Company, Inc., is recognized worldwide. Many of the port's 4,000 sailings a year of world trade in oil, grains, chemicals, general cargoes, and ores are carried by ships served by the organization.

J.L. Boyd, founder of Boyd-Campbell Company, Inc.

Tom M. Boyd, Sr.

W.L. BATES COMPANY

Since 1980 the W.L. Bates Company has been one of the most successful commercial, industrial, and ranch real estate firms in South Texas.

"I don't sell any better than anybody else, I guess. But I might work harder at it," says W.L. Bates. "And the harder you work, the luckier you get."

Real estate experts in the Corpus Christi market say Bates' 10-member sales force has become so recognized among major Texas and U.S. business developers that the firm receives more inquiries from large energy, industrial, and commercial prospects searching for new stores, offices, or manufacturing plants than the Corpus Christi Industrial Commission and the Chamber of Commerce—the city's principal promoters of new business and industry. Crediting his personal exposure for much of his success, Bates holds membership in a wide range of professional organizations and is active in many community projects.

Bates was born August 8, 1923, in Corpus Christi to the late W.L. Bates, Sr., and Agnes McAllister Bates, who moved to the city in 1911. His interest in real estate was motivated by F.M. Thomason, father of his childhood friend, Johnny, and he became a salesman for the realtor in 1946.

Below
W.L. Bates, president and chairman of W.L. Bates Company.
Below right
W.L. Bates in front of company's new building occupied in June 1982.

In 1948 Bates opened his own real estate agency in a small wooden building in the 4600 block of Leopard, which he shared with real estate investor D.W. Grant. His sales grew steadily until 1980, when Corpus Christi boomed with oil-related industry and business growth. In the following two years Bates' firm logged almost $200 million in sales—this included about 20 sales in excess of one million dollars each.

Prime property transactions negotiated by W.L. Bates Company include 3,000 acres of National Steel Corporation land on north Corpus Christi Bay Shore for $45 million, land for the $30-million Sunrise Mall Shopping Center on South Padre Island Drive, and 1,600 acres of El Paso Natural Gas land on the Portland shoreline.

Other major deals include acreage on Emerald Cove for a hotel site, property at North Padre Island Drive for another industrial park, the old Sears building on Leopard Street, The Mayflower Hotél site, the old Breakers Hotel site on North Beach, Sand and Sea Motel on Shoreline, many acres of the Sam Wilson estate on Mustang Island, and several large South Texas ranches.

The agency has had a part in the development or plant expansions of such firms as American Smelting and Refining (ASARCO), Berry Engineering, Exxon Company U.S.A., Padre Island National Seashore, Coastal States Petroleum Company, Baker Marine Corporation, Tenneco, Southwestern Refining, Champlin Petroleum, and others.

President of family-owned Coastal Bend Oil Company and Bacor Corporation, Bates also has extensive ranch and farm properties. He also holds interests in The 600 Building at Leopard and Upper Broadway and in the Wardner Ranch and Baldwin Farms.

Bates developed Corpus Christi residential areas of Tropic Isles, Donna Park, Hudson Acres, Kingswood, Oak Ridge, Jackson Heights, and was associated in the development of the Pernitas Point residential subdivision at Lake Corpus Christi.

Named Realtor of the Year in 1966, Bates is a past president of the Corpus Christi Board of Realtors. He also was a member of the Nueces County Park Board from 1968 to 1976, and served on the board of the Corpus Christi Better Business Bureau for nine years. Other duties have entailed activities on numerous Chamber of Commerce committees.

Bates established the Mr. and Mrs. W.L. Bates Ministerial Educational Fund at Brite Divinity School at Texas Christian University. He is past master counselor of the Corpus Christi Order of DeMolay.

The realtor has been involved in state and federal governmental agency studies and site acquisition teams for the Padre Island National Seashore and Mustang Island State Park. He was on the appraisals and acquisitions committee for the governments of the United States and Mexico on the Falcon Dam Project, and was a consultant on the development of the McAllen Foreign Trade Zone. Additionally, he has been an appraiser for the Texas Department of Highways, U.S. Internal Revenue Service, City of Corpus Christi, Nueces County, U.S. Department of the Navy, U.S. Department of the Interior, U.S. Small Business Administration, and others.

Bates drew up the first major industrial potential study for the Corpus Christi metropolitan area in 1963, and is a past chairman of the Corpus Christi Industrial Commission.

An avid orchid grower, for which he has won many prizes, he is a trustee, life member, and senior judge of the American Orchid Society. Also included in his many activities are membership in or directorship of the Urban Land Institute, Texas Industrial Development Commission, Texas and Southwestern Cattlemen's Associations, Texas and American Charolais Association, North American Quarter Horse Association, American Cattle Breeders Hall of Fame, Corpus Christi Area Convention and Tourist Bureau, First Christian Church Board of Deacons, Masonic Lodge No. 189, Alzafar Shrine Club, Texas Farm Bureau, 32nd-degree Masonic Order, Goodwill Industries, and

One of the many W.L. Bates-held interests is in The 600 Building at Leopard and Upper Broadway in downtown Corpus Christi.

National Riflemen's Association.

Bates is president and chairman of W.L. Bates Company. His son, Dan Bates, is vice-president and Earl Pennel, Jr., secretary-treasurer.

BRADLEYS', INC.

The year 1930 held few good tidings to citizens of Corpus Christi, who joined countless thousands across the nation in the Great Depression.

However, that year, on September 30, in a two-car-deep, one-car-wide garage on what was then known as B Street, a new enterprise took an optimistic venture into those shaky and troubled times. Founded as the Fixit Shop, it would prosper and emerge as one of Corpus Christi's major industries.

The firm began repairing domestic appliances, automobile electrical devices, and doing other odd-job, machine shop-type repairs. Original equipment included a few hand tools, an old Rahn-Larmon machine lathe built in the 1890s, and a pre-1900-vintage drill press. The first hoist was a chain block hung from a hackberry tree. Although V.A. "Dick" Bradley, Sr., Gail Bradley, and their father, H.L. Bradley, comprised the total initial work force, customer demand was there and the small quarters quickly became inadequate. The firm moved to a frame building at 1618 South Staples where emphasis was placed on automobile-engine repair and rebuilding. Electric motors and magneto repair and servicing soon became a significant part of business and the name was changed to Electro Mechanical Company.

Mrs. Marie Bradley, Gail's wife, and J.B. Funchus joined the management of the organization. Funchus devoted his activities to the electrical phase while Mrs. Bradley handled accounting and bookkeeping.

The company relocated to 603 South Staples a few years later, becoming Gulf Coast Armature Works. Another expansion to meet growing business needs prompted the firm's move to 1513 Leopard in 1937; it was then renamed Bradleys' Motor and Armature Works.

As Corpus Christi's heavy industries began to arrive—such as Southern Alkali, Corn Products, and Pontiac Refinery—the corporation developed a sales and distribution division. "V" belts and ropes, sheaves, electric motors, generators, and control systems manufactured under the BMAW name were supplied to industrial customers in an increasing world of electrical motors, large and small.

Bradleys' relocated to its present site at 1920 North Port Avenue in 1947. That final move began its most impressive years of expansion and business growth. More employees were added as work orders grew.

In 1946 Dick Bradley, Jr., joined the organization to add his youthful enthusiasm to the family operation. He encouraged the addition of more modern technology, shop expansions, and other improvements.

Warren Spanutius, an electrical engineer, joined the firm in 1967 as a co-partner with Dick Bradley, Jr. Spanutius' addition helped the company handle increased technical demands for larger and more complex products and services.

Today the original 8,000 square feet of shop on Port Avenue has been expanded to five times that amount. Bradleys' now is a recognized leader in all motor-repair fields and employs a staff of 50 persons.

Motors are rewound in a range from a fraction of a horsepower to 6,000-horsepower. Cranes in the plant can hoist pieces of equipment of up to 20 tons. The balancing facility can accommodate equipment weighing up to 20,000 pounds.

The second home of Bradleys' was at 1618 South Staples Street.

Bradleys' operated a third location at 603 South Staples Street.

Explosive growth in the refrigeration and air conditioning industries in the '50s and '60s brought diversification for Bradleys'. One of the largest hermetic rebuilding businesses in the nation at the time, it developed one of the trade's first production-line operations.

As parts for hermetically sealed compressors were difficult to obtain, the organization frequently met the challenge by manufacturing its own dies and parts. Consequently, a parts division evolved to supply parts to other rebuilders throughout the United States.

Today the corporation operates several business divisions and manufactures sewer-lift stations and packaged sewer-treatment plants for municipal and private industrial customers in many areas. It also supplies compressor parts such as connecting rods and valve plates internationally through a catalog agency.

Both Dick Bradley, Jr., and Warren Spanutius have been active in community and religious work. Bradley served as a member of the Corpus Christi City Council under the Jack Blackmon administration for two terms from 1967, and was the first president of the Independent Hermetic Rebuilders' Association. He was also president of the Southwestern Chapter Electrical Apparatus Service Association from 1958 to 1960.

In 1937 the firm moved to 1513 Leopard Street; it was then renamed Bradleys' Motor and Armature Works.

Spanutius headed the latter organization in 1982, and is a past national president of the Refrigeration Compressor Rebuilders' Association, composed of 100 firms in 50 states.

The present-day operation of Bradleys', Inc., offers a wide range of motor-repair functions.

H.E. BUTT GROCERY COMPANY

From its origins in 1905 to today, H.E. Butt Grocery Company has been in a constant state of growth, committing its energies to meet the requirements of the Texas communities H.E.B. serves.

Mrs. Florence Butt opened a small family grocery store in Kerrville during the year 1905. Her young son, Howard E. Butt, took over the family business in 1919. Howard initiated "one-stop" shopping by adding a butcher shop to the traditional grocery items. He expanded the business to small towns in the Hill Country, West Texas, and the Rio Grande Valley. The first three Corpus Christi stores were opened in 1931.

The headquarters for the fast-growing chain was moved to the Rio Grande Valley in 1928. In 1939 the company's offices were moved again, this time to Corpus Christi, as H.E.B. stores grew along the Coastal Bend.

Charles Butt, a graduate of the University of Pennsylvania's Wharton School of Finance, became president in 1971. During the 1970s, H.E.B. grew from 4,000 employees to 16,000.

Today there are 155 H.E.B. stores serving an area from just south of Dallas to the Mexican border. H.E.B. has emerged as a billion-dollar company, the nation's 14th largest supermarket organization, and one of the most innovative chains in the country. The success of H.E.B. can be attributed to the firm's emphasis on the development of its most important resource—its employees.

H.E.B. takes great pride in its manufacturing, warehouse, and distribution facilities, operating milk, meat, ice cream, cheese, and photo-processing plants as well as pastry and bread bakeries. All of these facilities utilize the most modern technology in the industry and provide H.E.B. stores with top-quality merchandise. As an example of the quality guaranteed with H.E.B. products, the American Cultured Dairy Products

The architectural design of H.E.B. stores has greatly changed since the 1940s, but the philosophy of providing customers the goods they desire, with friendly service, has remained the same.

Today H.E.B. stores average 45,000 square feet in size and service 16,000 customers per week, offering a pleasant atmosphere as well as convenient one-stop shopping.

Institute has ranked H.E.B.'s award-winning yogurt among the top three nationally for the past two years.

The newest addition to H.E.B.'s manufacturing facilities is the Photo Place, a photo-processing plant which opened in 1982. The plant was developed utilizing the concept of employees actually devising the methods and systems used in operating the plant. The Photo Place is one of only a few plants utilizing this participatory design approach.

The company's distribution centers employ over 1,800 people and cover over one million square feet. H.E.B.'s truck fleet travels over 44,000 miles per day—enough to circle the globe one and one-half times. Known for their skill and excellent safety records, H.E.B. drivers are always among the top 10 in state and national truck "roadeos," the contests which rate drivers on their driving skills and safety techniques.

H.E.B. Food/Drug stores have changed in a dynamic way from the 1905 store. Today H.E.B. stores average 45,000 square feet in size and service 16,000 customers per week. Utilizing a vivid color scheme, they are designed to offer customers a pleasant atmosphere as well as convenient one-stop shopping.

In addition to the standard departments of grocery, general merchandise, produce, service, and market, many H.E.B. stores offer their customers goods from specialty departments. These departments provide personalized service and include a hot bake shop, Western Chef Deli, and fresh plant and floral departments. Some stores provide a full-service pharmacy, open seven days a week for the customer's convenience.

Long a leader in public service, H.E.B. is a concerned participant in helping the communities it serves reach their goals. Despite its growth, H.E.B. has retained the flavor of the region it serves. Truly a Texas corporation, H.E.B.'s strength lies in its relationship with its customers and its employees.

CELANESE CHEMICAL COMPANY TECHNICAL CENTER

From small experiments, mighty laboratories grow. That happened at the Celanese Chemical Company's Technical Center (CCCTC) in Corpus Christi, a landmark facility for one of the giants of U.S. business.

An un-air conditioned, mosquito-filled World War II Army Quonset hut was the original laboratory and offices for the handful of staff which opened that pilot Celanese research lab on Clarkwood Road in September 1946. Today CCCTC's scientists share credit for developing 75 percent of the myriad of chemical processes operated by its worldwide chemical parent firm.

The Clarkwood technical center has been responsible for the majority of 200 U.S. patents issued for Celanese products and processes commercialized over the past 10 years. Celanese started its technical research center here 36 years ago as a result of the corporation's need for acetic acid.

Celanese had opened a Nueces County plant at Bishop to produce several chemicals or building blocks for numerous consumer product markets. Formaldehyde, acetaldehyde, and methanol headed the Bishop list of chemical streams. The technical center evolved from a corporate decision to separate research efforts from production with a goal toward an expanded and improved chemical line.

The first year, CCCTC researchers concentrated on development projects associated with the Bishop plant. But soon their program broadened to include chemical research of a more exploratory nature. In late 1949 work began on a new liquid-phase hydrocarbon oxidation process, the principal product of which was acetic acid. Within 18 months a successful process at the Clarkwood unit led to the erection of a new plant at Pampa, Texas, based on the work at the Corpus Christi Technical Center.

In 1952 large units were added to the Bishop plant for the expanded production of paraformaldehyde and trioxane, both based on processes developed at CCCTC. That same year a new process developed here produced pentaerythritol (PE). Celanese's Canadian affiliate at Edmonton, Alberta, went on-stream to manufacture the chemical. Another PE unit was later built at Bishop.

From that humble Quonset hut beginning, Celanese Chemical Company's Technical Center rapidly expanded to match the overall growth of the company. A $10-million expansion, completed in 1982, added 62 offices and 38 office-laboratories to swell the under-roof Technical Center space to 147,000 square feet. CCCTC employs 265 chemists, engineers, and related technical staff.

Celanese Corporation, founded in 1918, is a diversified world producer of chemicals, fibers, plastics, and special products. The corporation and its affiliates operate 80 plants with 47,000 employees in the United States and 17 other countries. Annual sales exceed three billion dollars.

The humble beginning, in 1946.

Celanese Chemical Company's Technical Center in Corpus Christi, after the 1982 expansion.

E.L. CALDWELL AND SONS, INC.

They started out making cypress water tanks to catch rainwater for Corpus Christi residents in 1916. Then they shifted to meet the needs of a blossoming agricultural region by pioneering rotary stalk- and brush-cutting equipment.

The father and his two sons continuously devised, invented, and changed with the times to become a key worldwide distributor of farm implements made in Corpus Christi.

E.L. Caldwell and Sons, Inc., today maintains a 13-acre manufacturing plant at 3204 Agnes which sells a wide range of farm products in every state and in more than 50 foreign countries. Members of the Caldwell family and other staff hold about 20 U.S. product patents and some 25 foreign patents. From a modest start with four employees almost seven decades ago, the firm's 100 employees today manufacture 38 separate products and 150 model variations to an international customer market involved in farming, ranching, airports, highway construction, parks, and municipalities.

Invention is the key to the success of one of Corpus Christi's oldest continuous businesses, according to F. Clay Caldwell, president of the firm his father founded. The company traces its roots to the hardware store operated by E.H. Caldwell, Clay Caldwell's grandfather, from 1890 to 1919.

E.H. Caldwell Hardware supplied everything that Corpus Christi's turn-of-the-century farmer or rancher needed. It sold the first barbed wire used in this part of the state, as well as pumps, pipe and well casing, gasoline engines, and air-motor windmills. It also made cartridges and carried assorted ammunition and gunpowder and supplies.

The family's eldest son, Edward L. Caldwell, studied agriculture at Purdue and Cornell universities and later joined his father's growing business as a traveling salesman covering a wide area of southern Texas.

When the 1919 hurricane destroyed the Caldwell Hardware Store and most of its merchandise, the elder Caldwell, then 70 years of age, retired. His son, E.L. Caldwell, had established the Caldwell Cypress Cistern Company about 1916.

The young Caldwell's observation of water-storage problems of the region led to his invention of a durable

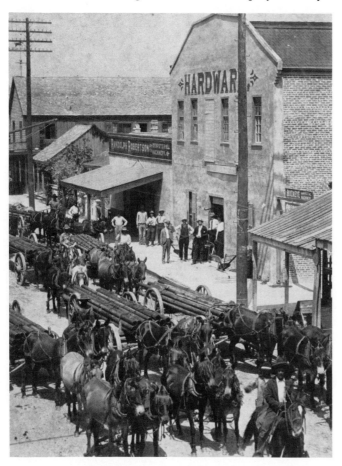

Casings for the first artesian wells drilled on the King Ranch were delivered by the E.H. Caldwell Hardware Store in 1890.

The original Caldwell Farm and Ranch Store on Chaparral Street in the early 1900s.

E.L. Caldwell and Sons, Inc., one of Corpus Christi's oldest and largest businesses, operates a worldwide farm and ranch implement production plant on 13 acres at 3204 Agnes Street.

Leaders of the worldwide Caldwell firm—the late E.L. Caldwell, Sr. (left), the late E.L. Caldwell, Jr. (center), and F. Clay Caldwell.

wooden water-holding tank. In those days people used metal tanks, which, because of local hard water and the salt air, were short-lived.

Caldwell's rugged water reservoir had staves cut two inches thick from the hearts of hardy cypress trees. These were held together with galvanized steel hoops. The tanks not only held water, they seemed to defy the passage of time.

A man of vision, Caldwell was one of the first to sense the seriousness of the encroachment of brush on pasturelands. In the 1920s Caldwell's range of manufacturing products expanded to include selling La Cross land-clearing plows and manufacturing seed-bed rollers.

In 1928 Caldwell invented a rolling cotton-stalk cutter that became an instant leader in the Texas coastal plains and later was widely accepted throughout the Cotton Belt. The cotton cutter chopped the stalks into short lengths, after which they could be plowed under or diced into the soil. Before Caldwell's stalk cutter, farmers raked and then burned cotton stalks. As a result, the land was losing its humus.

Caldwell earned his first U.S. patent for the rolling cotton-stalk cutter in 1932. The machine was the first truly successful cutter of its kind in this part of the country and contributed largely to the Caldwell firm's phenomenal business growth in the '30s and '40s.

Bulging at the seams from increased product line manufacturing, Caldwell's moved to its current site in 1945 and a large-scale product diversification program

was launched. Headed by a large rotary cutter model line, a huge export business emerged.

Today Caldwell products are heavily marketed in the United States, Central and South America, Europe and the Scandinavian countries, and elsewhere in overseas agricultural nations.

Caldwell also makes a wide line of earth-moving blades and even post-hole diggers. Another innovation is a flail cutter, which shreds the material it goes over and follows the contour of the land. The blades virtually cut vertically so they don't toss beer cans or rocks onto highways when rights of way are mowed.

When E.L. Caldwell, Sr., died in 1951, he was recognized as a man of foresight and limitless vitality and unselfish service. His contributions to the advancement of farming and ranching were incalculable.

Caldwell had made his sons, E.L. Caldwell, Jr., and F. Clay Caldwell, partners of the company in 1945. They continued the dedication and leadership patterns established by their father aimed at the improvement of farm and ranch operations throughout the world by designing and building machines for cutting brush, renovating land, and increasing soil fertility. Additional inventions, product line extensions, and modifications have all contributed to the success.

In 1978, through a sale of stock, Agrow Industries, Inc., owned by the Pritzker Family Trust of Chicago, became owners of E.L. Caldwell and Sons, Inc.

CENTRAL POWER AND LIGHT COMPANY

Progress in many areas of South Texas during the 1890s and early 1900s meant owning an electric iron or using a 12-candlepower light bulb in the parlor. Electric plants would chug to life only in the early evening, unless it was a Tuesday, which was often designated as "ironing day." At 11 p.m. the plant would shut down, but for its precious service, customers would pay flat fees, such as one dollar a month for each light bulb in some towns or 20 cents per kilowatt hour in others.

Laredo in 1888 became the first South Texas city to have electricity, with Corpus Christi and other large southern Texas towns following closely behind during the early 1890s. Soon, small power plants began appearing in even the tiniest communities as entrepreneurs sought to meet the steadily increasing demand for electrical power.

Ralph W. Morrison and Warner S. McCall were among these forward-thinking pioneers when they formed a partnership in 1910 and began acquiring utility properties. In 1916, the year they purchased the local electric companies in Uvalde, Alice, and San Diego, they decided to form the Texas Central Power Company, which became Central Power and Light Company (CPL) a decade later.

At first, each of their early locations had its own power plant, burning whatever was available—oil, gas, coal, or even wood shavings. All employees at that time were expected to know how to generate and distribute the electricity, collect the bills, wire customer's houses, build the lines, set the meters and transformers, sell appliances, and do anything else that was needed to serve the firm's customers.

One important reason a town wanted to have an electric company was to be able to run an ice plant. Morrison and McCall acquired their first ice facilities in Uvalde, Alice, and Marfa in 1917. In 1921 the success of their ventures led them to acquire the Texas Gas and Electric Company properties, which extended from Victoria to Del Rio.

The Corpus Christi ice plant and the electric company adjoining it also were acquired in 1921. Both had been destroyed in the 1919 hurricane, and they were placed back in service in 1923.

The quest for new business led the then-substantially sized company to purchase the ice plants in all the major towns in the Rio Grande Valley in the early 1920s, as well as an abandoned sugar mill in San Benito. The mill was converted into the firm's first "big" power plant, becoming La Palma Station, a facility that has remained an important part of CPL's system.

In 1925 Texas Central Power Company became a part of Middle West Utilities Corporation and changed its name to Central Power and Light Company. Its new pentagon-shaped symbol was painted on 45 ice plants, La Palma Station, and a number of small, isolated power plants throughout South Texas.

In addition to electricity and ice, CPL also owned two electric streetcar systems, one in Corpus Christi and the other in Laredo. Water and gas were other services provided to some South Texas communities, but by 1923 electricity had become the firm's main business.

Refrigeration in many Corpus Christi homes in 1930 depended on these ice delivery vehicles parked at CPL's Water Street warehouse and garage. CPL was in the ice-production business from 1917 to 1953.

By the end of 1927 the San Antonio-based company had 1,154 miles of transmission lines in service and many more under construction to serve more than 45,000 customers across the lower one-fifth of Texas.

The late '20s and early '30s ushered in a period of rapid expansion for CPL, with new local offices, water filtration, and ice plants along with steadily increasing appliance sales. Rates were reduced time after time as new, more efficient generators made electricity cheaper for CPL's customers.

The Great Depression, however, was as devastating to CPL as it was to every segment of the U.S. economy. Many cost-cutting measures were instituted, including employee pay cuts, and CPL's home office was moved from San Antonio to Corpus Christi. Bleak though the situation was, CPL never ceased providing electricity to its customers.

By CPL's 25th anniversary in 1941, the firm was serving 177 communities in South Texas. Twenty-four of these also had water service and 57 had ice service. CPL owned 28 power plants, 16 of which were regularly operated, with a total employment of 1,300 persons.

During World War II, CPL established a short-wave radio station, KRMV (Kilowatts Really Mean Victory), so that district engineers could communicate with service trucks and, in emergencies, with the local civilian defense office. Women took over many jobs vacated by military husbands and brothers. CPL's wartime efforts to maintain full electric service to the many military facilities that dotted the South Texas landscape won commendations from both the Army and Navy.

The postwar years began a period of intense growth. Between 1948 and 1958 CPL increased its kilowatt-hour sales by more than 300 percent, spending as much for new construction during this period as it had during its

Corpus Christi residents knew this building well from the late 1930s until 1955, because it housed CPL's local and district offices as well as its home office.

entire 30-year history. Electricity's success, however, doomed the company's ice business and all of CPL's ice plants were sold in 1953.

Natural gas had sparked CPL's expansion from its earliest days through the 1960s. But alternative energy sources today and for the future include nuclear, coal, and lignite, as well as natural gas. Today CPL serves 459,000 customers in 217 communities over 44 counties. To offer its services, the corporation requires 10 power plants and 2,444 employees.

Chief executive officers who have guided CPL from its ice-to-atoms growth over the years include W.S. McCall (1916-1925), Martin C. Insull (1925), James C. Kennedy (1926-1929, 1932-1939), E.B. Neiswanger (1929-1932), Lon C. Hill (1939-1954), J.L. Bates (1954-1964), E.S. Joslin (1964-1969), Barney M. Davis (1969-1974), R.W. Hardy (1974-1979), Durwood Chalker (1979-1980), William P. Sayles (1980-1981), and Merle L. Borchelt (1981-).

CPL's new $272-million coal-fired Coleto Creek Power Station near Goliad was built to help reduce rising fuel costs. Eight of the company's other power stations are natural gas-fired and one produces hydroelectric power.

CPL's Barney Davis Generating Station, located at Flour Bluff, is also the site of the Texas A&M Shrimp Mariculture Research Center. The ponds at the center of the picture use heated water from the power plant's cooling system to maintain the facility on a year-round basis.

CHAMPLIN PETROLEUM COMPANY

On Thanksgiving Day, 1937, while most folks were preparing for a turkey, cranberry sauce, and pumpkin pie dinner, a handful of employees of Pontiac Refining Corporation were readying for another occasion.

The event was the start-up of a new 4,000-barrel-a-day oil refinery on the Corpus Christi Ship Channel on Nueces Bay Boulevard. The owner and operator of the facility, Saul Singer, was in attendance for the auspicious occasion. Edwin Singer, at his father's request, joined the corporation as secretary and assistant manager in late 1937 to supervise, staff, and operate the plant.

For the next 23 years the little refinery cranked out products as periodic additions expanded the capacity of the facility. Then in April 1960, the Gulf Oil Foundation, a charitable institution founded by the Gulf Oil Corporation, purchased the Pontiac refinery from the Singer family.

Over the years the small facility had grown to a processing capacity of 54,000 barrels a day. In 1967 Celanese Corporation, then the parent organization of Champlin Petroleum Company, bought the refinery. Three years later the refinery and Champlin were purchased by the Union Pacific Corporation. Unprecedented growth was about to begin.

By 1972 the refinery had an additional 12,000 barrels-a-day capacity. In 1973 a $250-million expansion program began, which boosted its capacity to 125,000 barrels per day by early 1976. Modification of older units raised output capacity an additional 30,000 barrels a day by mid-1977.

The next major thrust for Champlin was in the petrochemicals field. In 1980 a $27-million cumene unit was completed at the refinery, which is capable of meeting 10 percent of the nation's demand for cumene, derivatives of which are used in building materials, plastics, laminates, and other products.

That same year marked the completion of the $700-million joint venture Corpus Christi Petrochemical Company ethylene complex. With the proximity of Champlin's refinery, which provides raw materials for the petrochemical complex, the 1.2-billion-pound-per-year CCPC is now fully operational and is operated by Champlin, a 37.5-percent-interest owner. A $260-million Champlin addition is also under way which will permit Champlin to process lower quality crude oil into higher value products such as regular and premium unleaded gasoline.

The company has come a long way since 1916, when an Oklahoma oil well sparked the beginning of Champlin Petroleum. Today Champlin is a fully integrated petroleum company, with 1981 revenues of four billion dollars. It is involved in the exploration and production of crude oil and natural gas; the refining, transportation, and marketing of petroleum products; and the manufacture of petrochemicals.

In addition to its operations in Corpus Christi, which provide permanent jobs to over 900 area residents, Champlin has refineries at Wilmington, California, and Enid, Oklahoma; owns or has interests in 33 natural gas processing plants; owns several pipelines; and has 850 retail service stations in the mid-continent area of the United States.

This was the start of Champlin Petroleum's 4,000-barrel-a-day processing unit in 1937.

Combined with sister Corpus Christi Petrochemical Company facility, Champlin Petroleum has a billion-dollar investment in Corpus Christi. This aerial photograph shows the Champlin refinery on Nueces Bay Boulevard.

CORPUS CHRISTI CHAMBER OF COMMERCE

As early as 1839 Corpus Christi had a one-man Chamber of Commerce in the person of Colonel Henry Lawrence Kinney, who advertised nationally and internationally for settlers to come to the "Naples of the Gulf."

However, the community's first authentic Chamber of Commerce— known as the Corpus Christi Commercial Club—was organized in 1905, when the city had a population of 6,900 persons.

Two years later the Commercial Club, under the leadership of its president, Joseph Hirsch, and its secretary, Roy Miller, sent a delegation of 60 persons to Houston to a convention of the Interstate Inland Waterway League of Louisiana and Texas. The first major project of the fledgling organization was to convince the U.S. Congress that Corpus Christi was a perfect site for a deep-water port.

Although the organization, renamed the Corpus Christi Commercial Association in 1917, was underfinanced and understaffed, it continued to push for an intracoastal canal and a deep-water harbor, industrial development, business expansion, tourists, and conventions.

In 1924 the newly formed Corpus Christi Chamber of Commerce agreed to assume the Association's obligations, assets, responsibilities, and functions. Henry B. Baldwin became the Chamber's first president on February 15, 1924, declaring to those present at the meeting that "this group of men (comprising the Chamber board) can do anything they set their minds on doing."

The formal organization of the Chamber was probably sparked by the realization of the principal goal of the old Commercial Association—opening the Port of Corpus Christi. Chamber directors helped raise $50,000 to finance a grand celebration for the opening of the Port in September 1926.

At this time, the office was moved from a building on Starr Street (near the site of the Federal Building) to the council chamber of city hall. It remained there until 1940, when it was relocated to the fifth floor of the Nixon Building (now the Wilson Building). In May 1951, $100,000 in contributions was raised to construct a building at 1201 North Shoreline Boulevard. In 1981 a $600,000 expansion and renovation project was completed, doubling the size of the original structure and providing space for the Corpus Christi Area Convention and Tourist Bureau, the Corpus Christi Business Development Commission, and the Coastal Bend Community Foundation.

Since the mid-1950s, the Chamber of Commerce has been an instrument through which Corpus Christi's business and professional leaders have invested time, talent, energy, and money to ensure the growth and progress of their community and area. Major projects have included attracting industry to this area; construction of the downtown seawall (early 1940s), the Harbor Bridge (1959), and the Padre Island and Nueces Bay causeways; establishment of the Naval Air Station (1941) and the Corpus Christi Army Depot (1961); construction of the Wesley Seale (1959) and Choke Canyon reservoirs (1982); designation of Padre Island National Seashore (1968) and Mustang Island State Park (1975); and the establishment of Corpus Christi State University (1973). All aspects of the quality of life—both economic and community—continue to be addressed by the Corpus Christi Chamber of Commerce.

From an operating fund of $30,000 in the 1920s, the Chamber's budget has grown to more than $420,000 in 1982—all voluntary contributions from the business community. Membership accounts total 2,200.

The Corpus Christi Chamber of Commerce is located at 1201 North Shoreline Boulevard.

CORPUS CHRISTI NATIONAL BANK

In 1890 Corpus Christi National Bank, the first national bank authorized to do business in Corpus Christi, opened its doors in a small one-story building just north of where La Quinta Royale Motor Inn stands today. David Hirsch was president of the fledgling bank.

The city's population numbered only 3,000 and was referred to as "The Naples of the Gulf." Although the bank was the city's only federally chartered institution, the scarcity of hard and soft money of those times was reflected by the fact that less than $5,000 was placed on deposit on opening day.

The Pioneer Bank (as it was called initially) was probably one of the very smallest in the United States. Early in 1891 the bank moved to a new two-story building erected by W.S. Rankin on North Chaparral. This property was acquired by the bank a few years later and underwent its first modernization in 1910. By this time the bank's resources had grown to slightly more than one million dollars.

During the next four decades Corpus Christi saw the inauguration of rail service to and from the Rio Grande Valley and the vital opening of the deep-water port. These two major events accounted in large measure for the increase of the population, which had reached 175,000 by the early 1950s.

First State Bank began operations on March 4, 1907, with Vincent Bluntzer as its president. In 1922 that bank

The Corpus Christi National Bank as it appeared in the 1890s at Chaparral and Schatzel streets.

The $35-million CCNB Center of Corpus Christi National Bank was opened in late 1981. Twin 12-story towers make it Corpus Christi's largest office building.

changed its name to State National Bank.

In 1956 stockholders of Corpus Christi National Bank and State National Bank approved a merger. The result was the formation of Corpus Christi State National Bank, with total assets of $89 million. At that time the combined bank had 150 employees and officers. A new building at Water and Schatzel was opened in 1960, and a 12-story tower providing both banking facilities and office rental areas was added in 1964.

In December 1973 Corpus Christi National Bank became a member of Federated Capital Corporation, a Houston multi-bank holding company. In 1978 Federated Capital and Mercantile National Corporation of Dallas merged and Corpus Christi National Bank became a member of the Mercantile Texas Corporation, fifth largest bank holding company in Texas with assets of $7 billion.

In a major commitment and vote of confidence for the Corpus Christi downtown central business area, the bank's directors approved construction plans for an additional 12-story office tower as part of a $35-million expansion project. Started in 1979, the tower and 850-car parking garage were opened in late 1981.

The new tower, coupled with a remodeled existing tower, are known as CCNB Center. They offer a total of 450,000 square feet of combined office space, largest of any office complex in the city today.

Corpus Christi National Bank boasts total assets of $600 million, with employees and officers numbering 500 persons. John H. Garner is president and chief executive officer while Richard King III, great-great-grandson of the founder of the King Ranch, is chairman of the bank board.

CURRIE'S NURSERIES INC.

Robert M. Currie's lifelong love for plants and flowers, which has grown into one of South Texas' largest nursery operations, began in San Francisco at the turn of the century.

Currie's keen interest in the beauty and pleasure of plants first came from what he learned as a boy in his mother's flower garden and roaming the wild outdoors of the California hillsides and mountains.

Today Currie's Nurseries Inc. (known as Currie Seed Company in the early days) is Corpus Christi's largest retail nursery and landscape business. Celebrating its 50th year, the firm operates on a total of six acres at three different locations and employs over 90 people. Currie's services range from retail vegetable and flower seeds, potted plants, trees, bulbs, insecticides, fertilizers, pottery, gardening tools, and assorted giftwares to residential and commercial landscaping.

Robert Currie literally started from the ground up. At age 18 he hired on with a California farm that produced flower and garden seed. By the time he was 28, Currie was production manager in Philadelphia for the largest mail-order seed house in the world.

In 1931, while on a business trip in Texas, Currie traveled through Corpus Christi and fell in love with the city. He and his wife, Mary Elizabeth, returned the following year to open his own seed store on Leopard Street. In 1938 Currie moved his seed business to 909 South Staples and opened a small 25-foot by 50-foot store. This location has expanded over the years and still serves as company headquarters.

Currie's son-in-law, J.B. Wright, who would later become company president, and his wife, the former Betty Currie, joined the business in 1943. J.B. soon saw the potential for a full-service nursery and began diversifying, expanding facilities and introducing a wide variety of nursery stock into Corpus Christi.

Currie's opened a second location at 5990 South Staples in 1978. This southside operation, with over 15,000 square feet under roof, was Wright's dream. With his over 35 years of nursery experience and the help of his son, J.B. Wright, Jr., who was raised in the business, they designed and constructed this modern, innovative garden center. It has been studied by a vast number of nurserymen and is considered one of the top retail facilities in the nation. A third operation was added at Aransas Pass in 1980.

Another innovation in retail nursery merchandising pioneered by Wright was adding Christmas merchandise to its product lines during the slow winter months. Since the mid-1950s Currie's has transformed its stores into Christmas wonderlands, filled with a wide range of Christmas-related merchandise. A tour through Currie's during the holiday season has become a yearly tradition for South Texas residents.

Currie's remains a family-owned and -operated business, with Mrs. J.B. Wright serving as chairman of the board. J.B. Wright, Jr., succeeded his late father as president and his sister, Carolyn Trammell, is treasurer. Currie's strives to maintain quality and service, while adding to the beauty of South Texas.

Posing in the original store in 1941 are Robert M. Currie (left) and J.B. Wright (right) with an employee.

Currie's newest store, at 5990 South Staples.

MAXWELL P. DUNNE FUNERAL SERVICE

Twenty-seven-year old Maxwell Peter Dunne pioneered an important, much-needed service to Corpus Christi when he borrowed $250 from a relative and opened his own business on October 10, 1908.

Today Maxwell P. Dunne Funeral Service remains one of the oldest family-owned and -operated businesses in Corpus Christi and the largest independent funeral home operation among 40 such firms in South Texas.

Born in Corpus Christi in 1881, Maxwell Dunne was one of three sons and three daughters of Lawrence and Alzade Stevens Dunne, Irish Catholics who emigrated from Ireland to make a new home in Corpus Christi in 1843.

The elder Dunne was a general merchant and so his son, Maxwell, quite naturally became a traveling appliance salesman. It was on a sales trip to Houston in 1905 that Maxwell Dunne met J.B. Earthman at church and the two struck up an eventful friendship. Earthman,

an embalmer, invited Dunne into his growing funeral business as an apprentice mortician.

Dunne liked the new trade and saw the need for its services, particularly since many communities (among them his native Corpus Christi) had no such professionals. Dunne remained with Earthman about three years, earned his professional license to practice, and then returned to Corpus Christi to enter private business. Dunne borrowed $250 from his uncle, Lee Stevens, and opened a funeral service in a small building in the 500 block of Starr Street, next to where the Federal Courthouse now stands.

Dunne thus became Corpus Christi's first professional embalmer and funeral director. Prior to that, caskets were made to order by carpenters or were sold in furniture and general merchandise stores. Bodies were prepared in homes, where they were viewed and mourned and were later borne by friends and relatives to cemeteries for burial.

Dunne's business was the first to provide a complete funeral service in Corpus Christi. Soon after opening, he purchased specially designed funeral equipment from Beynon Livery Stables. The items included the city's first hearse, ambulance, and several funeral carriages, all drawn by horses.

In 1916 Dunne opened the first chapel and parlor in the 100 block of Mesquite Street, where funeral services could be conducted and where bodies could rest in state and be viewed until interment. That same year he introduced the city's first motorized funeral vehicles and ambulance.

Maxwell P. Dunne, Sr., founder of Maxwell P. Dunne Funeral Service.

The first location of the funeral business, the 500 block of Starr Street.

The third establishment, at 720 Antelope, is shown here with the funeral auto fleet, circa 1932.

After the September 1919 hurricane, Dunne labored day and night to prepare the bodies of 600 persons who drowned or died from injuries received in the city's worst natural disaster. Dunne was responsible for identifying and providing official death records for many of the storm victims.

From 1908 until the mid-1940s, Dunne conducted complete funeral services not only in Corpus Christi, but traveled as far away as the Rio Grande Valley, Victoria, and Beeville areas to provide his skills.

Although he was hard working and his profession required many long hours, Dunne was also active in Corpus Christi civic and political affairs and in Boy Scout volunteer and leadership roles. He was a special investigator for the Nueces County district attorney's office for a number of years in the 1930s and 1940s.

Maxwell P. Dunne Funeral Service moved to its third home at 720 Antelope Street in 1926. It was the stately, three-story former E.C. Timon home, built in 1913. Dunne purchased it from Timon's widow, Josephine Bluntzer Timon, and converted it into a funeral home.

When Dunne died in 1948 his widow, Agnes Nikel Dunne, became president of the company, serving until her death in 1959. In June 1962 the firm moved into new, larger quarters at 1222 Morgan Avenue, which remains its current base of operations. A second funeral service branch was opened in Portland in October 1974.

Dunne's two sons inherited his interest and drive to participate in community and political service. One daughter, Johanna Dunne Roth, died in 1971, and the other, Virgin Dunne Pope, remains an officer and leader in operations of the family business today. A son, Maxwell P. Dunne, Jr., served as the firm's funeral director for a number of years. He was a justice of the peace from 1958 until his death in 1971.

Present owners of Maxwell P. Dunne Funeral Service are J. Quentin Pope and Mrs. Virgin Dunne Pope.

His other son, Patrick Joseph Dunne, also was an elected justice of the peace from 1954 to 1958. He was a member of the Corpus Christi City Council under Mayor Ellroy King from 1959 to 1961 and again under Mayor McIver Furman from 1965 to 1967.

In 1957 Patrick Dunne was named one of four outstanding justices of the peace by the Texas Law Enforcement Foundation. He was founder of the Serra Club of Corpus Christi, and a member of the St. Vincent de Paul Society and the Committee on Problems of Alcohol. Pope Pius XII named him a Knight of St. Sylvester.

Patrick Dunne was president of the funeral service when he died in 1980. J. Quentin Pope, grandson of the founder, became president and chairman of the board at that time. His mother, Virgin Dunne Pope, is executive vice-president, vice-chairman of the board, and treasurer. Sandra Pope LeMaire, granddaughter of the founder, is a vice-president and secretary. C. Michael Dunham is a vice-president and general manager.

E.I. DU PONT DE NEMOURS AND COMPANY, INC.

From its beginning in 1802 as a maker of black gunpowder along the banks of Delaware's Brandywine Creek, the E.I. du Pont de Nemours and Company has evolved into the world's largest producer of chemicals and allied products.

Eleuthère Irénée du Pont, the firm's founder, saw the need for a better product to replace inferior grades of gunpowder. His improved powder quickly became widely used by America's settlers as they struggled to open the wild frontiers of this land.

Quality products developed and manufactured over the succeeding years have borne the pioneering brand of the du Pont family, which today is a multinational enterprise with 1,700 product lines, 159 worldwide manufacturing sites, 137,000 employees, and annual sales of $15 billion.

From a producer of industrial chemicals by the millions of pounds and monoclonal antibodies measured in micrograms, Du Pont's diversified consumer market ranges from plastics to automotive finishes, from electronic connectors to X-ray films, and spans almost the entire spectrum of technology.

Du Pont's largest investment—of more than one billion dollars—is in its Texas plants. In 1945 its first operation opened along the Sabine River at Orange. It was part of the wartime effort to provide much-needed nylon for tire cord and parachutes. A Victoria plant, which produces ingredients for nylon, synthetic rubber, and plastics, has operated since 1951.

The Corpus Christi plant near Ingleside opened in 1973 as Du Pont saw the potential in opening a Freon® fluorocarbons plant on the Gulf Coast. Located on 1,560 acres on the north shore of Corpus Christi Bay, on La Quinta Channel, the facility began with a staff of 300

E.I. du Pont, founder of the giant worldwide chemical company.

employees. Today it employs 650 persons and has a local annual payroll of $24 million.

Products made at Du Pont's Corpus Christi plant are fluorocarbons, chlorocarbons, chlorine, caustic soda, hydrocloric acid, and cyclohexane. Another related operation, the Kel-Chlor Unit, converts some wastes from fluorocarbon manufacture into reusable products.

A 1981 merger with Conoco joined Du Pont with the ninth largest integrated oil company in the United States and the second largest domestic coal company.

Du Pont's deep commitment to safety has paid off. The firm is rated 17 times safer than the chemical industry as a whole and 68 times safer than all industry, according to National Safety Council data.

Du Pont has come a long way since its 1802 founding in America and its 1945 start in Texas. Future plans call for continued trailblazing behind the proven Du Pont slogan: "Better Things for Better Living."

Du Pont's Corpus Christi plant is one of six Texas manufacturing plants of the firm.

EXXON COMPANY, U.S.A.

Exxon Corporation began as Standard Oil Company of New Jersey on August 5, 1882. Exxon Company, U.S.A., a division of the organization, has been a major producer of oil and gas since the first significant petroleum discoveries were made in Texas around the turn of the century.

Since 1912—when the initial stirrings of the oil and gas boom erupted in Corpus Christi at White Point— Exxon, previously known as Humble Oil and Refining Company, has made many historic, economic, and technological contributions to the energy industry of South Texas.

Today, from its Houston headquarters, the company manages producing operations in 22 states and is the nation's largest producer of crude oil and natural gas liquids, with a daily output of almost one million barrels. It is also the largest domestic producer of natural gas.

Exxon was credited with the discovery of oil in Piedras Pintas field (in southern Texas), in 1925. Within two years the firm had completed a trunk pipeline from western Texas to Ingleside in San Patricio County, and had constructed terminals and storage facilities at deep-water shipping points at Harbor Island and near Ingleside. The company also operated one of the major early-day refineries on the Gulf Coast at Ingleside from 1927 until the early 1940s.

Today Exxon operates five refineries: Baytown, Texas; Baton Rouge, Louisiana; Bayway, New Jersey; Billings, Montana; and Benicia, California. These refineries and their plants manufacture 1,200 products, ranging from fuels and motor oils to special lubricants for use in the extreme conditions of outer space.

Corpus Christi is headquarters for Exxon's South Texas Production Division, one of five company production units. Organized in 1928 in San Antonio as the Southwest Texas Production Division, it was relocated to Corpus Christi in 1936 when the onshore oil boom intensified in that locality and surrounding areas.

In 1933 Exxon entered its first oil and gas lease arrangements with the King Ranch, a monumental event that was to accelerate into tremendous drilling activity in the '40s and '50s and continue into the '80s. The King Ranch Gas Plant, located 14 miles southwest of Kingsville, was constructed in 1960—the largest gas-processing and -cycling facility of its kind in the world. Situated on 150 acres, the plant was the center of Exxon's vast gathering system, in which gas was collected through 170 miles of lines from 13 producing fields.

Today Exxon Company, U.S.A., South Texas Production Division, employs 1,300 persons located in 40 counties, over a 43,000-square-mile operating area in southern Texas. It has been headquartered in the Wilson Tower in Corpus Christi since 1952.

This photograph shows one of Exxon's new offshore platforms operated off Matagorda Island.

Exxon's King Ranch Gas Plant is the largest of its kind in the world.

FIRST CITY BANK OF CORPUS CHRISTI

First City Bank of Corpus Christi boasts an impressive role in Corpus Christi's heritage. The "Hill" Bank comes from sturdy, pioneering stock—the legendary Driscoll family. They fought in the Texas Revolution and in the War Between the States and eventually acquired extensive land holdings.

Robert Driscoll, Jr., was a cattleman, banker, and civic leader who endeavored to provide fresh new life and financial growth to the Corpus Christi community. Driscoll's work and financial contributions led to the successful establishment of a deep-water port of Corpus Christi in 1926. He served as first chairman of the Nueces County Navigation District, the port's board of governors.

In 1928 Driscoll recognized the expanding needs of the area's residents and founded the Corpus Christi Trust Company, with the purpose of handling wills, trusts, savings, and real estate records. It opened in rented quarters on Schatzel Street. Original capital of the fledgling firm was $100,000, with Driscoll as its first president.

Soon Driscoll saw the increasing shops and businesses of every variety and led the decision to exercise the company's original charter privileges of opening checking accounts. He owned property at 801 Leopard and personally built the first "Hill" Bank at Leopard and Tancahua. The facility opened as a full-fledged bank on April 15, 1929. Named Corpus Christi Bank and Trust Company, it started with four employees and two officers. Driscoll, however, died three days before the grand opening. His sister, Clara Driscoll, acquired the controlling stock and succeeded him as bank president.

Miss Driscoll, nationally known for her philanthropies and public service, was acclaimed "Savior of the Alamo" for her leadership and financial efforts in purchasing the San Antonio Shrine of Texas Independence on behalf of the Daughters of the Texas Republic and saving the historic property from destruction. She later built the Corpus Christi Skyscraper, the Robert Driscoll Hotel, and left her fortune to operate the Driscoll Foundation Children's Hospital.

After the initial South Texas oil boom of the 1930s, the bank attained its first million dollars in assets. In 1939, 10 years after its opening, the bank doubled its quarters. Upon Miss Driscoll's death in 1945, A.E. Dabney, Jr., became president. In 1950 another major building

This is how the predecessor of First City Bank, founded in 1928, looked after a second remodeling in the early 1950s. The word "Company," which was part of the name of Corpus Christi Bank and Trust, was deleted in 1965.

expansion took place, again doubling the bank's size. After Dabney's death in 1963, James T. Denton, Jr., succeeded to the presidency and W.P. Pittman became chairman of the board.

Expansion occurred again in 1964 with the construction of a facility at Leopard and Tancahua. On July 14, 1973, the bank merged with First City Bancorporation of Texas, the 21st largest U.S. bank holding company. In July 1974 the bank was again enlarged. It was historically appropriate that the new home site was the remodeled Driscoll family hotel.

The bank changed its name to First City Bank of Corpus Christi in 1981. Construction also commenced on a new First City Plaza consisting of twin 16-story office towers. The $50-million project will add 520,000 square feet of new office space.

C. Ivan Wilson was promoted to president in 1970, and chairman of the board and chief executive officer in 1975. In 1981 Jace C. Hoffman was elected president, while Wilson remained chairman of the board and chief executive officer. From its humble beginnings in 1928, First City Bank has risen to assets exceeding $375 million with more than 300 employees.

First City Bank of Corpus Christi's current quarters is part of the former Robert Driscoll Hotel, a 20-story bank-office tower complex at Upper North Broadway, Antelope, Leopard, and Tancahua streets.

FLATO ELECTRIC SUPPLY COMPANY

Edwin Franklin Flato was a moving force in Corpus Christi's business, educational, municipal, and social growth and development from his arrival in 1904 until his death at 87 in 1972.

His activities and accomplishments are woven into the fabric of present-day Corpus Christi, ranging from service as head of one of the city's early businesses, as an organizer of the Port of Corpus Christi, and as Del Mar College trustee, to a term as mayor.

Flato was born August 13, 1884, in Flatonia, a small North Texas town named for his grandfather, F.W. Flato, a pioneer settler who was a sea captain in the early days of Texas. Flato came to South Texas shortly after the turn of the century when his father, Charles H. Flato, and Robert Kleberg, Sr., of the King Ranch entered a partnership in a Kingsville lumber business.

In 1905 Flato, then 21 years old, moved to Corpus Christi as a bookkeeper in a small lumber company. Within a year he had become president of Corpus Christi Hardware.

He married the former Winifred Westervelt in 1909. The couple's three sons, Franklin, Frederick, and Robert, were all active in the family business from early ages.

Flato was mayor of Corpus Christi from 1931 to 1933, during the depths of the Depression. He served on the board of regents of Del Mar College for 14 years and donated land for Del Mar Tech, where one of the center's first buildings bore his name. Flato was deeply involved in the opening and development of the Port of Corpus Christi and served as a director of the navigation district's board of managers for several years.

He was also a trustee of Southwestern Research Institute, a member of the board of the Area Development Committee, chairman of the executive board of the Corpus Christi Symphony Society, and president of Robstown Hardware Company. Flato served as a director of Corpus Christi State National Bank, Guaranty Title and Trust Company, the L.D. Garrison Lumber Company, and the Texas Mexican Railway Company.

His Edwin Flato Company developed Tropic Isles, a Flour Bluff subdivision adjacent to the Laguna Madre, in a unique, man-made canal residential area that was years ahead of its time.

Flato's hardware store expanded to include divisions specializing in sporting goods, automotive parts, plumbing, and heating equipment and electrical supplies. All but the electrical division was sold in the mid-1960s when the firm's name became Flato Electric Supply Company, a wholesale firm that today supplies 5,000 different items to residential and commercial construction customers, utilities, industries, petrochemical plants, and the general public over a 44-county South Texas region.

Franklin Flato, who took over management responsibilities from his father in 1939, remains president of the family-owned corporation. Henry McDowell is vice-president.

Edwin Franklin Flato, an active Corpus Christi citizen and founder of one of the city's early businesses.

THE FAMILY OF W.W. JONES

Few Texas bloodlines can proudly claim deeper, stouter roots that moved and helped shape Corpus Christi's mainstreams of business, trade, industry, tourism, and social progress than the historic Jones family.

Today the vast ranching holdings and minerals covering parts of five southern Texas counties continue to make the W.W. Jones Properties one of the largest privately held, family-owned enterprises in the area.

The Jones family owned and operated the 300-room Nueces Hotel, a Corpus Christi landmark, from 1913 to 1960. During its heyday the six-story Chaparral Street building, which sheltered many people during the 1919 hurricane, was the city's premier hotel and the center of civic and social activity. The St. Cecelia Orchestra played

William Whitby Jones, one of the leading financial entrepreneurs in the history of Corpus Christi, was born in Goliad, Texas, in 1857.

nightly for dancing during the summer months.

The family also owned the 10-story Jones Building, Corpus Christi's first major office structure, across the street from the hotel. It operated from 1930 until its sale in 1979. From 1937 to 1955 the large W.W. Jones family home in the 500 block of South Broadway housed La Retama Public Library.

The roots of the Jones family go back to Allen Carter Jones, a carpenter who was among the first American settlers in Texas. He was born in South Carolina about 1785 and later moved to Bell County in Texas. His son, Captain A.C. Jones, Jr., was born in Nacogdoches in 1830, the youngest of nine children. He fought in the Civil War and served as Goliad County sheriff before moving to Beeville in the early 1870s.

Acclaimed as "the father of Beeville," Captain Jones organized the First National Bank of Beeville in 1886. That same year, and again in 1890, he was mainly responsible for bringing two different railroads through Beeville, assuring the city's future growth and continued dominant role as an area trade center. His son, Colonel W.W. Jones, and his grandson, A.C. "Dick" Jones, followed in his footsteps as leading financial entrepreneurs, cattle and ranching operators, and community leaders. Beeville's A.C. Jones High School is on 10 acres and the Bee County College is on 100 acres of land, both parcels donated by the Jones family.

William Whitby Jones was born in Goliad in 1857 and started riding the range at age 12. Although his father wanted him to become a merchant or a banker, W.W. "Bill" Jones preferred cattle raising and racehorses. He rode long cattle drives to Kansas City through Indian territory, spending months along the harsh trail.

Operating his own ranch near Beeville, by the turn of the century Jones had acquired extensive ranchland, which today is the center of the Jones Properties covering energy and ranching interests in parts of Jim Hogg, Duval, Brooks, Starr, and Hidalgo counties. In establishing his vast landholdings, the six-foot, four-inch-tall giant of a man, who always wore a wide-brimmed hat, had several brushes with outlaws and cattle rustlers.

Colonel Jones, recognizing the opportunities in Corpus Christi, moved his home there in 1905 and began acquiring and developing property and lending his great energies and abilities to widespread businesses, banking, and community projects. He led the passage of a bill through the Texas legislature to form Jim Hogg County in 1913.

In addition to the hotel- and office-building operations, Jones served on the executive committee to secure a deep-water port with such other dynamic leaders as Robert Kleberg, Roy Miller, John Kenedy, and John Scott. He joined Richard King, Robert Driscoll, John Kellam, and Walter Timon as members of the port's first Navigation Commission in 1923. He also served as president of the Alice State Bank and First National Bank of Hebbronville, and was on the board of directors of National Bank of Commerce in Houston, Corpus Christi National Bank, and other banks.

Jones' oldest daughter, Lorine Jones Spoonts Lewis, served as the first female president of the Corpus Christi Chamber of Commerce in 1927-1928. She was the Chamber's only female president in its 57-year history until 1982. Mrs. Lewis planted three historic palms, known as The Three Sisters, on the patio of the Nueces Hotel. She also donated and planted a number of palms on Broadway Street and gave away thousands of palm

From 1913 to 1960 the Jones family owned the 300-room Nueces Hotel, a Corpus Christi landmark.

From 1937 to 1955 the large W.W. Jones family home, 500 South Broadway, housed La Retama Public Library.

seeds, hoping to make Corpus Christi the "City of Palms."

W.W. Jones' son, A.C. "Dick" Jones, born in 1884, followed his father to become one of the largest individual landholders and financiers of southern Texas by developing family property in several counties. He was an organizer and president of the South Texas Hereford Association and a director of the Texas and Southwestern Cattle Raisers' Association. When Jim Hogg County was organized, he was elected its first county judge.

The ideas and influence of the Jones family are carried on today by grandchildren and great-grandchildren. The Mestena Oil & Gas Company, organized in 1935 with the consent of W.W. Jones after rich discoveries of oil and gas, has been operated by W.W. Jones II of Corpus Christi, grandson of the founder, for the past 10 years.

Mrs. Donald Alexander was chairman of the board and president of Mestena Oil & Gas for many years until her resignation in 1969, when her nephew, Benjamin Eshleman, Jr., succeeded her as president. Upon his death in 1972, W.W. Jones II assumed leadership.

Corporate offices of the W.W. Jones Properties are in the Nueces Building, formerly the Jones Building.

139

KAFFIE COMPANIES

Kaffie Companies, a diversified group of investment operating firms with wide South Texas oil, ranching, and real estate holdings, started with a small lumber and building supply business in 1927. That year Harold Kaffie and his father, Dr. Leopold Kaffie, a physician, founded Kaffie Lumber and Building Company at 1319 Agnes.

The elder Kaffie had moved to Corpus Christi around the turn of the century, moving from Louisiana to engage in the private practice of general medicine. He married Jeanette Weil, a member of a pioneer Corpus Christi family, in 1910. Harold Kaffie was 18 when he joined his father in opening the new lumber business to supply materials for a family rental housing venture.

From 1928 to 1930, as the oil boom erupted in Corpus Christi, Harold Kaffie and his father seized the opportunity to furnish rough lumber, or "rig timbers," used by wildcatters throughout South Texas to build early derricks and other oil field structures. Kaffie Lumber also supplied other related products required for drilling wells.

Harold Kaffie (pictured) and his father, Dr. Leopold Kaffie, founded Kaffie Lumber and Building Company.

When Dr. Kaffie died in 1937, Harold Kaffie assumed full management of operations. He was constantly in the field, where he acquired an intimate knowledge of all phases of oil operations and the requirements of operators for oil field timbers, cement, casing, chemicals, drilling fluids, and drilling mud additives.

The Kaffie firm helped construct hundreds of temporary field camps that quartered oil work crews in the 1930s. Soon the oil industry in the area came to depend upon Kaffie to furnish its many operational needs in the competitive, richly rewarding quest for oil and gas.

With the increasing use and consequent development of drilling muds, Kaffie familiarized himself with the methods and techniques used in the supplying of muds and its handling from mine to mud pits. In 1949 Kaffie saw the need for bulk mud because of the oil field operator's manpower shortage and the conveniences that could result from its use.

So Kaffie pioneered bulk mud and engineered specially designed equipment to handle mud shipped from the mine in specific bulk-carrier railroad cars and from there to storage bins or directly into bulk transport convoys with weather-proofed tanks for delivery to the oil fields.

Kaffie's new firm, Bulk Barites, Inc., through its innovative operations, could mechanically handle drilling mud in bulk quantities. This system eliminated the old method of manually handling and mixing the product in sacks, which frequently produced waste, safety hazards, and delay, and required additional expenses of storage at the oil well site.

During the '40s and '50s, Kaffie's Bulk Barites was the largest handler of bulk mud in the United States. The

Rig tanks are seven feet square in cross sections and have a 75,000-pound capacity. Each rig tank will deliver the bulk mud from rates below 10 sacks per hour to a maximum of more than 600 sacks per hour.

A Bulk Barites, Inc., trailer unit with a 50,000-pound capacity. A fleet of these trucks services more than 100 storage bins in the South Texas area.

Kaffie family's related businesses employed about 400 persons and operated a fleet of more than 125 service vehicles. By 1956 Kaffie Lumber and Bulk Barites had combined to service more than 3,000 wells on land, in inland waters, and offshore in the Gulf of Mexico.

Harold Kaffie sold both the lumber company and the bulk mud firm in 1959 to Dresser Industries of Dallas. He then became executive director of sales for Magnet Cove Barium Corporation and was assistant to the president of Magcobar.

Harold Kaffie had acquired extensive real estate during his active business years. Often he accepted royalty interests on wells in exchange for supplies. He expanded these property holdings and ranching interests upon his retirement.

Kaffie also built and owned three office buildings in downtown Corpus Christi and on the bluff. All are still in use today. They are the four-story Jeanette Kaffie Building, the four-floor Sun-Texaco Building, and the seven-story Atlantic-Mobil Building.

Harold Kaffie died in August 1981. Today his sons, Charles and Harris, are partners in Kaffie Brothers, carrying on the multifaceted business empire their father and grandfather founded 55 years ago.

Kaffie Brothers owns interests in oil, gas, and uranium production in over 100 counties in South, Central, and West Texas. The family business also has ranching operations in Nueces, Jim Wells, and Jim Hogg counties; and controls extensive real estate, rental property, and varied banking investments. They also maintain one of the largest purebred Beefmaster cattle herds in the world.

The brothers also opened Kaffie Gallery at 525 South Carancahua in 1976. The gallery-studio was fashioned

"Mr. Gus," the offshore mobile drilling platform of the Glasscock Drilling Company, being serviced by the tender *Barbara Storm.*

from the 72-year-old house that once was their grandmother's home. Kaffie Gallery was started as a showcase for local potter William Wilhelmi, but it has evolved into a contemporary arts center for many worthy artisans.

In the true tradition of Harold Kaffie, who gave his energies and abilities to others, the gallery has provided the public a unique access to the works of local, regional, and national artists and their displays of pottery, tapestries, jewelry, collages, pastels, oils, watercolors, acrylics, and sculptures. Indeed, Harold Kaffie, an artist in his own right, enjoyed being able to return something to the city that had given him so much.

LOCKWOOD, ANDREWS & NEWNAM, INC.

It was in 1951 that Lockwood, Andrews & Newnam, Inc. (LAN), sent its first engineer to Corpus Christi to oversee the construction of a jet-aircraft runway designed for Corpus Christi Naval Air Station.

Thirty-one years later some 15 professionals staff the second of seven branches established in Texas by LAN since 1949. The Corpus Christi office offers a complete range of service in all facets of engineering, surveying, architecture, planning, and project management.

Not long after LAN's first engineer arrived in Corpus Christi, the firm moved full force into the city. Its first local project was a joint effort by the city of Corpus Christi and Nueces County. LAN conducted a survey for the city and county to assess the impact of relocating the ship channel to alleviate the traffic bottleneck of the old Bascule Bridge over the entrance to the port.

The King Ranch Dairy Barn Dam, built in 1952, was the first LAN/Corpus Christi project. In addition to the city/county work and the King Ranch project, the port study by LAN was the first of more than 40 endeavors involving the Port of Corpus Christi that the firm would undertake in becoming an important contributor to the major growth and development of the dynamic Coastal Bend region.

Lockwood, Andrews & Newnam, Inc., was founded in Houston in 1935. It has since grown into one of the largest full-service professional firms in the nation. It currently has 700 personnel in offices in Houston, Corpus Christi, Austin, Brownsville, Dallas, San Antonio, and Victoria, Texas; Denver, Colorado; and San Diego and Los Angeles, California.

Geogram, Inc., a wholly owned subsidiary of LAN, offers field surveying and engineering services to private interests, oil field and other industry, and others. Geogram maintains permanent offices in Corpus Christi and at all LAN's other Texas locations.

Typical LAN services to area cities, governmental units, and institutions have included engineering for airports, utilities, roads and bridges, drainage improvement and stormwater assessments, and coastal and marine works.

Unit 5 of Key Allegro is an example of LAN's contribution to residential and commercial development of the region. The firm specializes in effectively combining the skills of its planners, engineers, and other professionals to assure optimum use of land resources.

Professional service to area industry is an increasingly important part of LAN's local involvement. Celanese Corporation, Champlin Petroleum, Coastal States, Corpus Christi Petrochemical, E.I. du Pont, Exxon, Koch (Suntide), and Reynolds Metals are key representative industrial clients that LAN/Corpus Christi has served during the past decade. Among assignments for industry have been marine facilities, offsites and utilities, surveys, plant engineering, and environmental projects.

The future Port of Corpus Christi multimillion-dollar Bulk Materials Dock is a Lockwood, Andrews & Newnam project.

The King Ranch Dairy Barn Dam was one of LAN's first Corpus Christi area projects.

Key Allegro Island Estates, near Rockport, is an example of the firm's residential planning.

MAVERICK MARKETS, INC.

Maverick Markets, Inc., was established in 1961—the year President John F. Kennedy created the Peace Corps, Russia put its first man in space, and Roger Maris hit his 61st home run.

In June of that year Vice-President Lyndon Johnson visited Corpus Christi to inspect Padre Island as a potential site for a national seashore area. That same month Maverick Markets opened its five stores with 15 employees in Corpus Christi. Its president, Erich Wendl, also joined other convenience store executives that year in Kansas City to form the National Association of Convenience Stores (NACS). He served as the group's president in 1979.

By 1981 Maverick Markets was well-established as a national leader in the convenience store industry, with 104 stores operating within a 150-mile radius of Corpus Christi. There were stores located in 25 cities of South Texas ranging from Victoria and Port Lavaca on the north, Laredo to the west, and Brownsville to the south. On the national level, NACS had become a powerful force in the retail food industry; it numbered 300 members with more than 30,000 stores in the United States, Mexico, Canada, and Japan.

By its 10th-anniversary celebration in 1971, Maverick counted 39 stores with new openings in Victoria,

Laredo, and Alice. That year a tribe of lost Stone Age people, the Tasaday, were discovered in the uncharted tropical rain forest of the Philippines and *The New York Times* published the first installment of what was to be called "The Pentagon Papers."

Maverick Markets led the nationwide trend of rapid convenience store expansion during the next five years. By June 1976 the chain numbered 80 stores. This was the same time that Israeli paratroopers swooped down on Entebbe Airport in Uganda, Africa, to rescue 110 Israeli passengers and French crewmen from an Air France jet which had been hijacked by terrorists.

A native of Munich, Germany, Erich Wendl emigrated to the United States in 1953. He served in the U.S. Army, where in 1955 he became a naturalized U.S. citizen. Wendl has served as a president of both the Corpus Christi and the Texas Retail Grocers Association and was named 1975 Retail Grocer of the Year by the National Association of Retail Grocers of the United States. The highest honor of his career came in 1980, when his native Germany appointed Wendl an honorary consul for South Texas.

Wendl's philosophy of positioning Maverick Markets as "your next-door stores" has proven auspicious. The company provides jobs for almost 700 employees, most of whom are actively involved in the communities in which they work.

Erich Wendl, president of Maverick Markets, Inc., and honorary consul for the Federal Republic of Germany.

Maverick Markets was established in 1961 with five stores and 15 employees in Corpus Christi.

MEMORIAL MEDICAL CENTER

Memorial Medical Center officially opened on Memorial Day, 1944, as a tribute to the dead of World War I and II. The opening marked more than four years of planning and building, hampered by wartime shortages and heavy rains.

Architects designed the first four-wing, one-story building so that its pavilion-style structure took advantage of Corpus Christi's prevailing winds to abate the South Texas heat.

The hospital, the foremost public medical facility in the city at that time, had 94 ward beds and 15 private rooms when it opened. By 1982 Memorial Medical Center had steadily grown to become a 501-bed, postgraduate medical teaching, diagnostic, and medical trauma care center of a 12-county South Texas region. Its 1,700 employees, 450 nurses, and 389 physicians serve an annual patient admission load of 22,000.

The Corpus Christi community of 57,000 people desperately needed more hospital beds and medical treatment facilities in 1940. A survey commissioned by community leaders led to plans for the construction of a 250-bed public hospital at a cost of $1.4 million.

Early in December 1941, voters of both the city of Corpus Christi and Nueces County approved separate $500,000 bond issues for the new joint hospital. War soon broke out, however, and a shortage of construction labor and materials for the military effort delayed the actual hospital building start-up until 1943.

To aid in the construction, the Federal Works Agency granted $387,921 to the project. Attorney R. Richard Roberts was employed as coordinator; E.E. Harrison, general contractor, won the low bid to build it. H.L. Kokernot, president of the Baptist Foundation of Texas, donated 18.5 acres of land to the city for the hospital site at 19th and Morgan streets.

The Texas Legislature authorized the city and county to build and maintain the hospital and to levy taxes for its operation in May 1943. A groundbreaking ceremony was held on July 15, 1943.

Serving on the initial hospital managing committee were the Reverend W.C. Munds, J.E. Rhea, Frank Sparks, Mark A. Welsh, Ira Connell, Seab Stone, Floyd London, Dr. J.A. Garcia, Dr. McIver Furman, Herman Heep, O.N. Stephens, the Reverend J.H. Cozad, Robert McCracken, and Lon C. Hill. Comprising Memorial's first board of trustees were the Reverend Munds, chairman; Rhea, president; Welsh, vice-president; Connell, secretary; Sparks, treasurer; London and Stone, members; and M.G. Eckhardt, attorney.

The board adopted Memorial Hospital as the name of this joint city-county medical facility in September 1943. The medical staff was organized that November, with Dr. C.P. Yeager as its first chief of staff. Herbert Hammond was the first hospital administrator.

The original 48,000-square-foot, four-wing building remains in use today, housing the Samaritan Clinic and the Family Practice Model Unit. By December 1946 the hospital had added a 32-bed wing for polio patients, and air conditioning, a rare accommodation then, was placed in the operating and delivery rooms.

This artist's concept of Memorial Medical Center in the year 1995 provides a look into the future. The plan includes a helipad with jet elevator access to the emergency room, a 200-bed tower, intensive and coronary care facilities, and a new burn treatment center. A regional cancer treatment center is also planned.

Air-transported patients from a 12-county region and surrounding waters receive immediate emergency medical services at Memorial Medical Center.

Memorial Medical Center as it appeared in the early 1950s.

A case of poliomyelitis is rare today, but in the late '40s and early '50s, polio was rampant here. In 1951 polio reached epidemic rates, with Memorial Hospital treating almost 100 polio patients that year.

The story of Johnny Prestwich captured the heart of the city in 1953. The young London seaman contracted polio while his ship was docked in the Corpus Christi harbor. In a community effort that reaped national headlines, Prestwich was hospitalized in the MMC polio treatment facilities, with his mother from England by his side. He was then flown home in an iron lung aboard a plane from the Kingsville Naval Air Station.

The present shape of Memorial Medical Center began to take form in 1950, when ground was broken for what is now Memorial West. At that time, Memorial had 135 beds, including 23 bassinets. Memorial West, completed in 1952 at a cost of $1.2 million, swelled the bed capacity to 300. By 1955 the annual patient load had risen from 6,143 in 1951 to 12,308.

In 1960 hospital trustees approved a $6.5-million expansion which included the construction of an east wing tower, completed in 1965. The next addition was a $5.9-million improvement of the outpatient and emergency room services in 1978.

Memorial Medical Center launched the "Campaign for Progress," a five-year fund-raising project needed for a $40-million long-range building program, in 1982. This construction will include new intensive, coronary, and burn care units; a parking garage; a helicopter landing deck; a new power plant; relocation of 200 beds to a new patient tower; clinic parking facilities; and a

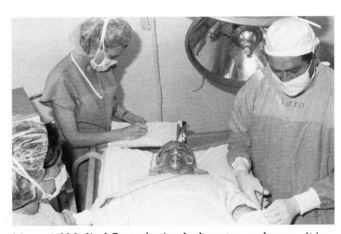

Memorial Medical Center's nine-bed, acute-care burn unit is the only officially designated burn medical treatment unit south of San Antonio.

cancer center.

President Wheeler B. Lipes heads the present administration, which operates under an annual budget of $54 million. More than 50,000 emergency room admissions will be serviced, 2,800 births will be recorded, over 12,000 surgeries will be performed, and more than 633,000 meals will be served in 1982.

Memorial Medical Center's board of managers includes Alvino C. Campos, chairman; Richard J. Hatch, chairman pro tem; and Robert L. Fordtran, M.D., Xico P. Garcia, M.D., George Peters, Oscar H. Reyna, and Weldon A. Rippy, members.

NUECES COUNTY HISTORICAL SOCIETY

The Nueces County Historical Society was organized in November 1952 for the purpose of preserving the local heritage. Established in Judge Noah Kennedy's office in the Nueces County Courthouse, a building constructed in 1914, its membership has always been open to the public. Dr. Floy Wise was elected the president, and the charter members were Wesley Agee, Aldine Brock Burton, Amelia Daimwood, Dr. William Hager, Dan Kilgore, and Bessie Stillwell.

The first complete narrative history of the local area was published in 1972 by the Nueces County Historical Society. The Society encourages young and adult members of the community to participate in research of local history and to publish individual historical works. The Society has published a monthly newsletter since March 1970, containing historical data of significance and interest.

The group cooperates with the Nueces County Historical Commission and Friends of the Courthouse, Inc., in accomplishing restoration and preservation projects. The Society meets monthly, featuring programs on local history. These meetings are always open to the public, as are Society-sponsored field trips to historic sites within a 150-mile radius of Corpus Christi.

Members of the Nueces County Historical Society assisted in the photographic research for Windsor Publication's *Corpus Christi: History of a Texas Seaport.* Monetarily, the Society is contributing to the restoration of the 1880 Nuecestown School at Hilltop Community Center and the 28th District Courtroom Museum in the 1914 Nueces County Courthouse.

Those who served as presidents in the past were Dr. Floy Wise, Sister Mary Xavier Holworthy, Hortense W. Ward, Dan Kilgore, Gene North, Vernon Smylie, Margaret Ramage, Dr. Richard Marcum, and Lee John Govatos.

Current officers of the Society are Margaret Walberg, president; Sally Robeau, first vice-president; Betsy Rodriguez, second vice-president; Margaret Ramage, third vice-president; Peggy Bickham, recording secretary; Ray J. Garcia, corresponding secretary; Thomas Murphy, treasurer; Lee John Govatos, parliamentarian; and Sandra Drescher, Mrs. Joe De Leon, Sr., Bobby Haegelin, and John Wright, directors. Elected May 6, 1982, were Kathy Boyd, first vice-president; Clara Davy, second vice-president; and Russell Reeb, Charles Davis, and Elsie Poenisch, directors.

Members of the Nueces County Historical Society outside the 1914 Nueces County Courthouse. Seated, front center, are charter members Aldine Brock Burton and Dan Kilgore. Seated directly behind them is founding member Judge Noah Kennedy.

TAYLOR BROTHERS JEWELERS

Taylor Brothers Jewelers, Corpus Christi's oldest and finest jewelry store, is one of South Texas' oldest family-owned businesses. It ranks as one of the largest independent jewelry-store operations in the Southwest.

Founded 55 years ago by brothers George and Sam Taylor, the firm has expanded considerably at its landmark downtown Corpus Christi location over the years to meet growing demands of its large clientele. It annually sells large quantities of diamonds, many precious gemstones, gold jewelry, valuable watches, silverware, and other gifts to customers throughout the United States.

The company opened in a small 25-foot by 50-foot building at the present site of the store at Mesquite and Starr streets in February 1928 in quarters formerly occupied by jeweler Carl Haltom; it was one of a group of stores built in 1927 on the Bingham property.

The Taylor brothers, a pioneer family who came to Texas with the original Stephen F. Austin colony of settlers, moved to Corpus Christi from upstate. Owners of four other jewelry stores in Texas, their local success soon necessitated expansion into adjoining business buildings such as the former Barry Hendrix drugstore, Bowen Printing, McGregor's Barber Shop, Harbins' Dress Shop, Mrs. Cheatams Millinery Shop, and others.

Today Taylor Brothers Jewelers covers one-fourth of a

Taylor Brothers Jewelers sells valuable, eye-catching showpiece jewelry.

city block. A feature of its operation is the front glass-showcase area, referred to by hundreds of Corpus Christi patrons as "The Wishing Well" because of its many valuable, eye-catching pieces of showpiece jewelry. The family purchased the Shoemaker property across the street from the main building several years ago, which provides free parking for customers.

Four registered gemologists are employed to advise customers in their selections and to offer gemstone and jewelry appraisals. Taylor Brothers also has jewelry- and watch-repair departments. For several generations the store has been a bridal center, providing full services for newlyweds.

Taylor Brothers offers the finest-quality merchandise, such as Rolex, Omega, Audemar, Piguet, Movado, and Corum watches; Hartmann luggage; Guerlain perfume; and Mikimoto pearls. Such names as Reed & Barton, Buccellati, Gorham, Wallace, Christofle, and other products grace its silverware shelves.

Brand names in china include Minton, Doulton, Worcester, Spode, Wedgwood, Royal Crown Derby, Lenox, Ceralene, and Limoges, plus fine porcelain pieces by Boehm and Cybis. The crystal department offers Lalique, Baccarat, Orrefors, Waterford, and others.

Taylor Brothers Jewelers is friendly, knowledgeable, courteous, and takes pleasure in serving its customers.

"The Wishing Well," a showcase of fine silverware and other quality gifts at Taylor Brothers Jewelers.

BILLY PUGH COMPANY, INC.

Billy Pugh grew up on the Corpus Christi waterfront during the income-lean times of the Great Depression. He did odd jobs as he worked on and around boats to help his father, John W. Pugh, who earned his living by piloting vessels to take people fishing or sightseeing.

When World War II called in 1941, Billy Pugh, still not yet an adult by chronological standards, joined the service of his country at 16. He chose the life he knew best—the sea—and enlisted in the Coast Guard. Two years later Pugh was one of the military's youngest chief boatswain's mates.

Discharged from military duty in the late 1940s, Pugh returned to his hometown and its bayfront as harbormaster for the city of Corpus Christi.

It was during the early 1950s that Pugh invented and manufactured a piece of marine safety equipment that was to make him a successful businessman and make his name a familiar one in millions of U.S. households and to others in numerous foreign countries. Billy Pugh would become well-known in the field of life-saving rescue equipment and earn a place in the Smithsonian Institution.

Pugh's successful turning point came in the '50s when "Mr. Gus," the revolutionary drilling rig designed and built by Corpus Christi oilman C.G. "Gus" Glasscock, was pioneering in the waters far offshore in the Gulf of Mexico. "Mr. Gus" made oil industry history as the first mobile rig to drill in waters of more than 100 feet deep.

But this forerunner of today's worldwide drilling activity had a problem that had to be ironed out. There

An astronaut is lifted to a helicopter during the Apollo space program in one of Pugh's land-air-sea rescue nets.

Rescue device inventor-manufacturer Billy Pugh sits in one of his famous creations that has made his name known worldwide.

was a vital need for improved equipment to lift its drillers from crew service boats to the top of the drilling rig platform in rough seas. The rig top was sometimes 90 to 110 feet above the choppy water's surface.

"They would dangle a two-inch pipe with a net hung on it over the side," Pugh recalled of the early personnel lift devices. "The men hung on it like monkeys and were pulled up and aboard."

In 1954 an offshore accident while men were transferring from boat to rig claimed two lives. Pugh offered his prototype, a 120-pound net that resembled a sea-going elevator. It could lift six men at one time. But most important, it transferred men more safely while attached to a crane atop the rig deck which raised and lowered the men to a boat below.

It was used on the "Mr. Gus" and the rest of the industry soon followed suit. So successful was Pugh's personnel carrier net that he began manufacturing duplicates and custom orders as a private business to meet the demands of the growing offshore oil boom. In 1959 Pugh also established a yacht and boat repair service center on the Corpus Christi L Head.

The sales success and wide acceptance of his offshore personnel safety net led Pugh in 1967 to design and offer a modified rescue basket or net suitable for one-man rescue operations. He saw a need in the U.S. space program to pluck astronauts from the water after their space capsules had returned to earth and had splashed down in the ocean. He also thought the military could utilize such a net to rescue stranded servicemen in the combat jungles of Vietnam. Pugh was correct in his visions on both counts.

A much lighter, 20-pound collapsible net that could easily be carried in a helicopter became known as the "Billy Pugh net." It made Pugh's name a famous one throughout the world as millions followed the details of America's space progress and moon walks on TV and in the print media.

The U.S. Navy signed a contract with Pugh in 1968 to purchase a number of his nets, which were used in naval rescue operations as well as in the Navy's key role of retrieving astronauts from their space journeys. The entire Apollo space program used Billy Pugh nets.

Later the U.S. Army and Marine Corps made Pugh's net a vital part of their life-saving rescue and safety operations. Thousands of U.S. servicemen may have been saved in Vietnam by helicopter air lifts with a Billy Pugh net.

Today the federal government remains Pugh's best customer, but foreign customers also buy and use Pugh

A one-man Billy Pugh land-air-sea rescue net is tested by a helicopter on the Corpus Christi bayfront. It was designed especially for the Army's Uhi Huey helicopter.

An offshore personnel transfer net lifts a worker from a boat to the top of a drilling platform by way of a crane hoist.

equipment. Civilians such as fire departments employ Pugh nets in emergency work, particularly in high-rise building fires.

Pugh sold the yacht-service portion of his business in 1977 and relocated the net and safety equipment manufacturing portion to 1415 North Water Street. Presently this manufacturing facility employs 90 persons.

Today Pugh nets are available in several sizes and models for offshore, industrial, military, and civilian operations. The nets range in weight from 20 to 380 pounds. Pugh also manufactures and markets related life-preservation equipment such as work vests, flotation jackets, raft-type floats, life-ring buoys, fast-throw rescue lines, litter frames for injured persons, safety belts, Jacob's ladders, cargo nets, ropes, distress signals, metal safety hooks, and marine lighting devices.

Two of Pugh's famous nets used in successful recoveries of astronauts are on display in the Smithsonian Institution in Washington, D.C. Others are found in the National Naval Air Museum and in various museums as part of the historic artifacts of this nation's space-age progress.

In addition to his Corpus Christi manufacturing facility, Pugh, with James E. Talley, operates an offshore supply base in Ingleside-On-The-Bay. This supply base consists of 1,900 linear feet of bulkhead and 20 acres of land, all utilized to service the offshore drilling and production activity in the Corpus Christi area. Pugh and Talley started this business from scratch in 1977, and now employ 50 persons, running one of the most functional and efficient offshore bases on the Gulf Coast.

SEASIDE MEMORIAL PARK AND FUNERAL HOME

Seaside Memorial Park and Funeral Home has emerged from a 10-acre private cemetery ground opened in 1936 to today's superbly landscaped park, chapel, and mausoleum complex. Situated on 100 acres, it is one of the largest perpetual-care facilities in Texas.

In 1979, when Reid Ryan built the new funeral home and chapel, he was fulfilling a promise made to his grandfather, William Roy Reid, to provide the finest in comfort and pastoral beauty to persons in time of bereavement.

The third-generation, family-owned Seaside Memorial Park and Funeral Home features atriums, skylights, fountains, a flower shop, memorial plaque and monument section, and pre-need funeral arrangement services. The garden and chapel mausoleums provide above-ground entombment in concrete, steel, marble, copper, and granite.

The first Catholic section, the Garden of Gethsemani, was opened in 1948, followed by the second Catholic section, the Garden of Resurrection, in 1978. The Jewish sections, the B'nai Israel and the Temple Beth El, were opened in the late 1940s. The Veterans' Memorial section was dedicated in 1951.

Today the three-board corporation of Seaside Memorial Park and Funeral Home is headed by Reid Ryan, president; his mother, Lorraine Reid Garcia, vice-president; and Fred Wakefield, secretary-treasurer. A staff of 50 persons is employed in the park complex, which holds in perpetuity the remains of many of the men and women who helped build Corpus Christi. Its directors have assumed care of the Nueces County Cemetery and county pauper burials since 1975.

William Roy Reid, who died in 1972, was a past president of the Texas Cemetery Association. He had been active in many community organizations and in state and national lumbermen's associations. His dreams and goals have been carried on by his grandson, Reid Ryan. "All people wish to die with dignity, to be buried with honor, and to be remembered with affection for the best of their past moments," Ryan says.

The Seaside Memorial Park and Funeral Home is one of the largest perpetual-care facilities in Texas.

The funeral home and chapel of Seaside Memorial Park and Funeral Home was built in 1979.

CORPUS CHRISTI BRICK AND LUMBER COMPANY

Born in Woodstock, Iowa, in 1892, William Roy Reid was a successful builder and residential subdivider in Houston before moving to Corpus Christi about 1940. He acquired a small lumber business which had been operating from a tiny frame building at 121 North Staples since 1924.

He developed several major south side Corpus Christi residential subdivisions as the city's population in the late '40s and '50s grew at a rate that was threefold greater than that for the entire state of Texas.

As residential construction boomed, so did the full-time building trades supplier, Corpus Christi Brick and Lumber Company. Under the leadership of Reid and later his grandson, Reid Ryan, the business expanded its product lines and realized spectacular growth.

Today Corpus Christi Brick and Lumber employs 70 persons. The firm, under 40,000 square feet of storage and display space, includes seven separate divisions: major appliances, lumber, hardware, paint, brick, television, and custom-doors.

Reid Ryan is president of the family corporation, which owns the building supply center. Lorraine Reid Garcia is vice-president. Jim Sherman is secretary-treasurer.

Recently a new store, Ryan's Sight and Sound, was established. This store fulfills the need for customers with the finest products in audio and video equipment.

Founded by William Roy Reid, the Corpus Christi Brick and Lumber Company is a major building trades supplier in Corpus Christi.

The names Corpus Christi Brick and Lumber Company and Seaside Memorial Park and Funeral Home are synonymous with quality. That's what William Roy Reid had foremost in mind in the early 1940s. A man of pioneering spirit, he dared to take business risks. He committed himself to vigorously serve and benefit the community and to do a better job. And he realized a dream.

Reid Ryan is proud of his companies' past successes and contributions. They are living monuments to his grandfather. But Ryan also looks forward to keeping pace with the modern diversity of the business world and the challenges of the future.

SPOHN HOSPITAL

There was no hospital of any kind in Corpus Christi when Dr. Arthur E. Spohn, a Canadian-born surgeon of Dutch-German ancestors, arrived here in 1895. Sick people were cared for in their homes where necessary operations were performed, often on dimly lit dining room tables.

A compassionate man who soon became known for his charities to the poor and for his medical services to both South Texas and Mexican residents, Dr. Spohn started a crusade in the community of 7,000 to construct a hospital before the new century had dawned.

Mrs. Alice Gertrudis King Kleberg and her husband, Robert Kleberg, joined by John and George Kenedy and Dr. Spohn and his wife, the former Sarah Kenedy, solicited and contributed a total of $6,000 to secure a tract of land on North Beach. Here the first building of what today is Spohn Hospital was constructed at a cost of $13,000. It was called Spohn Sanitarium.

After an application by Dr. Spohn, the Reverend Mother Madeleine of the Sisters of Charity of the Incarnate Word in San Antonio supplied Sister nurses for the new hospital. In March 1905, with consent of her

council, Mother Madeleine agreed to accept the hospital and operate it as a medical facility. The Sisters provided all the services required, from administration and nursing to cooking, cleaning, laundry, and even to raising their own vegetable garden, from which they fed their patients.

It was shortly after the hospital opened that Dr. Spohn, assisted by his associate, Dr. Alfred George Heaney, removed a 328-pound ovarian tumor from a young woman. The surgical feat earned the team national recognition in the medical ranks.

Earlier, on November 20, 1891, Dr. Spohn, who had trained at the Louis Pasteur Institute in Paris, France, had performed what was then recorded as "the first porro-caesarian delivery in a case of osteomalacia ever performed in the United States, saving both mother and child."

Dr. Spohn also was credited with being the first person to bring the Pasteur treatment of rabies to America. In 1870 he also was acknowledged for inventing a tourniquet for bloodless operations, which was adopted by a number of foreign military forces as a battlefield medical technique.

An annex to the Beach Hospital was added in 1906. It was the first Spohn Hospital expansion in a long series of additions and improvements that continue into the 1980s.

Dr. Spohn, first president of the Nueces County Medical Society he helped organize in 1901, was practicing medicine and surgery actively until shortly before his death in 1913 at age 68.

Spohn Hospital continued its mission of mercy on North Beach until the 1919 hurricane, when it was destroyed by tidal waters. A Sister, two patients, and two nurses were drowned in the storm. The hospital was surrounded by water after the hurricane and everyone was evacuated from it. The Sisters and patients were

Dr. Arthur E. Spohn, first president of the Nueces County Medical Society, founded Corpus Christi's first hospital on Corpus Christi's North Beach in 1905. Today it is the city's largest medical treatment complex.

The original Spohn Hospital, 1905.

moved to the John Gregory Kenedy, Sr., home on the Corpus Christi blufftop which is the present-day site of the Corpus Christi Cathedral. Kenedy was a brother of Mrs. Spohn. The Kenedy home was to serve as temporary quarters for Spohn Hospital for several years.

Mrs. Henrietta M. King, widow of Captain Richard King, founder of the King Ranch, donated a five-acre plot of land for a new Spohn Hospital. The first three-story unit of the new medical facility was completed in 1922 at Third and Ayers streets, the site of today's multimillion-dollar, 560-bed medical complex, which is Corpus Christi's largest medical hospital.

A 50-bed addition was completed in 1937. A five-story, 114-bed extension increased Spohn's capabilities in 1952. Two years later a professional school of nursing was established through the generosity of the James R. Dougherty, Jr., Foundation of Beeville.

In 1961 a $4.5-million, five-story addition was completed, increasing Spohn Hospital's capacity to 300 patient beds and 50 bassinets. The $410,000 Rachael Vaughan Radiation Therapy Center was opened in 1964. In 1974 the hospital launched a $28-million building program which was concluded in early 1982. Additions included a new 30-bed intensive care unit; a 10-story elevator tower; new radiology, day surgery, emergency, dietary, administrative, and other service facilities; an eight-story professional office building; a four-level parking garage; and a three-story, 102-bed medical-surgical patient expansion.

Today Dr. Spohn's dream, which started in a small frame structure on wind-swept North Beach, is a sprawling, modern bayfront medical plant covering seven acres.

Spohn Hospital's staff of 1,700 employees will assist more than 26,000 patient admissions in 1982. The facility will discharge more than 3,500 newborns, administer over 100,000 radiation X-ray examinations, serve 450,000 patient meals, attend to 16,000 emergency unit patients, and fill almost 70,000 drug prescriptions.

Sister Kathleen Coughlin is the current Spohn Hospital administrator.

The multimillion-dollar, 560-bed Spohn Hospital complex at 1436 Third Street covers seven acres with complete, diversified medical treatment facilities.

SWANTNER & GORDON INSURANCE AGENCY, INC.

Swantner & Gordon Insurance Agency, Inc., Corpus Christi's largest independent insurance firm, has been growing with the city and protecting its citizens and their property for almost a half-century.

The second-oldest local insurance firm began in 1936 when G.R. "Bob" Swantner, Sr., and Jamin Gordon cemented a business partnership that today accrues $10 million in annual premiums.

Swantner, born in Hazen, Arkansas, in 1900, was graduated from Creighton University in Omaha, Nebraska. He moved to Corpus Christi in 1929 to manage the insurance department of City National Bank.

Gordon, a native of Atmore, Alabama, was 23 years old when he left Alabama for the Rio Grande Valley of South Texas to try his luck in real-estate or insurance sales—professions of his father's. When he got lost in Corpus Christi on his way to the valley in 1927, he decided to stay and started selling cakes off of a truck. Four months later he was soliciting insurance.

At first Swantner and Gordon were competitors in selling general insurance. But on April 1, 1936, the competitive personalities of these two aggressive, well-liked professionals struck a bond.

Swantner & Gordon Insurance Agency originated in the old City National Bank Building at Chaparral and Peoples streets, with two women working in the office. The agency prospered and branched into mortgage loans in 1938.

In October 1941 construction began on the Swantner Building at 401 North Shoreline. It was the first private construction on Corpus Christi's newly created bayfront seawall-improvement program.

The original structure, spanning 40 by 120 feet, remains present-day headquarters for the 40-member staff. The two-story building has been extensively expanded and modernized several times to its current 8,000 square feet of space. A Swantner & Gordon branch also operates in Beeville.

Both partners were avid sportsmen—Swantner traveled to Africa, India, Tibet, South America, and other parts of the world in quest of wild game.

Past president of the Texas Mortgage Bankers Association and an organizer and director of First State Bank and Guaranty National Bank, Swantner also developed the residential subdivisions of Lindale, Lawndale, and Shoreline Estate. These included hundreds of homes in an area stretching from Louisiana to Texan Trail, along Ocean Drive, and between Staples and Alameda streets. He died in 1978.

Gordon, after retiring from active practice with the firm in 1968, took up oil painting as a hobby. He became a well-known artist for his seascapes, Americana scenes, and countryside works until his death in 1977.

The Swantner & Gordon Building was the first major private construction on the new bayfront after World War II building controls were lifted in the mid-1940s.

Jamin Gordon

J.R. "Dick" Swantner

G.R. "Bob" Swantner, Sr.

One longtime Swantner & Gordon insurance agent became internationally famous as a goodwill ambassador, both for Corpus Christi and the insurance firm. Buster Shely, the city's "Official Ambassador of Barbecue" earned worldwide headlines in the early 1950s when he learned that dignitaries of Corpus Christi College of Cambridge University in England wanted to observe their 600th anniversary by roasting an ox.

However, they didn't know how, as barbecued beef is a rarity in Britain. So Shely offered his chef's expertise and flew there to supervise the barbecuing and help make the celebration a success. He later was invited to mastermind the barbecue for 4,000 Shriners in Ontario, Canada, in 1962, and numerous other cookouts.

Shely retired from Swantner & Gordon after 31 years of employment in 1972.

In 1972 J.R. "Dick" Swantner, one of four children of the agency's cofounder, acquired the business. Realizing compound growth of 20 percent annually in sales since, the firm sells and services general property and casualty insurance, life insurance, employee benefit plans, and specializes in insurance programs for the energy industry

and large real estate projects.

Active in community affairs, Swantner is a two-time past president of the Corpus Christi Area Convention and Tourist Bureau, and donated the land for the site of the tourist bureau's initial building home at 603 South Shoreline. President of Swantner & Gordon, he is also a past director of the Independent Insurance Agents of Texas and past president of the Independent Insurance Agents of Corpus Christi. Dick Swantner is currently director of the First State Bank, Corpus Christi, a member of the education committee of Independent Insurance Agents of America, and president of the board of trustees of Texas Insurance Education Foundation.

A third-generation family member, Michael Swantner, joined the staff in 1981.

Dick Swantner, in concert with the other seven stockholders of Swantner & Gordon, has set a goal of $20 million in annual premiums by the time the firm reaches its milestone 50th-anniversary celebration in 1986, as the agency continues to professionally serve new generations of Corpus Christi's early families and their businesses and new arrivals as well.

TEXAS MEXICAN RAILWAY COMPANY

Long before there was a Good Neighbor Policy, there was a good neighbor railroad—the historic Texas Mexican Railway Company.

This pioneer line of south and southwest Texas has been cementing the bonds of amity with Mexico for 101 years, while also playing the part of a close and good friend to all the people it serves along its 157-mile right-of-way between Corpus Christi and Laredo. Early rails of the "Tex Mex" line helped the small fishing village of Corpus Christi blossom into one of the leading industrial ports of the nation by opening its gates of trade to Laredo and Mexico in the late 1800s.

The little railway, which had to fight for its life against competing ox-cart drivers and hostile Indians while it helped bring civilization to the southern Texas brush country, originated in 1856 when the citizens of Corpus Christi realized the need for a railroad link to tap the rich resources of Mexico as well as to move herds of cattle, sheep, and goats. However, there were not enough supporters or money to push the dream into reality until 1873 when Colonel Uriah Lott, a Corpus Christi merchant, organized a following to fight the competition of a new Rio Grande Valley line that threatened to ruin Corpus Christi's lucrative wool and hide business trade with Mexico.

Other supporters who joined Lott to form the Corpus Christi, San Diego, and Rio Grande Narrow Gauge Railroad Company were J.B. Mitchell, Perry Doddridge, N. Gossett, David Hirsch, George Evans, William Rogers, and Herman Chamberlain, all Corpus Christi residents; M.M. Levy and Henry Goldsmith of Laredo; C.W. Hurley, F.W. Shaffer, and Frank Davis of San Diego; and Leon Blum of Galveston. The new railroad association they organized won a charter in March 1875, after fighting off the powerful wagon lobby of the ox-cart freighting trade.

This steam locomotive, built in 1919 by Baldwin Locomotive Works, has 56-inch drivers and a total weight of 137,000 pounds.

The first spike was driven by Lott on Thanksgiving Day in 1876 near the Corpus Christi waterfront, and 25 miles of line were in operation by January 1877. The first locomotive, purchased by Captain Richard King of the King Ranch, made its inaugural run to Laredo in November 1891 with about 100 Corpus Christi passengers on board—creating a sensation on the prairie.

The railroad, which officially became the Texas Mexican Railway in June 1891, has been headquartered in Laredo since 1889. A passenger line until 1942, when it became unprofitable, the "Tex Mex" now annually hauls almost three million tons of assorted cargo. It employs 335 persons.

A.R. "Andy" Ramos, an employee of the company since 1936, has been president and general manager since 1978. Effective July 1, 1982, he was elected chairman and chief executive officer. Two leading Corpus Christi businessmen, banker Richard King III and real estate developer Jack Ryan, sit on the board of directors.

A series of Texas Mexican Railway boxcars entering Laredo, Texas, pulled by a General Motors locomotive.

TUBULAR INSPECTORS, INC.

Tubular Inspectors' in-plant inspection facility.

The J.I. Hailey No. 2 Yard, in Corpus Christi.

Tubular Inspectors, Inc., the newest member in Corpus Christi's "Partners in Progress," was organized February 25, 1981, by two natives of the city, Lanny Hollingshead and Bobby Gough. Friends since childhood, they had early dreams of being in business for themselves but went separate ways after graduation from W.B. Ray High School.

Hollingshead, after attending Del Mar College and completing a tour of military duty in Vietnam, returned to Austin to obtain a degree in international business from the University of Texas. Gough remained in Corpus Christi, earning a business management degree from Texas A&I University in Kingsville.

Meeting again seven years later in Corpus Christi in late 1980, the two friends collaborated for about six months on planning and financing their joint business venture. Opening at 1737 North Lexington Boulevard, Tubular Inspectors provided mobile electromagnetic pipe inspections in pipe yards, at well sites, and at other customer locations for the booming local energy industry.

The firm's initial staff included other key personnel such as area manager Cliff Bryan and David Figueroa, operations manager. From an initial employment force of 14 persons with a weekly payroll of $3,900, the company has rapidly expanded to its current staff of 140 technicians with a weekly $40,000 payroll. Modernized equipment and services offer such improvements as hydrostatic high-pressure testing of tubing and casing, ultrasonic inspection and prove-up, and automatic full-length cleaning and drifting of pipe.

A Houston branch operation, projected to be employing 150 persons by early 1983, was opened in February 1982. The following month the company leased a site on Interstate Highway 37 for two 12,000-square-foot buildings in which more than $2 million in new equipment was added for stationary, climate-controlled inspections of oil-patch tubulars and other improved services. A third branch operation was opened three months later at the Lone Star Steel Mill in East Texas.

By the end of 1983 Tubular Inspectors, Inc., expects to expand into other key markets in West Texas, Louisiana, Oklahoma, and the Rocky Mountain region.

The business is built on a long-lasting friendship and the similar working and free enterprise spirits of the two men. Dedicated to product quality and service, owners Hollingshead and Gough constantly study new methods and procedures to ensure their growth and position in the industry.

WHATABURGER, INC.

Whataburger, Inc., is one of the oldest and most successful quality fast-food restaurant chains in the United States today. "It's not just a hamburger—it's a Whataburger" dominates the corporation's advertising from coast to coast and throughout the rapidly developing Sunbelt marketplace.

Its primary product is the Whataburger®—a quarter-pound, 100-percent pure beef burger served on a five-inch bun. The customer may have his Whataburger "built to order," prepared with his choice of fresh lettuce, tomatoes, pickles, onions, salad dressing, ketchup, or mustard.

All Whataburger restaurants adhere rigidly to controlled standards of high quality, cleanliness, and service, with special commitment and dedication to quality products. Quality of the product and a concern for individual customer preferences have been the driving force behind the success of Whataburger and are the cornerstone of its corporate philosophy.

The corporation was founded by Harmon A. Dobson in 1950 in Corpus Christi. Harmon, a true entrepreneur and staunch believer in the free enterprise system, made his dream a reality: "Provide the public with the ultimate burger—the Whataburger."

The original buildings were small, portable structures designed to be moved to new sites if and when traffic and population changes occurred. The first franchise was granted in 1953. Success was immediate and volumes began to exceed the potential of the original restaurant. In 1961 the company designed a new permanent A-frame structure featuring the now-familiar orange-and-white striped roof. Volumes continued to grow and in 1966 an enclosed dining room was added to all A-frame restaurants. In 1974 new prototype-designed buildings were introduced which featured dining rooms

Left Whataburger, Inc., was founded by Harmon A. Dobson in 1950.
Right Grace W. Dobson, wife of the founder, is chairwoman of the board of Whataburger, Inc.

and drive-through facilities with the flexibility to accommodate various types of locations and cities with varied populations.

In 1967 the firm suffered a major setback when Harmon Dobson, the founder and chairman of the board, died in an airplane accident. Immediately Harmon's wife, Grace W. Dobson, assumed responsibility and kept the corporation moving forward. Under Mrs. Dobson's leadership a new management team was formed with Jim L. Peterson joining Whataburger, Inc., as president and chief executive officer. Peterson, a nationally known figure in the restaurant industry, set forth a master plan which has made Whataburger truly a leader in the food-service industry from coast to coast.

Peterson and his management team have been recognized for outstanding contributions in government affairs, marketing, advertising, building design, quality control, research and development, training, and community involvement.

Whataburger is what a burger should be!

Jim L. Peterson is the president and chief executive officer of Whataburger, Inc.

The present A-frame structure of Whataburger, Inc., was designed in 1961.

Corpus Christi Patrons

The following individuals, companies, and organizations have made a valuable commitment to the quality of this publication. Windsor Publications, the Nueces County Historical Society, and the Corpus Christi Chamber of Commerce gratefully acknowledge their participation in *Corpus Christi: The History of a Texas Seaport.*

Anco Sales Co.
Anslinger, Inc.
Baker Marine Corporation*
Dr. James L. Barnard, Sr.
Roger Bateman
W.L. Bates Company*
Judge Jack R. Blackmon
Boyd-Campbell Company, Inc.*
Bradleys', Inc.*
Brand Construction Co.
Braselton Construction Company
H.E. Butt Grocery Company*
E.L. Caldwell and Sons, Inc.*
Celanese Chemical Company Technical Center*
Central Power and Light Company*
Champlin Petroleum Company*
J.H. Chapman Construction Company
Coastal Bend Genealogical Society
Corpus Christi Brick and Lumber Company*
Corpus Christi Business & Professional Women's Club, Inc.
Corpus Christi National Bank*
Robert N. Corrigan, Jr.
Charles R. Cunningham
Currie's Nurseries Inc.*
Didear Van and Storage
Maxwell P. Dunne Funeral Service*
E.I. du Pont de Nemours and Company, Inc.*
Lillian Nail Edwards
Anita and Gene E. Eisenhauer
El Taxco Restaurant
Esenjay Petroleum Corporation
Exxon Company, U.S.A.*
First City Bank of Corpus Christi*
Federal Express Corp.
Flato Electric Supply Company*
B.E. "Buddy" Gates
Gold Key Realty
Jack & Sarah Graham
The Gulf Clipper
H.E.B.
Hayley Corporation
C.M. Henkel III, P.C.
Huff Foodtown Stores
Island Enterprises Inc.
Ivanne
The Family of W.W. Jones*
Kaffie Companies*
Henry P. Knolle Farms

Morris L. Lichtenstein, Jr.
Lockwood, Andrews & Newnam, Inc.*
McCaughan, Etheridge & Webb, Consulting Engineers
McKesson Drug Company
Mack Sales Inc.
Atlee and Allyne Magee
Richard D. Magee
Mathieu Electric Co., Inc.
Maverick Markets, Inc.*
Memorial Medical Center*
Munroe & Bass Corp.
Sid Murray Agency
Natural Gas Measurement Inc.
Naylor's Farm & Ranch Supply, Inc.
Martin and Miriam Nelson
Peat, Marwick, Mitchell & Co.
Marjorie L. Perkins
Peterson Development Company
Phillips' Merle Norman Cosmetic Studios
Port of Corpus Christi Authority
Power-Tech Company
Billy Pugh Company, Inc.*
Mr. & Mrs. Warren A. Rees
Robert and Sally Reynolds
Reynolds Metal Co., Sherwin Plant
John G. Seaman
Seaside Memorial Park and Funeral Home*
Ronnie Sizemore
Sizzler Family Steak House
Southern National Bank
Southwestern Bell Telephone Co.
Southwestern Refining Company, Inc.
Spann & Smith, P.C.
Spohn Hospital*
Robert L. Steel
Sterett Supply Company
Clemens Aram Struve
Susser Company
Swantner & Gordon Insurance Agency, Inc.*
Taylor Brothers Jewelers*
Texas Commerce Bank-Corpus Christi
Texas Commerce-Gulfway, N.A.
Texas Mexican Railway Company*
Thrifty Rent-A-Car
Thurman-Fondren Glass Company Inc.
Tubular Inspectors, Inc.*
U-Haul Co. of South Texas
Marion Uehlinger
Faires P. Wade
J. Rex Wayland
Whataburger, Inc.*
Dr. & Mrs. Lawrence H. Wilk & Family

*Partners in Progress of *Corpus Christi: The History of a Texas Seaport.* The histories of these companies and organizations appear in Chapter 8, beginning on page 113.

Chronology

1498 Amerigo Vespucci sailed the Gulf and made what is believed to be the first map showing the outline of the Gulf of Mexico.

1519 Spanish explorer Alonzo Álvarez de Piñeda sailed the Gulf while looking for a passage to the Pacific Ocean. He discovered the Mississippi River and landed at various spots along the Texas coast, mapping rivers, islands, and bays. Local legend says he gazed upon and named Corpus Christi Bay on June 24, which was the day of the Roman Catholic Feast of Corpus Christi.

1530 Alvar Núñez Cabeza de Vaca, treasurer for an ill-fated attempt to colonize Florida led by Panfilo de Nárvaez, was likely a visitor to Corpus Christi Bay while enslaved by Karankawa Indians. De Vaca escaped in 1534, and two years later arrived in Culiacán, Mexico.

1685 A colony was founded at Matagorda Bay by French explorer René Robert Cavelier, Sieur de La Salle. Fearing French encroachment on the Gulf Coast, Spanish troops passed northwest of present-day Corpus Christi on their way to eradicate La Salle's settlement.

1689 The ruins of La Salle's fort were found by Alonso de León as he explored the Gulf Coast region.

1720 Frenchman Jean Beranger sailed through Aransas Pass and set up camp on Copano Bay.

1747 Don José de Escandón planned a settlement to be named Villa de Vedoya on San Miguel de Archangel (Corpus Christi) Bay, but the colony never materialized.

1760-1764 In response to reports of an English expedition to the Gulf Coast, Blas María de Garza Falcón established Rancho Santa Petronila, five leagues southwest of the Nueces River.

1766 Colonel Diego Ortiz Parrilla explored the area and found no sign of an English presence. Parrilla wrote a report on the mission that contained the first mention of "Corpus Christi Bay," a name probably applied by the Falcón family.

1806 Encouraged by generous land grants from the Spanish government, by this time a number of Spanish ranchmen had settled in the Nueces area. Nicolas and Juan Ballí were given rights to Padre Island.

1830 Empresarios John McMullen and James McGloin founded San Patricio Colony.

1831 Captain Enrique de Villareal of Matamoros was given the title to Rincon del Oso by the Mexican government, covering land on which the city of Corpus Christi was later located.

1836 Texians captured Fort Lipantitlan on the Nueces River. The Mexican Army under General José Urrea swept the coast, overrunning Texians at Agua Dulce Creek, San Patricio, Refugio, and Goliad. The defeated Mexican Army stopped near Corpus Christi on its retreat to Mexico after Santa Anna's defeat at San Jacinto.

1839 Colonel Henry Lawrence Kinney and William Aubrey established a trading post on the western shore of Corpus Christi Bay and contracted to take over the Villareal grant.

1845 General Zachary Taylor's Army landed to prepare for war with Mexico. His U.S. flag in Corpus Christi was the first to fly over Texas soil. Texas voted to join the Union.

1846 Samuel Bangs, founder of the *Galveston News* and other early newspapers, started the *Corpus Christi Gazette,* which was short-lived. The first Post Office opened on May 22 with Aubrey as postmaster. The Texas Legislature authorized the formation of Nueces County.

1847 Corpus Christi was named county seat of Nueces County, and José de Alba was elected chief justice (county judge).

1848 Population 350. Colonel Kinney brought in a dredge to deepen the channel from Aransas Pass. *The Corpus Christi Star* began with John H. Peoples as editor. Mrs. de Meza opened a private school with tuition of $3 a month. For troublesome pupils, the fee was more.

1851 *The Nueces Valley* newspaper was founded by Judge B.F. Neal.

1852 Corpus Christi, which covered four square miles, was incorporated as a city with B.F. Neal as its first mayor. Colonel Kinney held the first State Fair of Texas, which contributed to his financial ruin. Captain Richard King and Gideon Lewis founded a ranch on Santa Gertrudis Creek. Kinney purchased land around the artesian wells dug by Taylor's Army and donated it to the city for a park, around which spas would open. On July 17, the Rivers and Harbors Act first recognized Corpus Christi as a seaport. The first jail was built.

1853 Nueces County erected a two-story frame courthouse on Mesquite Street.

1854 A yellow fever epidemic took a frightful

oll. George Washington Mockley, veteran of San Jacinto, secretary of war for the Republic of Texas, and emissary from General Sam Houston, died in Corpus Christi and was buried in Old Bayview Cemetery.

857 Trade with Mexico was interrupted by the "Cart War" between Mexican and American freight wagoneers. A lighthouse was installed at Buffalo and Upper Broadway.

862 Union ships bombarded Corpus Christi in an indecisive battle in which both sides claimed victory.

1863 The Union Army captured the Confederate fort on Mustang Island.

1864 Federal troops occupied Corpus Christi.

1865 Reconstruction governments were named in the city and state under military occupation.

1867 A yellow fever epidemic killed one-third of the population. Thousands of South Texas cattle moved up trails to Eastern markets. Border strife and lawlessness paralyzed the area.

1870 Population 2,140.

1871 City taxpayers voted a $25,000 bond issue to dredge a channel through the bay. The Fire Department was organized, and Incarnate

Word Academy was established.

1872 The *Gazette* was established by James R. Barnard & Son.

1874 The Morris and Cummings channel was dredged to eight feet, allowing the first steamship to dock at Corpus Christi. Lichtenstein's Department Store opened.

1875 Mexican bandits raided Nuecestown, killing three and inflaming the state with a reaction that ended much of the border strife.

1876 The *Gazette* became the city's first daily newspaper. The Corpus Christi, San Diego, and Rio Grande Railway was started, establishing the city's first railroad.

1877 The Reverend Solomon Melvin Coles started a private school for black children.

1880 Population 3,257.

1883 *The Free Press and Ledger* was consolidated to form the *Corpus Christi Caller*, with W.P. Caruthers, Ed Williams and Eli Merriman as editors. The first cotton was shipped from Corpus Christi.

1886 The city's second railroad, the San Antonio and Aransas Pass, was built.

1889 The boom promoted by Colonel E.H. Ropes set

In the 1880s one household necessity was a good saddle. The H. Keller store in Corpus Christi guaranteed all of its merchandise in this 1884 newspaper advertisement. Courtesy, University of Texas Barker Texas History Center, Austin

161

Above: The Corpus Christi Council of the Order Sons of America was photographed in the 1920s. This organization merged with other early Mexican American organizations in Texas to form LULAC. From the Archives of the League of United Latin American Citizens. Courtesy, University of Texas Mexican American Library Program, Austin

Right: Three Bonilla brothers, all longtime residents of Corpus Christi, have served as national president of LULAC. They are (from left to right) William, Tony, and Ruben Bonilla. Courtesy, William Bonilla

off a frenzy of speculation and growth before it collapsed in the financial panic of 1893.

1890 Corpus Christi Electric Company was organized.

1891 Southwestern Telephone and Telegraph Company bought out Corpus Christi Electric Company's telephone exchange. The *Corpus Christi Caller* went daily on June 1.

1892 A large downtown fire led to a bond election for a water system. Water previously had been obtained from a pond on Chatham's Ravine (in Blucher Park) or from rain cisterns.

1895 Spohn Hospital was established. Robert Fitzsimmons trained on North Beach for his world-championship prizefight with James Corbett.

1900 Population 4,703.

1906 A Confederate monument was dedicated in Bayview Cemetery.

1909 President William Howard Taft visited the city. La Retama Club acquired a library. A special act of the Texas Legislature formed the Corpus Christi Independent School District with 29 teachers.

1910 Population 8,222. The *Daily Herald* and the *Corpus Christi Caller* were consolidated. The U.S. Army designated Harbor

Island as the deep-water port for the area. Trolley cars replaced horse-drawn cars on city streets.

1911 The first causeway was built across Nueces Bay. The *Corpus Christi Caller* was bought by Mrs. Henrietta M. King, and the *Corpus Christi Democrat* was founded by J.W. Bauerfeind. On July 4 Oscar Brindley landed his Wright flying machine on the beach—the first airplane to land in Corpus Christi.

1912 The first streetlights were installed.

1913 A major gas field was discovered at White Point across Nueces Bay. Nueces Hotel opened. Mayor Roy Miller's civic improvements included gas, electricity, and paved streets.

1914 Bluff improvements were begun, and ground was broken for Nueces County Courthouse.

1916 A hurricane destroyed Nueces Bay Causeway and damaged the bayfront. The Army located Camp Scurry on the south edge of town. Prohibition was voted in a local election.

1917 The *Corpus Christi Democrat* was purchased by W.E. Pope and renamed *The Times.*

1918 World War I ended—35 Nueces County servicemen had given their lives.

1919 Corpus Christi was

devastated by a great hurricane.

1920 Population 10,522.

1923 Gas was discovered in Saxet Field just west of town, assuring the city and industries an ample supply of fuel. The Nueces County Navigation District was organized.

1924 Commercial Club became the Chamber of Commerce.

1925 South Texas Teachers College (later A&I) was established at Kingsville. The Little Theater, formed in 1924, presented its first play, Booth Tarkington's *Seventeen.* A gun battle erupted in front of Bessie Miller's place on Sam Rankin Street between Ku Klux Klan and anti-Klan forces. Four men were killed. Middle West Utilities Company bought Gulf Coast Power Company (formerly Corpus Christi Railway and Light Company) and changed the name to Central Power and Light Company.

1926 The Port of Corpus Christi opened.

1927 The Nixon Building opened. La Retama Club sold its libraries to the City of Corpus Christi for $1. The Corpus Christi Academy started classes.

1928 The first pipeline opened to Harbor Island. Corpus Christi High School was built at a cost of $320,916.

1929 The League of United Latin American Citizens was formed at Obreros Hall, combining the Order of Sons of America (Corpus Christi), Knights of America (San Antonio), and the Latin American Citizens' League of the Rio Grande Valley, with Ben Garza as chairman and its first president. The *Corpus Christi Caller* was bought by Marsh-Fentress and sold to Harte-Hanks.

1930 Population 27,742. The Jones Building (originally Sherman Building) opened.

1933 A hurricane struck, its tide coming up to the Federal Building. The Nueces Bay Causeway was knocked out again.

1934 Marcel and Conrad Schlumberger of Paris, France, came to town to demonstrate a system of electrically logging oil wells, a system that revolutionized oil exploration. A big well blowout on the Driscoll farm west of the city left a six-acre crater.

1935 By a vote of 317 to 45, Del Mar Junior College was created. The state established Kleberg Park, later Mathis State Park, now Lake Corpus Christi State Park. Highway 77 opened through the King and Kenedy ranches, and North Beach was annexed to the city.

1936 Centennial Art Museum was established in South Bluff Park with $4,000 from the state and

$2,000 from the county.

1938 Morris Lichtenstein and Sons purchased the old St. James Hotel and built a department store downtown. Mrs. Sam E. Wilson established the Ada Wilson Crippled Children's Hospital. Bayfront bonds were voted, launching a $2.2 million seawall and waterfront development program. Annexations increased the city's size from 7.45 to 13.26 square miles.

1939 The Post Office on the Bluff was dedicated, Corpus Christi Cathedral was built, and the Arts Community Center opened.

1940 Population 57,301. The Seawall was completed, and the Hug-the-Coast Highway opened from Brownsville to Orange.

1941 The Naval Air Station was dedicated, the red-light district was closed at the request of the Navy, and the first fliers were graduated at NAS. Warren Joseph Sherrill was killed on the USS *Arizona* at Pearl Harbor; Billy Brownlee was killed at Hickam Field on December 7. Sherrill Park and Brownlee Boulevard bear their names.

1943 Franklin D. Roosevelt and Mexican President Avila Camacho met at NAS.

1944 Memorial Hospital was organized. The Corpus Christi Art

Foundation was formed.

1945 Mayor Roy Self was elected on a platform to adopt a city-manager form of government. World War II ended; 400 county residents had died. Spurred by the war effort, the 12-foot-deep Intracoastal Canal, was opened from Galveston to Corpus Christi.

1946 The Corpus Christi Symphony was organized.

1947 The Clara Driscoll Foundation purchased 20 acres on South Alameda for a free clinic and hospital for crippled children. The Baptist Foundation purchased the Navy facility on Ward Island and established the University of Corpus Christi.

1949 The Intracoastal Canal was opened to Brownsville, and the Texas Legislature created the Lower Nueces River Water Supply District.

1950 Population 108,287. W.B. Ray High School opened, and Corpus Christi High became Roy Miller. Four-mile Padre Island Causeway (later John F. Kennedy Causeway) opened, bayfront beautification was completed, and Corpus Christi won Better Homes and Gardens' More Beautiful America contest with its bayfront landscaping.

1951 Nueces County bought the Harbor Island Causeway and ferry

system for $250,000.

1952 Wilson Tower and City Hall were completed. Del Mar Junior College became integrated after the local NAACP, headed by Dr. H. Boyd Hall, challenged school racial policies. Dr. Hall also helped desegregate Texas A&I College, lunch counters, parks, pools, and other public facilities and got jobs for blacks at the Post Office. The city celebrated the 100th anniversary of its incorporation.

1953 Seventy-four Nueces County men were killed before the Korean War ended.

1954 Dougherty School of Nursing opened. Memorial Coliseum was dedicated to the 400 soldiers from Nueces County who died in World War II.

1955 Corpus Christi schools became integrated following the U.S. Supreme Court ruling that "separate but equal" schools were unconstitutional. Ground was broken for Wesley Seale Dam. Spohn Hospital celebrated its 50th anniversary.

1956 The Corpus Christi Museum was chartered.

1959 The Overhaul and Repair Department at the Naval Air Station was closed, leaving 3,000 unemployed and causing a local recession. The 26-year-old battle to end the

"Bascule Bridge Bottleneck" ended with completion of Harbor Bridge over the ship channel. Tule Lake Lift Bridge also opened.

1960 Population 167,690. Corpus Christi International Airport was dedicated by World War I flying ace Eddie Rickenbacher. The Corpus Christi Arts Council was formed.

1961 The Army Maintenance Center (Army Depot) opened in buildings formerly occupied by Navy Overhaul and Repair Department. The Bascule Bridge was removed, and the second span of Nueces Bay Causeway was begun. Vice-President Lyndon B. Johnson visited the proposed seashore area of Padre Island. Flour Bluff was annexed.

1962 President John F. Kennedy signed a bill authorizing purchase of 80.5 miles of Padre Island for a national seashore area. Interstate Highway 37 to San Antonio was started. The Corpus Christi Museum became a city operation. Annexations of land west and south of the city increased its land area from 52 to 101 square miles.

1963 Corpus Christi School for the Retarded (Corpus Christi State School) was established.

1964 Corpus Christi Council of Garden Clubs

Mayors of Corpus Christi

opened Garden Center.

1967 Centennial Art Museum changed to Art Museum of South Texas.

1968 The ribbon was cut for Corpus Christi Museum, the first structure in Bayfront Plaza Park.

1969 The Main Post Office was built at Nueces Bay Boulevard and Buddy Lawrence Drive.

1970 Population 204,525. Hurricane Celia caused widespread wind damage.

1972 The Art Museum of South Texas, designed by Philip Johnson, was dedicated, and the Art Community Center was formed by the South Texas Art League, Corpus Christi Art Guild, Southwest Sculpture Society, Southwestern Watercolor Society, Art Association of Corpus Christi, Independent Artists, and the Flour Bluff Art Association. Land for Mustang Island Park was purchased from Mrs. Sam E. Wilson.

1973 University of Corpus Christi properties were transferred to the A&I University System.

1975 The Vietnam War ended; Nueces County had lost 125 men.

1976 Harbor Playhouse in Bayfront Plaza opened for the Little Theater of Corpus Christi with a performance of *1776*.

1977 County officials moved from the old courthouse to the new. A fountain was dedicated to the 199 Nueces County servicemen who died in Vietnam and Korea. Governor Dolph Briscoe signed a bill changing the name of A&I-CC to Corpus Christi State University.

1978 The U.S. Army Field Band and Soldiers' Chorus opened the Bayfront Plaza Civic Auditorium.

1980 Population 232,119. Nueces County population was 268,215.

1981 Interstate 37 was completed to San Antonio almost 20 years after the 140-mile highway was started. The $23-million Bayfront Plaza Convention Center formally opened.

1982 Choke Canyon dam gates were closed to create a new reservoir. The city's ground area was 155.84 square miles of land and 320.25 square miles of water, and Corpus Christi's 35-foot elevation was the highest on the Gulf Coast.

1852-1853	Judge B.F. Neal
1853-1854	E.R. Hopson
1854-1855	Henry W. Berry
1855-1856	B.F. Neal
1856-1857	Henry L. Maltby
1857-1858	Henry W. Berry (Resigned)
1858-1860	Reuben Holbein
1860-1863	Henry W. Berry
1863-1864	Dr. George Robertson
1864-1867	W.N. Staples
1867-1869	Colonel Nelson Plato
1869-1872	J.B. Mitchell
1872-1874	Perry Doddridge
1874-1876	Nelson Plato
1876-1877	William Headen
1877-1880	John M. Moore
1880-1884	John Baptist Murphy
1884-1886	George F. Evans
1886-1889	Cheston C. Heath
1889-1891	Henry Keller
1891-1903	Oscar C. Lovenskiold
1903-1907	Admiral Hiram H. Segrest
1907-1909	Dan Reid (Died in office)
1909-1913	Clark Pease
1913-1919	Roy Miller
1919-1921	Gordon Boone
1921-1931	Perry G. Lovenskiold
1931-1933	Edwin Flato
1933-1935	William Schaeffer
1935-1937	Henry R. Giles
1937-1945	A.C. McCaughan
1945-1946	Roy Self
1946-1947	Robert T. Wilson (Died in office)
1947-1949	Wesley Seale
1949-1953	Leslie Wasserman
1953-1954	Albert Lichtenstein (Resigned)
1954-1955	P.C. Calloway
1955-1959	Farrell Dee Smith
1959-1961	Ellroy King
1961-1963	Ben F. McDonald
1963-1965	James L. Barnard
1965-1967	McIver Furman
1967-1971	Jack Blackmon
1971-1973	Ronnie Sizemore
1973-1978	Jason Luby (Resigned to run for Congress)
1978-1979	Gabe Lozano
1979-	Colonel Luther Jones

Selected Bibliography

Books

Allhands, J.L. *Gringo Builders*. Dallas: Private Printing, 1931.

———. *Uriah Lott*. San Antonio: Naylor Company, 1949.

Bedichek, Roy. *Karankawa Country*. Austin: University of Texas Press, 1950.

Bollaert, William. *William Bollaert's Texas*. Edited by Eugene Hollan and Ruth Lapham Butler. Norman, Oklahoma: University of Oklahoma Press, 1956.

Bureau of Economic Geology, *Environmental Geologic Atlas of the Texas Coastal Zone—Corpus Christi Area*. Austin: University of Texas at Austin, 1976.

Caller-Times, The. *Corpus Christi, 100 Years*. Corpus Christi: The Caller Times Publishing Company, 1952.

Castañeda, Carlos E. *Our Catholic Heritage in Texas*. Austin: Von P. Voekmann-Jones, 1936.

Catschet, Albert S., *The Karankawa Indians, The Coast People of Texas*. Harvard University, 1891.

Coitt, Margaret L. *The Life History of the United States: The Sweep Westward*. New York: Time, Inc., 1963.

Davis, John L. *Treasure, People, Ships and Dreams*. San Antonio: Texas Antiquities Committee and the Institute of Texan Cultures of the University of Texas at San Antonio, 1977.

De Peña, José Enrique. *With Santa Anna in Texas: A Personal Narrative of the Revolution*. Texas A&M University Press, 1975.

Dobie, J. Frank. *A Vaquero of the Brush Country*. Little, Brown and Company, Inc., 1929.

Duaine, Carl L. *Caverns of Oblivion*. Manchaca: Packrat Press, 1971.

Durham, George, as told to Clyde Wantland. *Taming of the Nueces Strip*. Austin: University of Texas Press, 1962.

Fehrenbach, T.R. *Lone Star, A History of Texas*. New York: McMillan Publishing Company, 1968.

Hall, Lawrence Francis. *José Escandón on the Founding of Nuevo Santander: A Study in Spanish Colonization*. Ohio State University Press, 1926.

Hamilton, Holman. *Zachary Taylor: Soldier of the Republic*. Indianapolis: The Bobbs-Merrill Company, 1941.

Herbert, Rachel Bluntzer. *The Forgotten Colony, San Patricio De Hibernia*. Burnet: Eaken Press, 1981.

Hitchcock, Ethan Allen. *Fifty Years in Camp and Field*. Edited by W.A. Croffut. New York: 1909.

Holland, F.R., Jr. *The Aransas Pass Light Station: A History*. Corpus Christi: Private Printing, 1976.

Huson, Hobart. *Captain Phillip Dimmitt's Commandancy of Goliad*. Austin: Von Boeckmann-Jones Company, 1974.

———. *El Copano, the Ancient Port of Bexar and La Bahia*. Refugio: The Refugio Timely Remarks, 1935.

———. *Refugio, A Comprehensive History*. Houston: The Guardian Publishing Company, 1953.

Kilgore, D.E. *Nueces County, Texas, 1750-1800. A Bicentennial Memoir*. 1976.

Kilman, Edward W. *Cannibal Coast*. San Antonio: Naylor Company, 1959.

Lamar, Mirabeau Buonaparte. *The Lamar Papers*. Edited from the original papers by Charles Adams Gulick, Winnie Allen, Katherine Elliott, and Harriet Smither, Vols. III and IV. Austin: The Pemberton Press, 1968.

Lavender, David. *Climax at Buena Vista: The American Campaigns in Northeastern Mexico, 1846-47*. Philadelphia: J.B. Lippincott Company, 1966.

Lea, Tom. *The King Ranch*. Boston: Little, Brown and Company, 1957.

Linn, John J. *Reminiscenses of Fifty Years in Texas*. New York: 1883.

Meade, George Gordon. *Life and Letters of George Gordon Meade*. New York: Charles Scribner and Sons, 1913.

Morrell, Z.N. *Flowers and Fruits of the Wilderness: 46 Years in Texas and Two Winters in Honduras*. Reprint. Irving: Griffin Graphic Arts, 1966.

Morris, Richard B. *The Life History of the United States*. Vol. I. New York: Time, Inc., 1963.

Nance, Joseph Milton. *After San Jacinto, The Texas-Mexican Frontier, 1836-1841*. Austin: University of Texas Press, 1963.

———. *Attack and Counterattack: The Texas-Mexican Frontier, 1842*. Austin: University of Texas Press, 1964.

Newcomb, W.W. Jr. *The Indians of Texas, From Prehistoric to Modern Times*. Austin: University of Texas Press, 1978.

Nueces County Historical Society. *The History of Nueces County.* Austin: Jenkins Book Publishing Company, Inc., 1972.

Parkes, Henry Bamford. *A History of Mexico.* Boston: Houghton Mifflin Company, 1938.

Price, Glenn W. *Origins of the War With Mexico: The Polk-Stockton Intrigue.* Austin: University of Texas Press, 1976.

Price, W. Armstrong. *North Beach Study for the City of Corpus Christi.* Corpus Christi: 1956.

Reed, St. Clair Griffin. *A History of the Texas Railroads.* Houston: St. Clair Publishing Company, 1941.

Richardson, Rupert. *Texas, The Lone Star State.* New York: Prentice-Hall, Inc., 1943.

_____ ; Wallace, Ernest; Anderson, Adrian N. *Texas, The Lone Star State, Third Edition.* Englewood Cliffs, New Jersey: Prentice-Hall, 1970.

Smylie, Vernon. *A Noose for Chipita.* Corpus Christi: Texas News Syndicate Press, 1970.

Stephens, Ray A. *The Taft Ranch: A Texas Principality.* Austin: University of Texas Press, 1964.

Sutherland, Mary. *The Story of Corpus Christi.* Houston: Rein & Sons Company.

Syers, Ed. *Texas: The Beginning, 1519-1834.* Waco: Texian Press, 1978.

Webb, Walter Prescott and Carroll, H. Bailey. *The Handbook of Texas.* Vols. I and II. Austin: Texas State Historical Society. Ann Arbor: Edwards Brothers, 1952.

_____ . *The Texas Rangers, A Century of Frontier Defense.* Austin: University of Texas Press, 1935.

Williams, J.W. *Old Texas Trails.* Edited and compiled by Kenneth F. Neighbors. Burnet: Eakin Press, 1979.

Winsor, Bill. *Texas in the Confederacy: Military Installations, Economy and People.* Hillsboro: Hill Junior College Press, 1978.

Other Sources

Corpus Christi Board of Trade.

Corpus Christi Caller-Times files.

Corpus Christi Chamber of Commerce.

Louise Gravett (Interview, August 22, 1975).

This violinist is the daughter of Jerome Charlier, the Corpus Christi brass band director in 1890. She is dressed in an elaborate lace gown for a recital. Courtesy, Nueces County Historical Society

Acknowledgments

Dan Kilgore is the undisputed authority on Corpus Christi history. I have relied heavily on his knowledge, information, and suggestions for years, and this endeavor was no exception. It was he who kept me on the straight path in the search for historical accuracy.

My wife, Marjorie Kathryn (Ricky) Walraven—teacher, historian, and copy editor—used the skills of all three vocations on the manuscript and made a lazy scholar work.

Bill Walraven

The Nueces County Historical Society expresses sincere appreciation for assistance and cooperation in the pictorial research for this book to the following persons and institutions:

Barker Texas History Center, The University of Texas at Austin: Ralph Elder and Frances Rogers, assistant archivists; collections: Burton Dunn Scrapbook, Laura Dunn Sweatt, D.W. Grant Collection, Mrs. Mac Armstrong, Eli Merriman Scrapbooks, Rabb Collection—Natalie Horton; City of Corpus Christi; Corpus Christi Area Convention and Tourist Bureau; Corpus Christi Caller-Times: Publisher Edward H. Harte, Assistant to Publisher Laurie Evans, and the library staff; Corpus Christi Army Depot; Corpus Christi Cathedral Museum: Mrs. Robert Haegelin, director; Corpus Christi Magazine; Corpus Christi Minor Seminary: Claude E. Valentine, S.J., Librarian; Corpus Christi Museum: Director Albert Heine, Assistant Director Carroll Williams, Curator Martha Lynn Hill; Corpus Christi National Bank: Michael Harrison, vice-president; Corpus Christi Naval Air Station; First National Bank of Rockport: James Sorenson, Jr., president; Friends of the Courthouse, Inc.: Cecil Burney, chairman; Humanities Research Center, The University of Texas at Austin: Director Roy Flukinger, Mary Ellen MacNamara, and Sybil Miller; John E. Connor Museum, Texas A & I University, Kingsville: Director Jimmy Picquet and Curator Jim Powers; Institute of Texan Cultures, The University of Texas in San Antonio: Tom F. Shelton, library assistant; La Retama Library: Director Roger Pearson and Local History Librarian Margaret Rose; Nueces County Commissioner Court: County Judge Robert N. Barnes, and Commissioners Carl Bluntzer, Richard M. Orchard, J.P. Luby, and William McKenzie; Nueces County Historical Commission: Sally Robeau, Chairman; Nuecestown School Committee, Friends of the Courthouse, Inc.; Port of Corpus Christi: Director Harry Plomarity and Consultant Colonel Floyd H. Buch; Robstown Record: San Keach, publisher; Twenty-eighth District Courtroom Museum, 1914 Nueces County Courthouse; Texas Parks and Wildlife Magazine; Texas Highways Magazine; University of Corpus Christi Library; Violet Historical Society; Old Saint Anthony Catholic Church Museum: David and Barbara Kercher, director and curator.

The following deserve special appreciation and recognition for the professional quality of the photographic submissions of historical personages and events: J. Marie Digatono, Anita Eisenhauer, Lee John Govatos, Tom Hand, Doc McGregor, Ruel Robeau, Dean Thorpe, and Eugene Wukasch. Marjorie and Bill Walraven's assistance in correlating photos to the manuscript was invaluable. The society thanks the many citizens who contributed resource data, cherished photos, and miscellaneous memorabilia not included in this publication, and extends special thanks to County Auditor Thomas Murphy and his staff and the 150 members of the Historical Society who helped complete this project.

Sincere gratitude goes to the two assistant pictorial researchers, Sally Robeau and Anita Eisenhauer, who shared with us their professional expertise and infinite knowledge of local history. They spent tireless energy locating the scores of historical gems that portray the life and culture of our community throughout the years.

Margaret Walberg, President
Nueces County Historical Society

Index

Italicized numbers indicate illustrations

Partners in Progress Index

Titles in the
Windsor Local History Series

THIS BOOK WAS SET IN
PONTIAC AND EUROPA TYPES,
PRINTED ON
70LB. ACID-FREE WARRENFLO
AND BOUND BY
WALSWORTH PUBLISHING COMPANY
HALFTONE REPRODUCTION BY ROBERTSON GRAPHICS